国家级一流本科课程配套教材

跨文化交际
原理与应用

主编　余卫华　谌　莉

编者　曹　环　楼凌玲
　　　张　悦　王　敏

U0368739

清華大学出版社
北 京

内 容 简 介

《跨文化交际：原理与应用》是国家级一流本科课程"东方遇见西方：跨文化交际之旅"的配套教材。本教材采用全英文编写，希望在提高学生英语水平的同时培养他们的跨文化交际能力。教材的主要特点是在引入跨文化交际原理时采用案例进行分析和讲解，提升学生的学习兴趣，培养他们的问题意识和思辨能力，使其尽可能在轻松愉快的学习过程中获得更好的学习体验和学习效果。本教材另配有各章节习题、测试题及内容丰富的 PPT 课件，读者可登录 www.tsinghuaelt.com 下载使用。

本教材适用于高等学校跨文化交际类课程，也可供在智慧树平台学习该门课程的学生和对跨文化交际感兴趣的相关人士使用。

图书在版编目（CIP）数据

跨文化交际：原理与应用：英文 / 余卫华，谌莉主编. —北京：清华大学出版社，2022.8（2023.9重印）
国家级一流本科课程配套教材
ISBN 978-7-302-61444-9

Ⅰ.①跨… Ⅱ.①余… ②谌… Ⅲ.①文化交流—高等学校—教材—英文 Ⅳ.① G115

中国版本图书馆 CIP 数据核字（2022）第 136575 号

责任编辑：刘　艳
封面设计：子　一
责任校对：王荣静
责任印制：杨　艳

出版发行：清华大学出版社
　　　　网　　　址：http://www.tup.com.cn, http://www.wqbook.com
　　　　地　　　址：北京清华大学学研大厦 A 座　　　　邮　　编：100084
　　　　社 总 机：010-83470000　　　　邮　　购：010-62786544
　　　　投稿与读者服务：010-62776969, c-service@tup.tsinghua.edu.cn
　　　　质量反馈：010-62772015, zhiliang@tup.tsinghua.edu.cn
印 装 者：大厂回族自治县彩虹印刷有限公司
经　　销：全国新华书店
开　　本：185mm×260mm　　　印　张：18　　　字　数：384 千字
版　　次：2022 年 10 月第 1 版　　　印　次：2023 年 9 月第 2 次印刷
定　　价：75.00 元

产品编号：092630-01

前　言

跨文化交际是高校英语类专业核心课程，是"一带一路"和人类命运共同体环境下各涉外相关专业为提升学生的国际传播能力而开设的专业课程，同时也是大学英语的通识选修课程。本课程旨在提高外语学习者的跨文化交际意识，培养他们的跨文化交际能力，使其能灵活运用所学知识在今后的跨文化交际实践中有效应对不同的交际环境，提高他们传播中国文化、讲好中国故事的能力。相关教材中，概论型和论述语言与文化的居多，但是从学生跨文化交际能力视角出发，注重问题意识和思辨能力的培养，线上和线下学习相结合的应用型和案例分析型教材并不多。鉴于此，我们决定尝试编写出这样一本教材，并将该教材取名为《跨文化交际：原理与应用》。

本教材采用全英文编写，目的是希望学生通过基于内容的沉浸式学习模式学习该门课程，在提高学生英语水平的同时培养他们的跨文化交际能力。本教材的主要特点是在引入跨文化交际原理时引入案例分析，充分利用多种现实案例及多媒体手段增强学生的目的语学习兴趣，并采用问题探究和小组讨论等方式提升学生的反思能力，使他们尽可能在轻松愉快的学习过程中获得更好的学习体验和学习效果。

在课程体系上，本教材在对国内外同类课程的理论体系予以充分重视的同时，将案例分析、问题意识与理论体系有机结合，特别是在使用案例分析跨文化交际过程中遇到的相关冲突和问题时导入相关原理和理论，而绝非在讲解原理和理论时以问题来证明前者。本教材注重让学生通过团队合作的方式完成任务、解决文化冲突，促进自主性学习、过程性学习和体验式学习。教材每个章节都已经提供了含有解决方案的案例给学生作为参考，后面紧随的拓展案例则没有提供答案，要求学生根据前面的案例自己进行分析、应用和反思，目的是培养学生独立分析问题和解决问题的能力。

我们希望使用本教材的老师打破传统上以概念为主、过多地以理论推演为核心的教学模式，同时紧密结合学生的心理特点，运用教材中的诸多案例进行生动讲解，

开展直观教学，提高学生的学习兴趣和内在学习动机，尽量选择学生感兴趣的主题和最新的热点话题发问，着力凸显时代感与现代性。教学方法上建议教师采用直接法、情境法、探究法、任务型教学法以及暗示法等，将教学重点放在交际过程的问题意识上，以问题为抓手，以案例为核心，培养学生发现、思考和解决问题的学习习惯与能力，同时增强他们的团队合作意识和跨文化意识。评定该门课程成绩时可以结合过程性考核和终结性考核，并且采用以过程性考核和形成性评估为主的考核评估方式。

本教材的编写团队同时也是首批国家级一流本科课程"东方遇见西方：跨文化交际之旅"的教学团队。教材和课程均为团队里每一位成员团结协作的结晶。第一主编余卫华负责确定全书的整体编写框架、各章节的主要内容、全书的编写体例和规范等，同时提供主要文献并撰写前言，此外还负责与第二主编一起审校全书书稿及相关配套教学资源。其他编写人员的分工如下：谌莉编写第 1 章和第 8 章及 5.1 和 5.2 小节；张悦编写 2.3 至 2.5 小节及 3.1 至 3.3 小节；曹环编写第 6 章和第 7 章；楼凌玲编写第 4 章及 5.3 和 5.4 小节；王敏编写 2.1 和 2.2 小节及 3.4 小节。

为方便学生结合线上和线下开展学习，本教材提供了配套慕课，学生在智慧树网站搜索"东方遇见西方：跨文化交际之旅"课程，即可线上学习。本教材另配有各章节习题、测试题及内容丰富的 PPT 课件，读者可登录 ftp://ftp.tsinghua.edu.cn 下载使用。

限于编者水平，本教材难免会有疏漏之处，我们恳请专家和读者批评指正。

余卫华

2022 年 9 月

于浙江省绍兴市浙江越秀外国语学院

Contents

Chapter 1
Brief Introduction to Intercultural Communication

Chapter 2
Verbal and Nonverbal Communication

Chapter 3
Communicative Competence & Intercultural Competence

Chapter 4
Cultural Patterns

Chapter 5
Intercultural Communication in Various Social Contexts

Chapter 6
Cultural Bias

Chapter 7
Identity

Chapter 8
Globalization and Global Citizenship

Chapter 1

Brief Introduction to Intercultural Communication

Learning Objectives

After learning this chapter, you should be able to:

1. understand the concept of intercultural communication;

2. identify the two types of culture and the five dimensions of culture;

3. know the characteristics of communication and culture;

4. know the five elements in the communication process.

For those who work or live in the globalized world, it is sometimes amazing to see how people in other cultures behave. We tend to have an instinct that all people are the same "deep inside"—but they are not. Different countries have different culture. Culture crosses geographical limits and historical conditions in many ways. So culture differences are everywhere. They affect people's view of the world and their way of thinking. If we have some knowledge about intercultural communication, we can reduce anxiety, anger, or frustration. And we can be more effective when communicating with people from other countries.

Before we start this chapter, there are some questions for you:

(1) When we talk about Chinese culture, what is the first thing that comes to your mind?

(2) Are there any misunderstandings when you communicate with people from other countries? How do you solve the problem?

1.1 Defining and Describing Culture

There are important variations in the way societies organize themselves and interact with the environment, as well as in their shared conception of morality. Furthermore, we cannot deny many obvious cultural differences that exist between people, such as traditions, dress, and languages. Culture is a complex and vague concept, very hard to define. There have been at least over 300 different definitions of culture, but none of them seems to be able to tell us everything about culture. Yet there are some basic facts that most people can agree with. That is, culture is a set of values and beliefs, norms and customs, and rules and codes. It socially defines a group of people, binds them to one another, and gives them a sense that they have common characters.

1.1.1 Two Types of Culture

Culture consists of material culture and immaterial culture. The concept of material culture covers the physical expressions of culture, such as technology, architecture, art, etc., whereas the immaterial aspects of culture include principles of social organization, mythology, philosophy, literature, etc., all of which make up the intangible cultural heritage of a society (Macionis & Gerber, 2011).

Material culture is the physical evidence of a culture in the objects or architecture they make or have made. It refers to the touchable, material "things" that a culture produces—physical objects that can be seen, held, felt or used, examples of which are shown in Figure 1.1. Examining the tools and technology of a culture can tell us a lot about its examples of history and people's way of living.

The Classic of Rites, one of the "Five Classics of Confucianism"

Venus de Milo on display in the Louvre

A fake mask of the Punu Tribe, Gabon, West Africa

Figure 1.1   Examples of Material Culture

Immaterial culture, or non-material culture, is the thoughts or ideas that make up a culture. They do not include any physical objects or artifacts. Any ideas, beliefs, values, or norms that may help shape a society can be defined as immaterial culture.

1.1.2 Five Dimensions of Culture

Although culture is a complex and vague concept which is very hard to define, we can approach the study of culture through five different dimensions.

1. Culture as Heritage

Heritage is the most typical symbol of culture. For example, the Great Wall and the Imperial Palace are the symbols of Chinese culture, while the London Bridge represents British culture, and the Statue of Liberty stands for American culture.

2. Culture as Product

Product is also culture. For example, silk and Chinese paintings represent

Chinese culture, while KFC (Kentucky Fried Chicken) and Hollywood movies symbolize American culture.

3. Culture as Behavior

People's behavior often reflects their culture. For example, Chinese people often shake hands or pat on the shoulder when meeting their friends; Japanese people bow a lot; American people are more likely to hug; and the French are fond of kissing their friends on the cheeks.

4. Culture as Relation

Culture is also deeply rooted in people's relations to each other and to oneself. For example, Chinese people are in favor of relationships with close social distance, while Westerners tend to enjoy more privacy.

5. Culture as Value

Culture is also embedded in people's values or beliefs, such as Confucianism and Taoism for Chinese people, Christianity for most Westerners, and Islam for people from Islamic countries.

In a word, heritage, product, behavior, relation, and value represent specific cultural phenomena and they have their distinctive features which make them different from each other. Thanks to those differences, we have culture diversity which makes our world more colorful.

Case Study: The Culture of Shaoxing

In this case, what can be taken as the heritage, product, behavior, relation, and value of Shaoxing?

Shaoxing is a city in Zhejiang, near Shanghai and Hangzhou, famous for its traditional Chinese bridges, boats, architecture, yellow rice wine and a huge number of textile and cloth factories. With a history of thousands of years, the city is well-known for the abundant tourism resources, including cultural relics like the Mausoleum of Yu the Great（大禹陵）and many residences of famous figures in Chinese history. These historical attractions and residences, including Anchang Ancient Town（安昌古镇）with old streets and bridges, add much charm to this city. It is recognized as one of the famous historical and cultural cities in the country. Moreover, as a city to the south of the Yangtze Delta, the natural scenery here is totally charming and varied with a beautiful landscape of numerous green hills and clean waters. Shaoxing is sometimes called the "Oriental Venice" (东方威尼斯). People live by the water, with the water, and love the water. In the parks, the tune of Shaoxing Opera can be heard now and then.

Shaoxing is also known variously as the "City of Bridges", "City of Calligraphy", and "City of Scholars". The most well-known historical and cultural figures are Yu the Great, Goujian, and Lu Xun. Yu the Great is an ancient hero in prehistoric times, whose most remarkable accomplishment was taming the flood. Goujian was the king of the Yue Kingdom in ancient China who endured self-imposed hardships to realize his ambition. Lu Xun is a well-known writer with his famous words "Fierce-browed, I coolly defy a thousand pointing fingers; head-bowed, like a willing ox I serve the people." Shaoxing has its unique cuisine like Huixiang beans and stinky toufu. People there prefer yellow rice wine than other kinds of wine and they also have unique personalities. Nowadays, they still keep traditional customs like the sacrificial ceremony of Yu the Great, attaching great importance to their ancestors and families. When you live there and get along with its people, you will soon know the difference.

We can have a glimpse of Shaoxing's culture from the five dimensions of culture. The Mausoleum of Yu the Great and Anchang Ancient Town are Shaoxing's heritages. The city's representative products are the yellow rice wine, Huixiang beans, and stinky toufu. People of Shaoxing have unique behaviors such as drinking yellow rice wine and appreciating Shaoxing Opera. They attach great importance to their ancestors and families. This fact can be taken as relation. The spirits of Yu the Great, Goujian, and Lu Xun are examples of culture as value.

Your hometown has its own culture. Now it's your turn to list all the things that you think can be described as the form of the culture. Try to group them according to the five dimensions of culture.

1.1.3 Characteristics of Culture

1. Culture Is Everywhere and Nowhere

Culture is a convenient abstraction, like some well-known concepts, such as gravity in physics. We never see gravity, yet we see things falling in regular ways.

Similarly, although culture is everywhere, nothing or nobody alone is sufficient for catching its full picture. We can only feel it, recognize it, experience it, learn it or create it in various ways.

2. Culture Can Be Both Tangible and Intangible

Most of material culture such as architecture, paintings, is tangible, which can be easily seen, felt, or noticed, while the immaterial culture like religion or literature is intangible. Tangible cultural heritages are physical places or objects we can touch, like Mount Tai or West Lake. Intangible cultural heritages include:

1) oral traditions and expressions, like languages;

2) social practices, rituals and festive events, like the Spring Festival;

3) performing arts, like folk songs, Peking Opera, or lion dancing;

4) knowledge and practices concerning nature and universe, like the traditional Chinese medicine (TCM) or acupuncture (针灸);

5) traditional craftsmanship, like paper cutting or embroidery (刺绣).

3. Culture Can Be Both Static and Dynamic

Some symbols of culture can be kept for a very long time. For example, traditional Chinese culture advocates such moralities as benevolence, righteousness, courtesy, wisdom, and trust. As time flies, Chinese culture has also developed and integrated with other cultures in some aspects. More and more young people celebrate Western holidays such as Valentine's Day and Christmas. Another example is that German people today generally seem eager to adopt new words from other languages, especially from American English, while many French people are resistant to it for fear of "corrupting" their own language.

4. Culture Can Be High or Popular

High culture means it can be shared by the upper class of the society. On the other hand, popular culture is the subculture shared by everyone or the mass of the society. Take music as an example. Rock and roll and rap are regarded as popular music, while classical music and symphony belong to high culture.

5. Culture Can Be Material or Spiritual

The food products such as McDonald's and sushi are one of the symbols of American culture and Japanese culture respectively. The Hollywood movies and

Bushido (武士道) spirit can also embody American culture and Japanese culture separately.

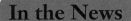 

In the News

As this article illustrates, Hanfu is not just a piece of clothing, but an expression of the national spirit and cultural heritage. The return of Hanfu shows that culture can be both static and dynamic.

Hanfu Connects People with Traditional Cultural Roots

As more and more young people are wearing *Hanfu*, the traditional clothing of the Han ethnic group, industries of *Hanfu* manufacturing and traditional Chinese culture thrive.

Ran Dan is a huge fan of *Hanfu* in Beijing. "I started to know *Hanfu* in 2011 when I accidentally saw some *Hanfu* photos and was completely stunned by its beauty. Soon I had my first set of *Hanfu*. At present, I have more than 50 sets of *Hanfu*, and over 80 single pieces," Ran shared her fascination with *Hanfu*.

Unlike other people who wear traditional ethnic clothing on special occasions, however, Ran wears *Hanfu* on a daily basis.

"Many people think *Hanfu* is inconvenient in daily life. In fact, there are many styles of *Hanfu*. Wide and long sleeved *Hanfu* may not be convenient, but narrow sleeved ones will not affect work at all," she said.

So far, the *Hanfu* market is estimated to have more than two million consumers across China, and the total market value of the sector has reached around 1.09 billion yuan (US$ 154 million).

With the increased popularity, stores renting *Hanfu* rose rapidly. From April to August this year, the number of *Hanfu* rental stores in Beijing increased from 3 to more than 20, as media reported. In addition, online sales of *Hanfu* surged

by 146% year on year and sales of traditional Chinese style creative jewelry increased by 94% year on year, according to an e-commerce platform.

"Students are the largest group of customers of *Hanfu* across China, but we also target adults as our customers," said Dao Ding, who runs an online *Hanfu* store which has cooperated with more than 20 brick-and-mortar stores and has 45,000 fans on media video app Douyin.

Female customers dominate the *Hanfu* market, said Dao Ding, adding that the male to female ratio of its customers was 1:5.

Overseas students and ethnic Chinese are also *Hanfu* lovers. "Overseas students have a deep national and cultural identity with the motherland as they live in a foreign country," Dao Ding explained.

In addition, many people had a deeper understanding of traditional culture through *Hanfu*, said Dao Ding.

When promoting *Hanfu*, traditional culture promotion and inheritance are also promoted. This is also what many *Hanfu* cultural associations have been doing.

Hanfu Beijing, a *Hanfu* association in Beijing, is among them. Established in 2009, the association is the largest and longest existing *Hanfu* cultural association in Beijing, with 600 registered members.

Associations like Hanfu Beijing have organized a variety of activities, including traditional festival activities, publicity performances, etiquette activities and internal training activities.

"*Hanfu* is a part of traditional culture that cannot be ignored. The return of *Hanfu* that we advocate is not about calling on people to wear *Hanfu* and live the life of the ancients. We expect more people to explore the cultural significance behind *Hanfu*," Ran explained.

"*Hanfu* is not just a piece of clothing, but an expression of the national spirit and cultural heritage. We believed *Hanfu* is more than a decoration for external beauty; more importantly, it enriches our minds," said the person in charge at Hanfu Beijing.

1.2 Culture and Communication

1.2.1 Defining and Describing Communication

As we come in contact with people from cultures different from our own—in our neighborhoods, schools, or workplaces—we begin to understand communication as a transactional process. Viewing communication as a transactional process means that we develop a mutually dependent relationship by exchanging symbols.

This definition suggests several facts about communication. First, communication is a process. As such, it is symbolic, continuous, irreversible, and unrepeatable. We'll examine each of these one by one.

Communication is symbolic—we use symbols (verbal and nonverbal) to stand for things. For example, the word "chair" stands for, or symbolizes, something we sit on. It is not the actual chair. Also, one symbol may have many meanings. When someone says "chair", does he or she mean a beach chair, an easy chair, or a rocking chair? This leads to an important truth about communication: Meanings are in people, not in words. Put it another way, words do not have meanings, people make them do. We use symbols—words and behavior—to create meanings. In order for us to communicate effectively, we must have common meanings for these symbols. Otherwise, it will cause many troubles in our daily life.

Imagine how difficult communication becomes when people from different cultures come together. Not only are their languages different, but the same gesture can mean different things. The meaning of patting a child on the head in the United States is a gesture of affection. But in Thailand, this action might damage the spirit of the child, because people in Thailand believe that the spirit of a person lives in his or her head.

Communication is not only symbolic, but also a process which has no beginning or end. In other words, it is continuous. All the communication we have done affects the communication we are engaged in right now. For example, when we meet with a new teacher, even if we have never met each other at the beginning of the course, all our previous experience of communicating with other teachers and the teacher's experience with other students affect the communication between the two of us. And when we see him or her, our clothes, hairstyle, facial expression, tone of voice,

and so on, all communicate. Thus nonverbal symbols as well as verbal symbols communicate.

In addition to being continuous, the communication process is also irreversible and unrepeatable. Once we have said or done something, we cannot take it back. If we hurt our friend's feelings, we can say that we are sorry, but we can't unsay what we have said or undo what we have done. This fact reminds each of us to think carefully about what we communicate. We can't go back. We can say the same thing over and over again, but that does not mean communication is repeatable. Time has passed and we have said it before. So saying it again does not repeat the exact same communication.

Second, the fact that communication is a transactional process means participants are both the source and the receiver of the message at the same time. As we send messages, we are also receiving them from the other and interpreting them and sending messages back to him or her. He or she is doing the same. We are not in a ping-pong game in which we sometimes send the ball, wait for the other to return it to us, and then hit it back again to him or her. Actually, we are receiving ping-pong balls from him or her at the same time—the voice tone, the words, the facial expression of him or her, and so on. And he or she, of course, is doing likewise. We don't just stand waiting for the ping-pong ball to reach us. We are sending various types of messages to the other as we receive them from him or her.

The third characteristic of communication is that it has both a content component and a relationship component. The content component is the information expressed while the relationship component suggests how the information should be interpreted in terms of the relationship between the participants of the communication. If a man says "I love you!" to a woman in a loving tone, the relationship message of the content is that he cares for her. But if he says the same content in a sarcastic tone, the relationship message shows that he doesn't really care about her. In general, the content message is verbal and the relationship message is nonverbal.

1.2.2 Relationship Between Culture and Communication

The relationship between culture and communication is complex and interrelated. In short, all communication happens within some culture; they act on one another. It can be explained from three aspects.

First, culture affects our verbal language. For example, in English, we have one word for "you"; in German, "du" is the form of "you"; in China, we say "ni" or "nin" for "you".

Second, nonverbal language is also affected by culture. For example, for European Americans, standing close to someone signals close or warm friendship; while in Middle Eastern cultures, standing close does not necessarily mean warm friendship.

Third, culture affects our identity. For example, in Chinese culture, mother's father is called *Waigong*, and father's father is called *Yeye*. Grandchildren are called differently: A son's daughter is *Sunnü*, and a daughter's daughter is *Waisunnü*. Because of the importance of relationship in terms of the different ranks or levels of Chinese culture, how each member is addressed shows his or her role and status in the family.

All in all, communication is the carrier of culture and thus influences the structure of culture. In turn, culture is demonstrated in our communication since culture tells us how we should talk and behave appropriately. Thus, culture is affected by and affects communication.

When we consider our world from this perspective, the need for acceptance, understanding, and education becomes obvious.

For Your Information

Chinese Names

The full name of a Han Chinese is composed of two parts: the surname and the given name, while the opposite of the arrangement of names is widely practiced in many other countries outside Asia.

Today, there are more than 8,000 Chinese surnames, of which 3,000 surnames are used by the Han Chinese. Among these names, *Li*, *Wang*, and *Zhang* are the most commonly heard, given to millions of Chinese.

The surname is generally composed of one character or syllable, such as *Zhang*, *Wang*, *Li*, or *Zhao*, among which *Li* is the most popular. There are also two-syllable surnames, or compound surnames, such as *Ouyang* (欧阳), *Zhuge* (诸葛), *Sima* (司马), and *Gongsun* (公孙).

A given name usually has two words but also can have just one syllable. A full Chinese name always has two or three characters, but sometimes it can also have four if there is both a compound surname and a two-syllable given name.

Since ancient times, a full name with a one-syllable surname and a two-syllable given name has been the norm in China.

Traditionally, a Chinese surname is often passed down through the father, and Chinese women always retain their family name even after marriage.

Case Study: "Yes" Is Not the Answer

There are some questions to help us analyze this case:

(1) What happened in this case?
(2) What's the reason?
(3) How should we solve the problem?

Some years ago, I went to the Philippines to organize an international meeting. The people responsible for the organization were four Europeans (from Italy and Switzerland). We worked together with some people coming from Manila. At the international meeting, about 300 people arrived from all continents. We had a meeting with the local members of the staff. We looked at the program of the meeting together, and we organized some logistical aspects (we had another meeting previously). After that, each one of us left the session with something to do. The staff from the Philippines had something to prepare for the following day. During the session, they were very kind and always answered "yes" to all our questions (they smiled all the time).

The following day, we waited for the Philippines' staff and their work. They came but they had not prepared their part of work. We could not understand. So we repeated to them all the details, and we asked them to bring us the work (what they had to do) in the afternoon. Unfortunately, in the afternoon the Filipinos came but, once again, they had not prepared the job. It was strange, and some of us became nervous. What happened to these people? They looked very kind but they did "nothing" at all. They answered "yes" but they brought us nothing.

The day after we had a meeting with them. We said very kindly that it was impossible to work for and advance the international meeting without their local help. The meeting, 300 people, needed the Philippines' staff to be efficient. But they were not. We brought them some examples: When we needed a computer and we asked for it "as quickly as possible", they answered "yes", but the day after we were still waiting for the same computer.

During this meeting, there was a typical tension between the European organizers and the Philippines' staff. It was logical for the organizers to receive what they had requested. It was not logical for the staff. The European organizers found the Philippines' staff very unprofessional people, while the staff found the organizers very nervous people.

As mentioned above, all communication happens within some culture, and they act on one another. In the Philippines, "yes" was a certain type of kind answer (as for OK), but it did not mean "OK, I will do it", "I do it now", or "I have it". Another problem was about "time". Filipinos took their time and were never on time; they did all things without stress. It was their style of life, not Europeans'. So the tension appeared.

In order to solve the problem, the European organizers can change the timing, the appointments (fewer meetings during the day). They can change the breaks (longer than before). Taking a long break sometimes is an occasion to solve a problem, to discuss an idea, to find a solution. It is a different way to manage a meeting like that.

The case above is just one example of the impact of cultural differences on intercultural communication. There are numerous other examples. For example, the surname comes after the given name in English. If a person's name is "Will Smith", "Smith" is the surname and "Will" is the given name. On the contrary, the given name usually comes after the surname in China.

Now it's your turn to brainstorm some different expressions in English and Chinese, and think about the reasons for them.

1.3 Defining and Describing Intercultural Communication

1.3.1 Definition of Intercultural Communication

Intercultural communication is a field of study that looks at how people from different cultural backgrounds try to communicate with each other. Culture decides

how individuals encode messages, what kind of medium they choose to transmit them, and the way messages are decoded or interpreted. Every nation has its own characteristics. It's mainly through its culture that we first begin to know the nation and its characteristics. So we cannot say that this culture or custom is right and that is wrong. Equal respect should be attached to every culture in the world, even to those that are not in existence any longer.

The world is becoming smaller and smaller. More and more foreigners come and go around us every day. When we are in the same country, the same city, or even the same neighborhood, cultural collision is expected to be more serious. If we want to avoid this situation, one important thing is to get some basic knowledge about other cultures so as not to misunderstand some actions or habits of the foreigners. On the other hand, people nowadays are more likely to go overseas for experiencing culture diversity. They can broaden their horizons and develop themselves for all kinds of reasons. Especially, with current process of globalization, people who own different perspectives on cultures stand at a more competitive position in the world. If they can combine positive culture elements from different cultures for their self-development, it would be a competitive advantage in their future career.

1.3.2 Five Elements in the Communication Process

Normally, the communication process involves five interrelated elements: the context of the communication, the participants, the messages being communicated, the channels through which the communication occurs, and the verbal and nonverbal responses known as feedback.

1. Context

Context refers to the conditions which make up communication, including physical, historical, psychological, and cultural conditions. As the saying goes, "When in Rome, do as Romans do." In other words, following the communication norms of the context is the first priority for any successful intercultural communication. For example, when greeting someone for the first time, we often shake hands with each other in China, while we need to put our palms together in Thailand, as shown in Figure 1.2.

In China

In Thailand

Figure 1.2 Greetings in China and Thailand

2. Participants

Participants refer to the senders and receivers of messages during the communication process, especially for face-to-face communication. As senders, we form messages and attempt to communicate them to others through verbal and nonverbal symbols. As receivers, we process the messages sent to us and react to them verbally and nonverbally.

Three important variables related to participants may affect communication: relationship, gender, and culture. Undoubtedly, cultural difference is a major barrier in intercultural communication, but we should not neglect the other two variables. For example, males and females can sometimes experience difficulty sharing meaning because they approach the world with different perspectives. For another example, people often behave differently in workplace relationships and in family relationships.

3. Messages

Communication takes place through the sending and receiving of messages. Messages include the elements of meanings, symbols, encoding, and decoding. The meanings can be transferred or shared with others through messages comprising verbal and nonverbal symbols. The encoding and decoding processes include nonverbal cues, which significantly affect the meaning created by the participants in a communication transaction. Conflicting meanings are created when the verbal symbols are contradicted with the nonverbal cues. For example, if a foreign customer says "Yes, I'm very interested in your products", the meaning we decode will be very different if the person leans forward and looks interested or yawns and looks away.

4. Channels

Messages are transmitted through a variety of sensory channels. We may use

sound, sight, smell, taste, touch, or any combination of these to carry a message. Face-to-face communication has two basic channels: sound (verbal symbol) and sight (nonverbal cue). However, people can communicate by any of the five sensory channels. A fragrant scent or a warm hug may contribute as much to meaning as what is seen or heard. Some channels are more effective in communicating certain messages than others, and the nature of the channel selected affects the way a message will be processed. For example, what kind of message do we get from someone who comes to a business meeting wearing a T-shirt and jeans?

5. Feedback

As receivers attempt to decode the meanings of messages, they are likely to give some kind of verbal or nonverbal response. This response, called feedback, tells the sender whether the message has been heard, seen, or understood. If the feedback tells the sender that the communication was not received or was misinterpreted, the person can send the message again, perhaps in a different way, until the listener receives the meaning the sender intends to convey. For example, when we greet a friend on a noisy street by waving our hands but fail to get his or her attention, we can call his or her name loudly instead. In the case of intercultural communication, if we have to do some shopping in a foreign country and the shop assistant does not understand our language, we can simply point to the goods we want.

Case Study: Attitude to Politics

We can approach this case from these questions:

(1) In this case, what are the context, participants, and channels?
(2) Are there any problems in encoding and decoding messages for Nastya? What are they?
(3) What is the feedback of Mr. N? How should we treat this kind of feedback?

It was Nastya's first coming to France. The purpose of her stay in Metz is a two-month internship at the Faculty of Humanities, Arts and Culture of the University of Lorraine (Université de Lorraine). Before the trip, Nastya had a choice—to live in a hotel or a family. At last, she decided to stay in a family, because she would have a much higher level of French if she had to constantly communicate on various topics with native speakers.

The arrival in Metz was quite good. Nastya was met at the railway station by the head of the host family, Mr. N. There were no problems in communication during the first few days. On weekends, Nastya and the family members walked a lot around the city. During conversations the topics raised were on culture, art, nature of Russia and France, the sights of the capitals of the two states. Nastya talked about the university, where she studied in Moscow, and she also shared her plans for the future.

Difficulties in communication began later. Nastya wanted to ask Mr. N about his attitude towards the politics and economy of his country. To start the conversation, she decided to share her thoughts on the difficulties of Russian economic development. Wishing to draw attention to the issue under discussion, she criticized the European Union's sanctions policy in general and France in particular in relation to Russia. Mr. N did not support the topic of the conversation. He refused to continue it, saying that this topic did not interest him and he was not going to discuss it with a foreigner. Nastya lost her temper and did not return to the topic.

From that moment on, there was no need to dream about getting close with the family members. Nastya spent all her days at the university, trying to spend as little time as possible in the house. She regretted that she had not stayed at the hotel. It seemed to her that in an environment that has so many youths, communicating with those from other countries who came, like her, to an internship in Metz, it would have been easier for her to discuss topics related to international events. (From Intercultural Content of a Foreign Language Fexbooks. Concept, Texts, Practices, by Tareva et al., 2017)

Apparently, this case is full of mutual misunderstanding and rejection of representatives of different cultures in life circumstances. As we know, the communication process involves five interrelated elements. When we communicate with others, we should pay attention to the physical, historical, psychological, and cultural contexts. In this case, Nastya should not neglect that she lives in a host family in France which is one of the members of the European Union. She should have noticed that the cultural and historical contexts are different in France and Russia. Also, she should have taken the participants into consideration. Mr. N is the head of the host family and he is a French. Criticizing the host's nation is not a good idea, even if her intention is to discuss issues. Thirdly, there is a problem in the process of encoding and decoding messages. When the European Union's sanctions policy is mentioned after the difficulties of Russian economic development, it is natural that Mr. N takes it as a kind of blame and feels offended. Feedback is another element we should pay attention to. When Mr. N refuses to continue the topic, he has sent negative feedback

to Nastya. Maybe the best thing for Nastya to do is to say "sorry" rather than losing temper.

If you were Nastya, what would you do to solve this problem? Try to write a letter to Mr. N. Here are some suggestions for you:

- Show your appreciation to Mr. N for the help he provided;
- Make an apology for what happened that day;
- Show your willingness to know more about the family and the country, etc.

Summary

The first question we should ask ourselves while studying this course is: What is intercultural communication? It is a field of study that looks at how people from different cultural backgrounds try to communicate with each other. Then here comes the next question: What is culture? It consists of material culture and immaterial culture. Material culture is the physical evidence of a culture in the objects and architecture while immaterial culture, or non-material culture, is the thoughts or ideas that make up a culture. They do not include any physical objects or artifacts. Culture is everywhere and nowhere, tangible and intangible, static and dynamic, high or popular, material or spiritual. However, we can still approach the study of culture through five different dimensions: culture as heritage, culture as product, culture as behavior, culture as relation, and culture as value. Successful intercultural communication involves five elements: context, participants, messages, channels, and feedback. If we know these characteristics, approaches, and elements involved in the process of intercultural communication, the cultural gap would not be the obstacle to the civilization of human beings. It ought to be the motivation of us for going farther.

Exercises

Questions for Review

1. What are the five elements in the communication process?

2. What are the characteristics of communication?

3. What is the relationship between culture and communication?

4. What are the five dimensions of culture?

5. What are the characteristics of culture?

Problems and Application

1. Identify the examples of five dimensions of culture in two movies, for example, *Armageddon* (《陨石大冲撞》) and *The Wondering Earth* (《流浪地球》). And compare the differences between Chinese culture and the culture of another country. You can take the table below as an example.

Five Dimensions of Culture	Heritage	Product	Behavior	Relation	Value
Chinese Culture	The Great Wall; Peking Opera	Chinese paintings; silk	shaking hands	close social distance	Confucianism; Daoism
Japanese Culture	geisha girl (艺妓); sumo (相扑)	sushi; sake (清酒)	bowing	close social distance	Shinto (神道教); Bushido

2. Try to analyze the following case with the knowledge of the five elements in the communication process.

Invitation by a Stranger

In January, I attended a course on racism that bore the title "Fighting Against Racism in Switzerland" supported by the Swiss government. During the lunch break, which we spent in a nearby restaurant, I was sitting near a young man from Chad (乍得) who had already been living in Switzerland for several years. When it was time to pay for our meals, this person paid for my drink. Quite spontaneously, I reached for my wallet with the intention to pay him back but he refused and stopped me with a brisk gesture that betrayed some kind of anger from his part. Even if it was just a bottle of mineral water, I didn't feel right to let him pay for me.

This state of affairs made me feel awkward and strengthened my determination to pay him back; so during the coffee break I offered him a cappuccino but it was obvious by then that he was a little bit upset if not offended. I started to talk about this misunderstanding openly, in a very carefree manner, in order to shed some light on this communicative dilemma. He told me that Europeans are a bit too cold and detached and

shouldn't be so formal. I explained to him that I couldn't avoid feeling bad and the desire to pay him back stemmed from a natural social reflex, which made me feel that I should do it to be polite.

The fact that he was an immigrant certainly didn't help; this led me to question his financial situation: His paying for me had produced some kind of guilt in me at the time. Also, my social background, or my personal approach to situations in general, had produced a sense of awkwardness in me because we hadn't spoken that much prior to the incident. Although I would normally accept this gesture from a friend or a close acquaintance, I couldn't do the same with a perfect stranger. In describing this situation, I am possibly understanding it better: The young man just wanted to show his sympathy and his gesture was just part of his desire to start a new friendship. I reacted following my social code and ended up misunderstanding the young man's intention.

Chapter 2

Verbal and Nonverbal Communication

Learning Objectives

After learning this chapter, you should be able to:

1. define verbal and nonverbal communication;

2. compare and contrast verbal and nonverbal communication;

3. supply examples of major types and functions of nonverbal communication;

4. identify and employ strategies to help interpret verbal and nonverbal messages.

How can you address a stranger properly? Why do some people like to move their hands when talking on the phone? If someone avoids eye contact while talking, is this person lying to you? To answer all these questions, we must know the concepts of verbal and nonverbal communication.

When talking about communication, we would probably immediately think of verbal communication, namely the words that we say to express information. While verbal communication is important, humans had relied on wordless cues for thousands of years before developing the capability to communicate with words. Think about how we cannot help doing gestures when having a conversation on the phone even though the other person cannot see us. The fact that nonverbal communication is processed by another part of our brain makes it more instinctual and involuntary than verbal communication. Instead of taking nonverbal communication as the opposite or separate topic of verbal communication, it's more accurate to view them as operating side by side—as part of the same system. However, they still have significant differences. One of the most important ones is that there are grammar rules that structure our verbal communication, but no such official guides exist to govern our use of nonverbal signals. Likewise, there are no dictionaries and thesauruses of nonverbal communication as there are of verbal symbols. That is why nonverbal communication can be ambiguous sometimes and relies very much on context. These are some characteristics that differentiate verbal communication from nonverbal communication. In this chapter, we will discuss in greater detail the functions and major types of nonverbal communication before concluding with some guidelines on how to improve some aspects of our communicative competence.

2.1 Introduction to Verbal Communication

Communication is the act of conveying intended meanings from one entity or group to another through the use of mutually understood signs and semiotic rules. The act of communication among human beings has been subject to consistent evolution and upgradation from time to time. In prehistoric times, people used to communicate with their fellow beings through grunts, barks, and roars just like animals. But gradually they developed an elaborate set of sounds to express their feelings and convey their messages. Now it is the systematic use of language that differentiates human beings from animals. Only human beings have been blessed with the gift of language.

The languages used by human beings do differ from other codes used by them to communicate among themselves. Human language has the properties of recursiveness and creativity which suggest that there are signals within signals but each signal has its own significance. In any language, with a definite set of graphic symbols and their corresponding phonological symbols it is possible to form and communicate an infinite number of messages.

2.1.1 Role of Language in Verbal Communication

Because of the various functions it can perform, language has a great role in communication. Whatever codes we use to convey our message within a fixed frame of reference in a given language, it serves different functions. The basic functions of language can be grouped into three categories: descriptive, expressive, and social.

1. Descriptive Function

Under descriptive function, we can include travel log (description of places), biography, autobiography, and writing about other people, diary and personal letters, and technical and scientific works. We can also include the verbal description of people, places, and things under this function. While attempting descriptive writing or speaking, it is essential that the writer or speaker has obtained all necessary information about the object of writing or speaking.

2. Expressive Function

Under expressive function, we have interjections, exclamations, and special words and phrases for emphasis. Using interjections, we can express satisfaction, excitement, surprise, pain, hurt or disgust. In order to lay emphasis, we either use a word with a stress or an extra word or phrase to add emphasis (e.g., You have never been fair to us at all.). We also use question tags, rhetorical questions, auxiliary "do" or fronted negation (Starting a sentence with a negative word, e.g., Never have I seen a fool like you.) to put emphasis on a statement or a particular idea.

3. Social Function

Under social function, we have examples like greeting people; bidding farewell to people; giving a command or order; asking a question; making a request;

advising; offering a suggestion; expressing agreement or disagreement; accepting or declining an invitation; expressing wishes, thanks, apologies, regrets, condolences, etc.; sending seasonal greetings; offering help; giving instructions; expressing obligation, certainty, etc. Under each function, we have multiple sub-functions. For example, under the function of "request", we have "request for permission", "request for help", "formal request", "informal request", etc. When we choose a particular language function, we need to use the code that is appropriate for that function. The words, structures, and sentences used to perform a particular function do differ from those used to perform another function. While expressing a polite request, for instance, we use "could" or "would" whereas for formal requests we use "may" and for making informal requests we use either "can" or "will".

The word order in an assertive sentence is different from an interrogative or an imperative sentence. In an assertive sentence we follow the normal sentence pattern (e.g., Rahim is a sincere boy.), but in an interrogative sentence we have an inverse order (e.g., Is Rahim a sincere boy?), and in an imperative sentence we do not have a visible subject (e.g., Do this work at this moment.). Likewise, for sentences expressing suggestions we have quite different structures (e.g., Why don't you go to the police station? How about joining a new party next week? Let's have a picnic at this weekend. You had better consult a doctor.).

One more important point should be noted in regard to the use of language for communication. The language we use should be simple enough for the receiver to understand the intended message but at the same time it should not be jerky. Too many short and simple sentences in a passage also spoil its beauty. If we use long and complex sentences packed with a lot of ideas, the receiver/addressee will be confused and the message will not be properly transmitted. Therefore, the best way is to maintain a balance between the two. Short sentences connected with suitable connectors impart clarity, conciseness, and grace to a passage and make it worth reading/listening.

While performing a particular language function, we actually have a purpose in our mind. In order to see the purpose turned into action, we need to use the words, structures, and sentences that are grammatically correct, socially acceptable and meaningful. Moreover, we must try to understand whether the receiver has the same competence as us to receive the message, process it, understand the importance inherent in it and wherever possible, provide the necessary feedback to us regarding the effectiveness of the message being transmitted.

2.1.2 Receptive and Productive Language Skills

Within a linguistic community, one is said to be a successful communicator if he or she has mastered the basic language skills, the receptive and productive skills required to make effective use of a language for performing different activities and satisfying various purposes. Under receptive skills we have the listening and reading skills whereas under productive skills we have speaking and writing skills. To be a good communicator, one should be able to have a balanced knowledge of both the receptive and productive skills. Unless we are able to listen to people with patience, we won't be good speakers. In order to speak well, we must listen to how individual words are pronounced, how sentences are pronounced with proper pauses and what tonal modulations are adopted in long speeches. These skills help us speak the words and sentences with proper accent, stress, and intonation, and make our speech intelligible to others. Not only this, listening to great people also helps us pick out the important ideas in the talk and filter out the irrelevant ones. Similarly, if we are not able to read well, we will not be able to write well. All good writers are voracious readers. Reading new books helps us get new ideas and understand unique and attractive ways of presenting old ideas and integrating the new and old to bring out the best.

The receptive skills and the productive skills are interdependent. It is a general assumption among people that unless one is a good speaker of a language, he or she cannot be a good communicator. But speaking skills are just one fourth of the set of skills required for the use of language for both personal and professional communication. Listening skills, reading skills and writing skills are equally important. In order to communicate properly, we should be able to use the language automatically in response to the needs of various contexts. This linguistic behavior is conditioned by the context where we are communicating with others to connect to them. While talking or writing to our relatives or friends, we follow the rules of language but we are relaxed and do not bother to be polite. But when talking or writing to our officers in the office, teachers at school, and other people on official occasions, we try to be as formal and polite as possible so as not to offend them. The former situation is informal and the latter is formal.

2.1.3 Need for Using Bias-Free Language

Being sensitive to the context is not the whole thing. We also need to be aware of the biases we might be susceptible to. When the act of communication is being transacted within a community, there is little chance of the message being misinterpreted or misunderstood. On the other hand, in case of inter-community or intercultural communication, there might be interruption in the transmission of the message due to class/caste-based bias, racial/ethnic bias, disability bias or gender bias, etc., which are called socio-cultural biases. Being the citizens of an open and globalized world, we should be sensitive to the issues that affect the lives of common people. Both in spoken and written communication we should avoid words and expressions that may hurt people belonging to a certain gender, caste, class, religion, race, or ethnicity. It is always wise to use neutral language that does not favor a particular community at the cost of another. Instead of saying "salesman" or "saleswoman", it is better for us to use "salesperson" which includes people from both genders. Likewise, it is better to use the phrase "all communities" than "people belonging to the scheduled caste, scheduled tribe, general and other backward categories". Nowadays, a new trend has started coming up. We have started using the word "actor" to mean both the "actor" and the "actress". It is heinous to call people by the disabilities they suffer from. If we call someone blind, we directly attack his or her disability and remind him or her of the pain that he or she has been suffering from. But if we call the same person "visually challenged", we just hint at his or her disability but with a lot of respect, in a more polite and mild tone. In the same manner, we can use "hearing impaired" for the deaf people, "speech impaired" for the dumb people and "differently-abled" for the physically handicapped people.

2.1.4 Types of Verbal Communication

By verbal communication, we mean the type of communication that is rooted in language. Verbal communication among human beings is possible at both the spoken level and the written level and it is possible through different formats.

Some people believe oral communication is more effective for its several important features. It has to be candid, clear, complete, concise, concrete, correct, and courteous. It is useful because it saves time and money and it is more forceful than other modes of communication. With oral communication, it is possible to convey different shades of meaning; the listener can get immediate clarification from the speaker and the speaker can get immediate feedback from the listener. It can be effective in both face-to-face communication and public interactions or public speaking.

The disadvantages of oral communication often reduce its effectiveness. It is not possible to connect to distant people without the aid of technical devices. It is not possible to transmit long messages through oral communication. If it is not being recorded on any technical device like a tape recorder or video recorder, it is not easy to reproduce the oral communication between two persons as evidence. That's why it does not have legal validity as people can keep on changing their oral versions from time to time.

Hall (1976) claimed that human interaction can generally be divided into low-context communication (LCC) and high-context communication (HCC). In low-context communication, the emphasis is on how intention or meaning is expressed through explicit verbal messages. In high-context communication, the emphasis is on how intention or meaning can best be conveyed through the embedded contexts (e.g., social roles or positions, types of relationship, intergroup history) and the nonverbal channels (e.g., pauses, silence, tone of voice) of the verbal message.

In general, LCC refers to the communication pattern characterized by a direct verbal style, matter-of-fact tone, transparency, assertiveness, and sender-oriented values (i.e., the sender assumes the responsibility to communicate clearly). In the LCC system, the speaker is expected to be responsible for constructing a clear, persuasive message that the listener can decode easily. The value priority in the LCC system is saying what you mean and meaning what you say as a mode of respect for verbal honesty and personal accountability. In comparison, HCC refers to the communication pattern characterized by an indirect verbal style, tactful nonverbal tone, diplomatic talk, self-humbling speech, and receiver-sensitive values (i.e., the interpreter of the message assumes the responsibility to infer the hidden or contextual meanings of the message). In the HCC system, the listener or interpreter of the message is expected to "read between the lines" and infer the nonverbal subtleties that accompany the verbal message. The value priority in the HCC system is not saying anything that will hurt the other's feelings as a mode of interpersonal sensitivity for other-centric consideration.

Case Study: Need a Ride?

Read the two conversations below and think about the two questions:

(1) What's the difference between these two conversations?

(2) What's the reason for the difference?

Conversation One

Alaine: We're going to the Orange Bowl in Miami this weekend.

Patrick: What fun! I wish I were going to the game with you. How long are you going to be there? [If she wants a ride, she will ask.]

Alaine: Three days. By the way, we may need a ride to the airport. Do you think you can take us?

Patrick: Sure. What time?

Alaine: 10:30 p.m. this coming Saturday.

Patrick: All right. No problem.

Conversation Two

Essie: We're going to the Orange Bowl in Miami this weekend.

Daniela: What fun! I wish I were going to the game with you. How long are you going to be there?

Essie: Three days. [I hope she'll offer me a ride to the airport.]

Daniela: [She may want me to give her a ride.] Do you need a ride to the airport? I'll take you.

Essie: Are you sure it's not too much trouble?

Daniela: It's no trouble at all.

The first conversation happens between two Irish Americans and the second two Latinos. They have different verbal patterns.

In the Latina conversation, requests for help are likely to be implied rather than stated explicitly and directly. Indirect requests can help both parties to save face and uphold smooth harmonious interaction. When Daniela detects a request during a conversation with Essie, she can choose to offer help, pretend she does not understand the request, or apologize that she cannot take Essie to the airport with a good reason. An implicit understanding generally exists between two high-context communicators. They do not need to overtly state their request or use an overt "no" to state their opinion, thus hurting the feelings of the other high-context communicator.

China belongs to the countries of high-context communication. Can you share your talking patterns in your family and your school?

2.2 Verbal Communication Skills

2.2.1 Effective Verbal Communication

Effective verbal communication skills include more than just talking. Verbal communication encompasses both how we deliver messages and how we receive them. Communication is a soft skill, and it's one that is important to every employer. Employees who can convey information clearly and effectively are highly valued by employers. Employees who can interpret messages and act appropriately on the information that they receive have a better chance of excelling in the job.

Effective verbal communication in the workplace depends on the relationship between communication partners and the workplace context:

- Verbal communication in a workplace setting takes place between many different individuals and groups such as co-workers, employers, employees, customers, clients, etc.
- Verbal communication occurs in many different contexts, including training sessions, presentations, group meetings, performance appraisals, one-on-one discussions, interviews, sales pitches, and consulting engagements.

2.2.2 Examples of Verbal Communication Skills in the Workplace

Here are some examples of effective verbal communication skills employed in different workplace contexts.

1. Verbal Communication for Employers

The best employers don't merely tell their employees what to do and expect them to listen. Instead, they employ active listening skills to understand the needs and perspectives of their employees, engage in verbal negotiation to address and defuse disputes, and capitalize upon opportunities to praise individual and team achievements.

What should employers do?

- Advise employees regarding an appropriate course of action.
- Show assertiveness.
- Convey feedback in a constructive manner emphasizing specific, changeable behavior.
- Discipline employees in a direct and respectful manner.
- Give credit to employees.
- Recognize and counter objections.
- Show an interest in employees, asking about and recognizing their feelings.
- Speak calmly even when you're stressed.
- Terminate staff.
- Train employees to carry out a task or role.
- Use affirmative sounds and words like "uh-huh", "got you", "I understand", "for sure", "I see", and "yes" to demonstrate understanding.
- Use self-disclosure to encourage sharing.

2. Verbal Communication for Team Members

Open and constant lines of communication are vital to team success, particularly when completing quality- and deadline-critical projects. One of the most important team-building skills, strong verbal communication, helps to ensure that issues will be spotted and resolved in formative stages, averting costly escalation.

What should team members do?

- Convey messages concisely.
- Encourage reluctant group members to share input.
- Explain a difficult situation without getting angry.
- Explain that you need assistance.
- Paraphrase to show understanding.

- Pose probing questions to elicit more details about specific issues.
- Receive criticism without defensiveness.
- Refrain from speaking too often or interrupting others.
- Request feedback.
- State your needs, wants, or feelings without criticizing or blaming.

3. Verbal Communication with Customers

To have one-on-one communication with customers, it's helpful for the sales professional to have a gift of gab. Their conversations need to be focused upon identifying and addressing their customers' needs, and using their verbal talents to encourage consultative dialogs will ensure positive client relations.

What should a sales professional do?

- Anticipate the concerns of customers.
- Ask for clarification.
- Ask open-ended questions to stimulate a dialog.
- Calm agitated customers by recognizing and responding to their complaints.
- Emphasize benefits of a product, service, or proposal to persuade an individual or a group.
- Notice nonverbal cues and responding verbally to verify confusion, defuse anger, etc.

4. Verbal Communication for Presenters

Public speaking is a talent that is honed through both practice and formal training. Speaking articulately and persuasively to a live audience involves:

- enunciating each word you speak clearly;
- introducing the focus of a topic at the beginning of a presentation or interaction;
- planning communication prior to delivery;
- projecting your voice to fill the room;
- providing concrete examples to illustrate points;
- restating important points towards the end of a talk;
- selecting language appropriate to the audience;
- speaking at a moderate pace, not too fast or too slowly;
- speaking confidently but with modesty;

- summarizing key points made by other speakers;
- supporting statements with facts and evidence;
- tailoring messages to different audiences;
- telling stories to capture the audience;
- using humor to engage the audience.

 7Cs of Communication

The 7Cs of communication is a checklist that helps to improve the professional communication skills and increases the chance that the message will be understood in exactly the same way as it was intended.

- Clear: The message should be clear and easily understandable to the recipient. The purpose of the communication should be clear to the sender that only the receiver will be sure about it. The message should emphasize a single goal at a time and shall not cover several ideas in a single sentence.

- Correct: The message should be correct, i.e., correct sentences should be used, and the sender must ensure that there are no grammatical and spelling mistakes. Also, the message should be exact and well-timed. The correct messages have a greater impact on the receiver and at the same time, the morale of the sender increases with the correct messages.

- Complete: The message should be complete, i.e., it must include all the relevant information as required by the intended receivers. The complete information gives answers to all the questions of the receivers and helps with better decision-making by the recipient.

- Concrete: The communication should be concrete, which means the message should be so clear and particular that no room for misinterpretation is left. All the facts and figures should be clearly mentioned in a message so as to substantiate to whatever the sender is saying.

- Concise: The message should be precise and to the point. The sender should avoid lengthy sentences and try to convey the subject matter in the least possible words. The short and brief message is more comprehensive and helps in retaining the receiver's attention.

- Considerate: The sender should take into consideration the receiver's opinions, knowledge, mindset, background, etc. in order to have an effective communication. In other words, the sender must relate to the target recipient and be involved.

- Courteous: It implies that the sender should take the feelings and viewpoints of the receivers into consideration and make sure that the message is positive and focused on them. The message should not be biased and should include the terms that show respect for the recipient.

2.2.4 Steps to Improve Your Verbal Communication Skills in the Workplace

Improving our verbal communication skills will help us avoid misunderstandings at work. Take the following steps:

- Be prepared: Before we start a conversation, figure out what information we want to provide. Then decide on the best way to relay it to our recipient. For example, do we need to do it face to face or just by a phone call?

- Choose our words carefully: Use vocabulary our recipient can easily comprehend. If he or she doesn't understand our words, our message will be lost.

- Speak clearly: Be aware of our volume and rate of speech. Speaking too softly will make it difficult for anyone to hear us, but shouting can be very off-putting. Speak slowly enough to be understood, but not so slowly that we bore the listener or put him or her to sleep.

- Use a proper tone: Our voice may reveal our true feelings and attitude. For example, if we're angry or sad, it will be shown through our tone. Try to stay in control, and avoid revealing more than we want and distracting the listener from our message.

- Make eye contact: The listener will better be able to connect with us if we maintain eye contact throughout the conversation.

- Check in with the listener periodically: Get feedback to make sure the listener understands us. He or she must "get" what we are trying to say. While we are speaking, observe his or her facial expressions and body language, or simply ask for verbal confirmation that he or she understands us.

- Avoid distractions: Background noise will distract our listener and make it hard for him or her to hear what we are saying. Find a quiet place to talk. If we are speaking to someone by phone, go to a quiet area and make sure he or she is in one as well. If that isn't possible at the moment, arrange to talk when it is quiet.

Communication is a very useful skill in all aspects of life. To be a successful communicator, we have to know how to communicate effectively to get our message across and be understood by others. Daily conversations, messages, small talk, greetings, smiles, nods, electronic means, hand tricks, etc., all are ways to communicate with others. For the most part, these are enough to pass information, or just show an attitude. But when discussing important things, making significant decisions, or having sensitive negotiations, we need effective communication skills.

- Recognize our goals: Identify our object for communication. Each must be conveyed in the ways that are suitable and applicable to a particular situation. So we need to identify our goals and plan what to say accordingly. If necessary, we can write down our goals and provide supporting reasons or arguments to back up our statements.

- Know our audience: Whether we are speaking to a group or a single individual, we need to know specific things about our audience that will increase our ability to meet their needs and help them receive our message positively. The audience can be a labor union, our family members, school teachers, or our sweetheart, who require a different approach, language, and degree of preparation. Respect the needs and communication requirements of our audience and they will reward us with their attention. Possibly they will applaud, and more importantly, their action will be in response to our message.

- Know our message: Once we know our goals and audience, draft our message. We have to know our subject inside and out. We have to know how our target audiences are likely to respond, what they want to hear, and what we are actually going to tell them. Move to shorten the gap between expectation and reality. In this way, our audience will know we have taken the time to prepare for them, and they will respect for it.

- Function with the best manners: Kindness and courtesy will go a long way. We can say good news badly, and we can convey bad news well. Be careful of our choice of words, tone of voice, inflection, facial expressions, and body language. Everything should work together to reinforce our message. It is important to be tactful, sincere, kind, and courteous. When the message has a tendency to be unwelcome, be sure to relay it with other modest ways. There is no need to increase somebody's anger by being impolite.

- Know our limits: Determine the length of time that is acceptable for us to talk and do not overstate we are welcome. Remember "KISS"—"Keep It

Short and Simple". Once we have conveyed our message, assure our audience to determine they are still willing to listen, and then we can add more to help convince them about our message. It is better to leave our audience hungry than to make them sick of us. If we turn our audience off us, they will most likely close their mind to our message as well.

Communication is a skill we develop after birth, but it is about how to communicate effectively that we need to learn more as we grow older. Keep practicing and keep learning; there is no doubt that we can be a professional communicator someday.

Case Study: An Interaction Failure

This is an interaction between a supervisor from the United States and a subordinate from Greece. Here are some questions to help you analyze the case:

(1) Why are the interpretations so different from each other?
(2) The misunderstanding comes obviously from the fact that the American supervisor wants the employee to participate in decisions, while the Greek subordinate expects to be told what to do. What should they have done?
(3) What do you think we should do to avoid such problems in communication when participants hold different cultural expectations?

American: How long will it take you to finish the report? [I asked him to participate.]

Greek: [His behavior makes no sense. He is the boss. Why doesn't he tell me?] I do not know. How long should it take?

American: [He refuses to take responsibility.]

Greek: [I asked him for an order.]

American: You are in the best position to analyze time requirements. [I press him to take responsibility for his own actions.]

Greek: [What nonsense! I better give him an answer.] 10 days.

American: [He lacks the ability to estimate time; this estimate is totally inadequate.] Take 15. Is it agreed you will do it in 15 days?

American: [I offer a contract.]

Greek: [These are orders.] *15 days.*

(In fact the report needed 30 days of regular work. So the Greek worked day and night, but at the end of the 15th day, he still needed one more day's work to finish the report.)

American: Where is the report? [I am making sure he fulfills his contract.]

Greek: [He is asking for the report.] It will be ready tomorrow.

American: But we agreed that it would be ready today. [I must teach him to fulfill a contract.]

Greek: [The stupid, incompetent boss! Not only did he give me wrong orders, but he does not appreciate that I did a 30-day work in 16 days.]

(In the end, the Greek hands in his resignation.)

In this dialog, what one actually means is interpreted differently by the other and neither of them seems to be aware of that. Generally speaking, the American supervisor uses a straight talk approach in dealing with the work problem, whereas the Greek subordinate uses a face talk approach. If both had a chance to understand the differences in their communication styles, they might arrive at a better understanding of each other. They might also learn to be more culturally sensitive in their interpretation process. They should try to be more respectful of each other's styles and work more adaptively in achieving a common goal in their interaction.

Imagine you were the Greek, what would you do to solve this problem?

2.3 Introduction to Nonverbal Communication

Have you ever tried to conceal your surprise, suppress your anger, or act joyfully even when you were not? For most common people whose career does not involve a lot of acting or manipulation, it may be quite difficult to control or suppress these feelings. Contrary to common beliefs, some studies have claimed that 90% of our meaning system is derived from nonverbal signals, but more recent and reliable findings claim that it is closer to 65% (Guerrero & Floyd, 2005). This powerful kind of communication, which is involuntary and somehow arbitrary in most cases, is often referred to as nonverbal communication.

2.3.1 Definition of Nonverbal Communication

Unlike verbal communication, which is mostly transmitted through sounds and picked up by our ears, nonverbal communication involves all five of our senses. To further understand nonverbal communication, we need to distinguish between the vocal and verbal aspects of communication first. The vocal element of verbal communication is the words spoken—for example, "Come back here." But the speaking rate, volume, and pitch of saying these words, fall into the range of nonverbal communication. Nonverbal communication includes both vocal and nonvocal elements. The nonvocal elements of nonverbal communication commonly refer to body languages such as gestures, facial expressions, and eye contact. The relationship between the vocal and nonvocal elements of communication can be further explored in Figure 2.1 (Hargie, 2011). To sum up, nonverbal communication is the process of generating meaning using behavior other than words. As we learn about each type of nonverbal signals, we should keep in mind that nonverbal cues often work in concert with each other, combining to repeat, change, or contradict the verbal message being sent.

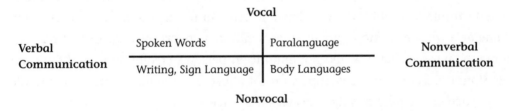

	Vocal		
Verbal Communication	Spoken Words	Paralanguage	**Nonverbal Communication**
	Writing, Sign Language	Body Languages	
	Nonvocal		

Figure 2.1   Vocal and Nonvocal Elements of Communication

2.3.2 Types and Features of Nonverbal Communication

1. Paralanguage

The vocal elements in communication is called paralanguage. We all know that voices vary in their vocal elements such as pitch, volume, rate, tone, and verbal fillers; what we might not know is that these elements provide important context for the verbal content of speech. They can help communicate the intensity of a message. For example, a louder voice is usually thought of as more intense, same as a higher pitch. Vocal elements can also lead others to form impressions about one's emotional state, credibility, and intelligence. For instance, a slow speaker could bore

others and lead their attention to wander while a fast delivery can also distract the audience from the message, as it may be too difficult for them to follow the speaker.

Even verbal fillers, such as "um", "like" and "ah" can help a person keep the floor during a conversation if he or she needs to pause for a moment to think before continuing with verbal communication. We might have heard about the rumor that using verbal fillers such as "like" and "you know" can make our English sound more like native speakers. This is true to some extent, because verbal fillers are sometimes needed in the English-speaking world to help avoid the awkward silence because of the speaker's having nothing to say in between thoughts. However, overuse of such expressions might show that the speaker is poorly educated and not fluent in thinking and speaking.

Typical patterns could be found in how people perceive others' personalities based on the speakers' vocal features, as it is shown in Table 2.1 (Knapp & Hall, 2010). Generally speaking, we perceive nasal voices negatively and assign negative personality characteristics to them (Andersen, 1999); on the other hand, we find voices that employ vocal variety and that are not monotone, lower pitched (particularly for males), and do not exhibit particular regional accents much more pleasing. Like the use of verbal fillers, there is no one-size-fits-all rule to follow or fixed sample to mimic when it comes to real communication. A voice at a low volume or a whisper is more proper when sending a covert message or flirting with a romantic partner, but it would not enhance a person's credibility if used during a professional presentation. It is important to adjust vocal features based on specific settings such as the relationship between the speakers.

Table 2.1　Stimulated Vocal Cues and Personality Stereotypes

Simulated Vocal Cues	Speakers	Stereotyped Perceptions
Breathiness	Males	Younger, more artistic
	Females	More feminine, prettier, more petite, more effervescent, more high-strung, shallower
Thinness	Males	Did not alter the listener's image of the speaker, no significant correlations
	Females	Increased social, physical, emotional, and mental immaturity; increased sense of humor and sensitivity
Flatness	Males	More masculine, more sluggish, colder, more withdrawn
	Females	More masculine, more sluggish, colder, more withdrawn
Nasality	Males	A wide array of socially undesirable characteristics
	Females	A wide array of socially undesirable characteristics

(Continued)

Simulated Vocal Cues	Speakers	Stereotyped Perceptions
Tenseness	Males	Older, more unyielding, more cantankerous
	Females	Younger, more emotional, more feminine, more high-strung, less intelligent
Throatiness	Males	Older, more realistic, maturer, more sophisticated, more well adjusted
	Females	Less intelligent, more masculine, lazier, more boorish, more unemotional, uglier, sicklier, more careless, more inartistic, more naive, humbler, more neurotic, quiet, more uninteresting, more apathetic
Increased rate	Males	More animated, more extraverted
	Females	More animated, more extraverted
Increased pitch	Males	More dynamic, more feminine, more esthetically inclined
Variety	Females	More dynamic, more extraverted

2. Kinesics

Kinesics refers to body movements and posture, which could give away our true thoughts and intentions. Gestures are the most commonly recognized cues of body language. If the gestures used have a specific agreed-on meaning, they are referred to as emblems, such as the thumbs-up sign. Of course, the meanings of emblems are not necessarily agreed-on universally. If their meanings can be interpreted within an area, they are qualified as emblems of a certain kind. On the contrary, if the gestures do not typically have meanings of their own and are used more subconsciously to illustrate the verbal message they go with, they are known as illustrators. For example, a lot of us use hand gestures to show the size or shape of an object while describing it.

It is common to find that many of us subconsciously click pens, or shake legs, fiddle with phones or engage in some self-touching behaviors like scratching, twirling hair, or fidgeting with fingers or hands during classes, meetings, or while waiting. These gestures are called adaptors (as shown in Figure 2.2) because they help to ease part of the tension resulting from uneasiness, anxiety, or a general sense that we are not in control of our surroundings. Most of the adaptors happen unconsciously, but it does not mean that we cannot use them to our advantage. If we have trouble dealing with the pressure in public speaking occasions, carry a bottle of water or a pen in our hand and twirl it slightly when we feel stressful rather than twirling our hair or clothes, which may be perceived as inappropriate in public. We will find it extremely helpful in making our speech smooth and fluent.

Figure 2.2   Signs of Common Adapters

3. Haptics

Haptics refers to touch behavior that conveys meaning during interactions. Touch can be welcoming, threatening, or persuasive. Think of how the touch of a friend or family member has the power to comfort us in moments of sorrow when words alone cannot. Now, change the person who touches us to a total stranger. This positive power of touch is highly likely to be countered by the risk of it turning into threats due to its connection to sex and violence. However, if the stranger is a doctor or tailor, our feeling could be entirely different. Why is that? There are several types of touch, including functional-professional (as shown in Figure 2.3), social-polite, friendship-warmth, and love-intimacy (Heslin & Apler, 1983). For example, barbers, doctors, and security screeners touch us in ways related to a goal or part of a routine professional interaction, which makes it less threatening and more expected. On the other hand, a handshake and a pat on the shoulder are examples of touch at the social-polite level to help start interactions and show that others are included and respected.

Figure 2.3   Common Ways of Functional-Professional Touch

At the friendship-warmth level, touch interactions are important because they serve to maintain relationship and communicate care and concern. Friendship-warmth touching also varies greatly. For example, too much touch can signal romantic interest while too little touch may signal distance or unfriendliness.

Therefore, friends should negotiate their comfort levels at times to ensure appropriateness. At the love-intimacy level, touch is more personal and is typically only exchanged between significant others, such as best friends, close family members, and romantic partners. Touching faces, holding hands, and full frontal embraces are examples of touch at this level.

4. Chronemics

Chronemics studies how time can influence communication. In this sense, time can be classified into several different categories, including biological, personal, physical, and cultural time (Andersen, 1999). Biological time affects people in ways that when our natural rhythms are disturbed by certain scheduling abnormalities, our physical and mental health as well as our communicative competence and personal relationships may suffer as a result. Think about how quickly time passes when we are doing something interesting. How we experience time based on our mood or interest level is how we perceive personal time. Nothing could better capture the essence of personal time than Albert Einstein's famous explanation of the term "Relativity" (相对论).

Physical time refers to the fixed cycles of days, years, and seasons, which can also affect our mood and psychological states. Take season for example. Some people who experience seasonal affective disorder can experience emotional distress and anxiety due to the changes of season, primarily from a warm and bright season to a dark and cold one. Cultural time refers to how a large group of people view time. Polychronic people who do not view time as a linear progression hence keep more flexible schedules and may engage in several activities at once. On the contrary, monochronic people tend to schedule their time more rigidly and do one thing at a time.

Besides, an individual's feeling of time also varies based on whether this person is future- or past-oriented. People with past-time orientations may want to reminisce about the past, reunite with old friends, and put considerable time into preserving memories in scrapbooks and photo albums. On the contrary, people with future-time orientations may spend the same amount of time making career and personal plans, writing out to-do lists, or researching future vacations, potential retirement spots, or what book they are going to read next.

5. Proxemics

When we are content with and attracted to someone, we say we are "close" to him or her. When we lose connection with someone, we may say he or she is "distant" . That is a clue to show how space influences the way people communicate and behave.

Proxemics refers to the use of space and distance within communication. The amount of space we keep between each other during communication is the major sign to show how we feel towards the other party at that particular time.

Take the Americans for instance. Scholars have found that Americans, in general, have four zones in terms of personal space: public zone, social zone, personal zone, and intimate zone (Hall, 1968). Touching to eighteen inches means intimate, which is right for closest friends, family members, and romantic partners, and indicates closeness and trust. Eighteen inches to four feet is personal, which means still close but keeps another at arm's length for most of our friends or acquaintances. Four to twelve feet is social, which is used for the kind of communication that occurs in professional or casual interaction. While more than twelve feet is considered as public, which occurs in situations where two-way communication is not desirable or possible such as engaging in formal speech.

The way the Chinese perceive proxemic zones of personal space is quite different from the Americans. The distance between the Chinese concerning social counteractions is actually closer than that between the Americans, especially when it comes to social and public zones as it is demonstrated in Table 2.2 (Li, 2002). However, it is important to point out that, as the U.S. population grows ever more ethnically diverse, any broad label would probably be an oversimplification.

Table 2.2　Comparison of American and Chinese Distances of Zones of Space (cm)

Zones	Chinese	Americans	Environment	Relationship
Intimate	0–30	0–45	Most intimate activities	Couples, parents and children
Personal	30–70	45–120	Face to face interaction	Friends, acquaintances, relatives
Social	70–250	120–360	Formal interactions, business and social event	Co-workers, commercial relations
Public	> 250	> 360	Public speaking related	Students and teachers, performers and audience

As we can see, nonverbal communication is a powerful tool, and what we say is not the only thing that is important. Although we are never explicitly taught about how to use body language, we learn it through observation and practice as we grow up and we do it automatically. It is fair to say that nonverbal communication is primarily biologically based while verbal communication is mostly culturally based. Everything, from pitch to volume, eye contact to facial expressions, gestures to handshakes, etc. says something to others. In a word, we are speaking to everyone even when we do not say a word.

2.4 Functions of Nonverbal Communication

Nonverbal communication has a distinct history and serves separate evolutionary functions from verbal communication. The fact that some nonverbal communication signs have the same meaning across cultures while no verbal communication systems share that same universal recognition somehow proves that nonverbal communication is primarily biologically based while verbal communication is primarily culturally based. Some scholars even believe that nonverbal communication evolved earlier than verbal communication and served an early and important survival function that helped humans later develop verbal communication. While some of our nonverbal communication abilities, like the sense of smell, lost strength as our verbal abilities increased, other abilities, like paralanguage and movement, have grown alongside verbal complexity.

2.4.1 Conveying Meaning

A primary function of nonverbal communication is to convey meaning by reinforcing, substituting for, or contradicting verbal communication. For example, facial expressions can reinforce the emotional states we convey through verbal communication such as smiling while telling a funny story. Messages have been shown to be better remembered when nonverbal signals affirm the verbal information exchange. Most of the times we tend to do it unconsciously, such as pointing to an object or direction during discussion. In the aspect of reinforcing, both complementing and repeating are used to make messages clearer. The difference between complementing and repeating is that complementing always happens simultaneously with verbal communication. For example, if we say we are hungry, we might rub our stomach. However, repeating can be sequential, which means there could be a delay between the verbal and nonverbal communication. For example, we say "no", and then we shake our head afterwards.

Nonverbal communication can also substitute for verbal communication. For example, people usually clench teeth or fists to show endurance or anger, and cover face with hands to show sadness or shame. The difference between reinforcing and substituting is the existence of verbal cues. If we just wave our hand to mean "Hi" or "Bye", it is substituting. Yet, if we say "Hi" or "Bye" while waving our hand, it is complementing. Substitution is often used when verbal communication is not

effective. For example, babies who have not yet developed language skills make facial expressions to generate meaning. Substitution can be done in a variety of ways. Nonverbal communication is useful in quiet situations where verbal communication would be disturbing. For example, we may use a gesture to signal to a friend that we are ready to leave the library. Crowded or loud places can also impede verbal communication and lead people to rely more on nonverbal messages. Getting a server's attention with a hand gesture is more polite than yelling "Hey you!" Besides, there are just times when we know it is better not to say something aloud. If we want to point out a person's unusual outfit or signal to a friend that we think his or her date is a loser, we are more likely to do that nonverbally. As the old saying goes, "Some things are best left unsaid."

In addition, nonverbal communication can convey meaning by contradicting verbal communication. If a person verbally expresses a statement of truth while simultaneously fidgeting or avoiding eye contact, opposing or conflicting messages are sent. When mixed messages are received, we often perceive nonverbal communication to be more credible than verbal communication. For example, a person may say, "I'm sorry" in a humble tone but follow that up with a roll of his or her eyes, which could indicate the person does not really mean it. Mixed messages on the part of receivers can be sent deliberately to confuse or show sarcasm. It may also happen subconsciously when lying. For example, we may say "I did not do it" while rubbing the nose or pulling at the collar. Persistent mixed messages can lead to relational distress and hurt a person's credibility in professional settings. Moreover, if we are unable to solve the discrepancy, we are likely to react negatively and potentially withdraw from the interaction (Hargie, 2011).

2.4.2 Regulating Conversational Flow

Vocalics, which makes up a significant part of nonverbal signals, helps us cue others into our conversational intentions. If we use vocal rather than nonvocal elements to modify a verbal message, it is often either to accentuate or moderate. Accentuation refers to the amplification of verbal messages. For example, when we speak louder, we are adding emphasis to the verbal message. Apart from increasing volume, we can also move forward, slow down, or stamp. Moderating is the opposite of accentuating as it looks to reduce attention, remove emphasis, and distort it in various ways to make the verbal message more difficult to understand, such as reducing volume, speeding up, or being incoherent.

Nonverbal communication can also help us regulate our conversations, so we do not end up constantly interrupting each other or waiting in awkward silence when taking turns to speak. A rising pitch typically indicates a question, and a falling pitch indicates the end of a conversational turn. We can also use a falling pitch at the end of a speech to cue applause and prevent awkward silence if the speaker just ends up with a "That's it" or "Thank you".

Other nonvocal elements can also regulate our conversation flow to show conversational order. For example, if someone puts both elbows on the table and inhales, it is saying that he or she is about to speak. A person touching another person's arm can signal that he or she wants to talk next, interrupt or signal the person being touched that it is time to calm down. We can also show the end of a speech by stopping using hand gestures or shifting eye contact to the person who will speak next (Hargie, 2011). In contrast, repeating a hand gesture or using one or more verbal fillers can extend our turn even though we are not verbally asking for more time at the very moment.

2.4.3 Affecting Relationships

Immediacy behavior, tie signs, and expressions of emotion are just three of the many examples that illustrate how nonverbal communication affects our relationships. Other than conveying meaning, expressing emotions, and regulating conversational flow, nonverbal communication can also affect relationships in forms of immediacy behavior. Immediacy behavior, both verbal and nonverbal, plays a significant role in bringing people together or pushing them apart, which has been identified by some scholars as the most important function of nonverbal communication (Andersen & Andersen, 2004). Nonverbal behavior such as smiling, nodding, making eye contact, and occasionally engaging in social, polite, or professional touch is a good way of lessening real or perceived physical and psychological distance between communicators. It can also create rapport, or a friendly and positive connection between people.

Tie signs (as shown in Figure 2.4) are nonverbal cues that communicate intimacy and symbolize the connection between two people. These relational indicators can be objects such as wedding rings, tattoos that are symbolic of another person or the relationship, actions such as sharing the same drinking glass, or touching behavior such as handholding (Andersen & Andersen, 2004). Kisses and hugs, for example, are considered as tie signs, but a kiss on the cheek is different

from a kiss on the mouth and a full embrace is different from a half embrace. Touch behavior is the most often studied tie sign and can speak a lot about a relationship based on the area being touched, the length of the touch, and the intensity of the touch.

Figure 2.4   Common Tie Signs to Show Intimacy

While verbal communication is our primary tool in solving problems and supplying detailed instructions, nonverbal communication is our primary tool for communicating emotions. Touch and facial expressions are two primary ways we express emotions nonverbally. Take facial expressions for example. With all the various muscles that precisely control the mouth, lips, eyes, nose, forehead, and jaw, it is estimated that human faces are capable of displaying more than ten thousand different expressions to show both positive and negative emotions. For instance, we can express most of the negative emotions by increasing tension in various muscle groups: tightening of the jaw muscles, furrowing of the forehead, squinting eyes, or lip occlusion. In contrast, positive emotions are revealed by the loosening of the furrowed lines on the forehead, relaxation of the muscles around the mouth, and widening of the eye area. Despite its versatility, much research has supported the universality of a core group of facial expressions to express happiness, sadness, surprise, fear, contempt, disgust, and anger. Love is a primary emotion that we express nonverbally and that forms the basis of our close relationships. No single facial expression for love has been found; it is expressed through prolonged eye contact, close interpersonal distances, increased touch, and increased time together, among other things. Given our limited emotional vocabulary, nonverbal expressions of emotion are central to our relationships.

Case Study: Close or Far?

Xu Lei was about to take the elevator to get to the 23rd floor for a job interview. After the door opened, Xu Lei found that there was already a woman in the elevator in the back. As Xu Lei always liked to stand in the back to lean against the elevator wall, he walked towards the back to the corner facing the woman. To his surprise, as he approached the corner, the woman in the back also changed her position to the corner in the front facing Xu Lei diagonally. Wanting to leave a good impression on the people working in the building, Xu Lei said "Hi" to her, and the woman greeted back. However, as they continued the riding, Xu Lei noticed a sense of awkwardness starting to grow. Why did the woman in the back change her position? Was it Xu Lei's greeting that froze the atmosphere?

Most people know that awkward feeling when they shuffle into an elevator with other people and try not to make eye contact. According to a study made by Dr. Grey Lee from the North Carolina State University, there is actually a pattern of how people would stand in elevators. If one is all by himself or herself in the elevator, the standing position is usually random, and the person can do anything he or she likes. If two strangers are in the elevator, they would normally take the two corners facing diagonally. As more and more people get into the elevator, people would continue to change their positions to ensure maximum distance from each other. And people would normally stop talking, stand still and avoid eye contact in the elevator. The more people there are, the more silent and solemn it would be in the elevator (Shi, 2013).

We learned in the earlier session that distances could also influence communication by indicating intimacy after introducing the four zones—public, social, personal, and intimate. Quite a few situations could lead to our personal and intimate zones being breached by others against our will sometimes, even if such space is normally only reserved for the closest friends, family members, and intimate partners. Waiting for a crowded elevator is one of such cases, where such breaching is inevitable. What will happen if our space is violated? Unexpected breaches of personal space can lead to negative reactions; sometimes it could even lead to criminal or delinquent behavior, known as a "mob mentality" (Andersen, 1999). If this type of density is predicted beforehand, such as a crowded concert or a subway during rush hour, it is highly likely that people will make various communicative adjustments such as moving, crossing arms, or avoiding eye contact to manage the space issue. If the situation continues to get worse, people may even rely on certain degree of verbal communication to reduce immediacy by showing that they are aware that a breach has occurred and are not interested in any further closeness. For example, people may make comments about the crowd by saying things like "We're really packed here like sardines".

Now, it is your turn to analyze a case.

A couple were riding in the elevator with a stranger. Where do you think these three people would stand? Please draw a map of their standing positions and give your reasons. What would happen if a boy and his mother come in? Redesign your picture by adding the number of strangers until the total number reaches seven and state your reasons for drawing like this.

You can begin by evaluating the relationship between the groups of people and assessing the distance they would maintain based on that. Always remember to ensure maximum distance between strangers.

In the News

Where You Stand in the Lift Reflects Your Social Status

A study found that people decide where they stand based on a micro social hierarchy, established within seconds of entering the lift. Rebekah Rousi, a Ph.D. student in cognitive science, conducted an ethnographic study of elevator behavior in two of the tallest office buildings in Adelaide, Australia. As part of her research, she took a total of 30 lift rides in the two buildings, and discovered there was an established order to where people tended to stand. In a blog for Ethnography Matters, she wrote that more senior men seemed to direct themselves towards the back of the elevator cabins.

She said: "In front of them were younger men, and in front of younger men were women of all ages." She also noticed there was a difference in where people directed their gaze half way through the ride. "Men watched the monitors, looked in the side mirrors (in one building) to see themselves, and in the door mirrors (of the other building) to watch others. Women would watch the monitors and avoid eye contact with other users (unless in conversation) and the mirrors," she writes. The doctorate student concluded it could be that people who are shyer stand toward the front, where they can't see other passengers, whereas bolder people stand in the back, where they have a view of everyone else.

2.4.4 Expressing Identities

Nonverbal communication expresses who we are. Many things relating to our identities such as the groups to which we belong, our hobbies and interests, etc. are all conveyed nonverbally through the way we set up our living and working spaces, the clothes we wear, the way we carry ourselves, and the accents and tones of our voices. Our physical body features as well as our level of attractiveness leaves impressions on others about who we are. Height, for example, has been shown to influence how people are treated and perceived in various contexts.

Aside from our physical appearances, objects and possessions that surround us, such as our clothes, jewelry, and space decorations, also reflect our identities. Clothing expresses strongly who we are, or even, who we want to be that day, which in turn shows people who we want to be associated with, and where we fit in. For instance, Jewish men may wear a yarmulke (圆顶小帽) to display outwardly their religious belief while Scottish men often wear kilts in traditional festivities to specify their culture. People may show themselves with accessories and high-end fashion in order to attract partners they are interested in. In this case, clothing is used as a form of self-expression in which people can flaunt their power, wealth, sex appeal, or creativity.

Other than using more invasive and costly measures such as cosmetic surgery, we can also temporarily alter our height or looks. For example, we can wear different shoes or colored contact lenses or simply change the way we carry and present ourselves through posture or eye contact. Even the tone of our voice can be altered to present ourselves as warm or distant depending on the context.

For Your Information

The Chinese Costume—*Qipao*

Qipao is a body-hugging one-piece Chinese dress for women, made fashionable by the upper-class women in the 1920s in Shanghai. During the Qing Dynasty, Manchu women typically wore a one-piece dress that retrospectively came to be known as the *Qipao* because certain groups of the Manchu communities are referred to as the Banner People, namely *Qiren* (旗人) in Mandarin. In about 1925 it started to be a new fashion item for women of the

Han ethnic group. The original *Qipao* was wide and loose which covered most of the woman's body, revealing only the head, hands, and the tips of the toes. With the passage of time, though, it was tailored to become more formfitting and revealing, which put more emphasis on women's body line. The length of *Qipao* was also reduced from ankle to above the knee.

The "standard" style of *Qipao* was formed in Shanghai during the 1920s by the upper-class women who were urgently seeking something to show their new taste. *Qipao* briefly lost its followers during the revolutionary times due to its connection to the bourgeoisie. With the trend of reevaluation of Chinese traditional culture, Chinese women started to pay attention to *Qipao* again. In the 1960s, actress Nancy Kwan made *Qipao* briefly fashionable in Western culture due to the movie *The World of Suzie Wong*. *Qipao* is also commonly seen in beauty contests, along with swimsuits. In contemporary China, the meaning of *Qipao* has been revisited again. It now embodies an identity of ethnic Chinese, and is thus used for important diplomatic occasions. In the 2008 Summer Olympics, the medal bearers wore *Qipao*. In November 2014, *Qipao* was chosen to be the official attire for the political leaders' wives in the 22nd APEC meeting in Beijing. With the growth of the Chinese economy, *Qipao* has experienced a renewed popularity in the Western world. In the 2011 movie *One Day*, Anne Hathaway, an American star, wore a set of dark blue *Qipao* as an evening dress, which was appreciated by viewers.

The style of *Qipao* has evolved over the decades and is still worn today. It was influenced by the culture of the time and has indeed also influenced the current culture and society.

More to Study

Your Body Language Shapes Who You Are

At the TED Global 2012 conference, social psychologist Amy Cuddy gave the talk "Your Body Language Shapes Who You Are" in which she explained in detail how power posing can affect the level of hormones resulting in the gaining of personal confidence. Her talk has gained great popularity among the viewers, even being crowned one of TED's most watched talks ever, yet it also received quite a few critics from peer scientists. Watch the talk and try to state your own opinion concerning the effects of postures. If you are interested, you could continue to read the article written by Ranehill Dreber titled "Assessing the Robustness of Power Posing: No Effect on Hormones and Risk Tolerance in a Large Sample of Men and Women". You can also find Cuddy's rebuttal article in the passage "Inside the Debate About Power Posing: A Q&A with Amy Cuddy". Both the video and the articles could be found on the website.

2.5 Guidelines to Improve Nonverbal Competence

It is without a doubt that language proficiency is valuable for successful communication to happen. However, it is not enough to know the grammar and vocabulary of that language, especially if intercultural communication is involved. People enjoy interacting with others who are skilled at encoding and decoding verbal and nonverbal messages. As we age, we tend to think that we will become better at communicating as we practice and internalize social and cultural norms related to sending (encoding) and interpreting (decoding) information, but it is not necessarily true.

People do not always say what they want to say. In addition, people do not mean what they say sometimes. At times, it requires people to read between the lines. However, as we have already learned, we receive few, if any, official instructions on nonverbal communication, which may cause great trouble when we try to "read other people's minds". Competent communicators understand how to use (or avoid) touch, proximity in physical space, and paralinguistic sounds to convey their intended meanings. They also know how to use politeness strategies in making requests, which is a principle of pragmatics. In addition, competent communicators can avoid insults and gaffes by not using gestures that may mean quite different things in a host culture as opposed to their home culture.

Research shows that education and training in communication, especially nonverbal communication, can lead to quick gains in knowledge and skill. As nonverbal communication plays an important part in the communication process,

we can all benefit by improving our nonverbal communicative effectiveness.

The most important guideline when we try to decode nonverbal communication is to realize that there is no such thing as nonverbal dictionary. Although some books may have many valid "rules" of nonverbal communication, those rules are always relative to the individual, social, and cultural contexts in which an interaction takes place. The second guideline for decoding nonverbal communication is to acknowledge that certain nonverbal signals are related. The third guideline is that rather than using a list of specific rules, it is more recommended to develop more general tools that are useful and adaptable to interpret nonverbal cues under various specific contexts.

While it is important to recognize that we send nonverbal signals through multiple channels simultaneously, we can also increase our nonverbal communicative competence by becoming more aware of how it runs in specific channels. Although no one can truly offer us a rule book on how to send and receive every type of nonverbal signal effectively, the following advice may help us communicate better with specific nonverbal messages under a less academic perspective.

1. Vocalics

People often decode personality traits from a person's vocal quality. Verbal fluency is one of the strongest factors influencing persuasiveness and this is especially true when it comes to communicating in a second language. Verbal fillers are often used subconsciously and can negatively affect our credibility and reduce the clarity of our message when speaking in situations that are more formal. One way to catch the overuse of verbal fillers is to monitor our talking by using the recording application on our phone and play it to our ears. Then we can try to eliminate the unneeded verbal fillers. Beginners can often reduce their use of verbal fillers noticeably over just a brief period.

Vocal variety enforces the engagement and understanding of both the listener and the speaker. As a result, having a more expressive voice that varies appropriately in terms of rate, pitch, and volume can help us achieve communication goals related to maintaining attention, effectively conveying information, and getting others to act in a particular way.

2. Eye Contact

We are all familiar with the fact that when feeling interested or excited a person's pupil will dilate. Eye contact is the primary nonverbal way of indicating engagement or interest. The length of a gaze, the frequency of glances, patterns of fixation, and blink rates are all especially important cues in nonverbal communication.

Eye contact is useful for starting and regulating conversations. To make sure people are available for interaction and to avoid being perceived as rude, it is usually a clever idea to "catch their eyes" before we start talking to them. Likeness between speakers increases as mutual gazing increases. Therefore, if we are talking to someone, make sure to engage in eye contact for 60%–70% of the time; but if we are the listeners, increase that to 90% to show that we are listening. Avoiding eye contact or shifting eye contact from place to place can make others think we are being deceptive or inattentive.

3. Facial Expressions and Posture

We can use facial expressions to manage our expressions of emotion to intensify, diminish or cover up what we are feeling. They can also be used to express or simulate an emotion that we are not feeling. Smiles are especially powerful as immediacy behavior and a rapport-building tool. They can also help to disarm a potentially hostile person or de-escalate a conflict (Metts & Planlap, 2002).

The head leaning over and being supported by a hand can typically be decoded as a sign of boredom, the thumb supporting the chin and the index finger touching the head close to the temple or eye a sign of negative evaluative thoughts, and the chin stroke a sign that a person is going through a decision-making process. In terms of seated posture, leaning back is usually decoded as a sign of informality and indifference, straddling a chair a sign of dominance (but also some insecurity because the person is protecting the vulnerable front part of his or her body), and leaning forward a signal of interest and attentiveness.

4. Gestures

Gestures send messages about our emotional state. Since many gestures are spontaneous or subconscious, it is important to raise our awareness of them and monitor them. Be aware that clenched hands may signal aggression or anger, nail biting or fidgeting may signal nervousness, and finger tapping may signal boredom. Keep in mind that adaptors can hurt our credibility in more formal or serious interactions. It is useful to figure out what our common adaptors are and monitor them so that we can avoid leaving unfavorable impressions.

On the other hand, making common illustrative gestures while speaking can help our verbal communication to become more engaging. Although it does not always mean a person is being honest, displaying palms is unconsciously encoded and decoded

as a sign of openness and truthfulness. Conversely, crossing our arms in front of the chest is usually decoded as a negative gesture that conveys defensiveness. Verbal communication is enhanced when a good listener allows the time for reflection on the subject in discussion while letting other people interject and have the floor. When we have something to say, instead of verbal injection or abrupt interrupting which may seem rude, we can use nonverbal signals like leaning in or using a brief gesture like subtly raising one hand or the index finger to signal to another person that we would like to soon take the floor. It is without a doubt that cultural differences of possible nonverbal cues need to be taken into consideration while we do so.

5. Touch

Consider the status and power dynamics involved in a touch. Offering a solid handshake can significantly help communicate confidence and enthusiasm that can be useful on those important occasions. The first rule of a good handshake is to stand up and look the other person in the eye before shaking hands. It is not smart to grab into the other person's palm or be a bone crusher. Besides, always shake with our right hand and do not have our left hand in our pocket. We typically decode people putting their hands in their pockets as a gesture that indicates shyness or discomfort. People often subconsciously put their hands in their pockets when they do not want to take part in a conversation. However, displaying the thumb or thumbs while the rest of the hand is in the pocket is a signal of a dominant or authoritative attitude. If we want to appear to be more powerful to show our dominant position, make sure to stand on the left, so when we shake someone's hand, our hand will stay on top. Nevertheless, we cannot always be on the left, if we are on the wrong side, we can still appear to be dominant during handshaking by wrapping our hands all over the other person's hand.

Culture, status, gender, and age can all influence how we send and interpret touch messages. In professional and social settings, it is normal to give other people a handshake. However, touching others on the arm or shoulder with our hand may be slightly more intimate. The following are some types of touch to avoid (Andersen, 1999):

- Avoid interrupting touches such as hugging someone while he or she is talking to someone else.
- Avoid startling or surprising another person with your touch.
- Avoid touching strangers unless being introduced or when helping.
- Avoid moving people out of the way with only touch—pair your touch with

a verbal message like "Excuse me".

- Avoid combining touch with negative criticism. For example, a hand on the shoulder during a critical statement can increase a person's defensiveness and seem condescending or aggressive.

Summary

It is fair to say that improving one's nonverbal communicative competence is the first step towards successful communication. Since nonverbal communication is more ambiguous than verbal communication, we must learn to interpret these cues as clusters within contexts. In short, we cannot read people's nonverbal communication like reading a book. Moreover, there are no A-to-Z guides that capture the complexity of nonverbal communication (DePaulo, 1992). When we are listening, pay attention to other people's intonations, as well as facial expressions and other body language, making sure we do not miss anything sent voicelessly to eliminate the possibilities of being misled. Incongruent nonverbal cues are helpful when the message we decode does not match up with the speaker's intent. Do not forget to get more information from multichannel nonverbal clues before jumping at any conclusion in these cases. Meanwhile, being conscious of our own physicality and feelings means to monitor the nonverbal signals we sent that may be perceived as incongruent: Do our gestures match our words? Alternatively, do they give away about what we are really thinking about? To better train ourselves with self-monitoring, we can record ourselves with a video camera or an audio recorder to see how we communicate nonverbally, or just practice improving our nonverbal communicative skills in front of a mirror.

Following the suggestions to become a better encoder of nonverbal communication will lead to better decoding competence. Yet, as with all aspects of communication, improving our nonverbal communication takes commitment and continued effort. Once the first effort is put into improving our nonverbal encoding and decoding skills and those new skills are put into practice, we are encouraged by the positive reactions from others. As we get better at monitoring and controlling our nonverbal behavior and understanding how nonverbal cues affect our interaction, we may show more competence in multiple types of communication.

Exercises

Questions for Review

1. What are the 7Cs of communication?

2. How can you improve your verbal communication?

3. What is the role of language in verbal communication?

4. What types of verbal communication are there?

5. Can you explain the meaning of paralanguage? What aspects does it cover/study?

6. What do emblems usually refer to? What is the name for a certain gesture that helps to ease part of the tension resulting from uneasiness or anxiety?

7. Can you list at least two nonverbal signs that show inconsistency within a speaker's message?

8. If some people clench teeth or fists to show endurance or anger without saying anything, what kind of function do the nonverbal signs play? Can you list any other examples of this function?

9. Can you briefly describe the difference between complementing and repeating?

10. When a person verbally expresses a statement of truth while simultaneously fidgeting or avoiding eye contact, what kind of message does the nonverbal cue send? Which channel of information is more trustworthy? Why?

Problems and Application

1. You are working as an intern in an international trade company. Yesterday afternoon, your supervisor asked you to pick up a VIP guest Mr. Yao from the airport and take him to the hotel. Knowing how important the guest is, you arrived at the airport early to leave a good impression on him. Soon you saw Mr. Yao coming towards you. Because of nervousness, you stretched out your left hand to shake hands. Mr. Yao looked a little surprised to see your behavior. Which part of your action is not appropriate according to the rules of hand shaking? How can you fix the problem?

2. You have been invited to attend a job interview this morning at 8 o'clock in a big Japanese trade company. Halfway on your trip there, you find out that you have left your resume at home, which is supposed to be handed in during the interview, but you have an electronic version in the USB drive in your bag. If you go back home and pick it up, you would be five minutes late for the interview. What would you do to solve the problem? Why?

Chapter 3

Communicative Competence & Intercultural Competence

Learning Objectives

After learning this chapter, you should be able to:

1. define communicative competence and intercultural communicative competence;

2. provide examples of nonverbal differences in greetings under various cultural contexts;

3. identify and compare characteristics of high-contact culture and low-contact culture;

4. employ strategies to overcome culture shock and develop intercultural communicative competence.

Why would overseas students often gain a few extra pounds in their first year abroad? How can you avoid offending foreign friends when inviting them to dinner? Which countries prefer bowing to handshaking? To answer all these questions, we must know the concept and connotation of intercultural communication.

As the world becomes more and more globalized, people communicate across cultures more frequently now than ever before. Since different cultures may vary in their religions, customs, rules, and rituals in all aspects of life, an intercultural communicator needs to have at least intercultural awareness as well as communicative competence to build up his or her intercultural communicative competence in order to engage in intercultural communication between different cultures successfully. For example, foreign newcomers to a family party for a wedding anniversary might meet some troubles if they fail to notice that lilies are appropriate in China as gifts for eternal love, yet they are used in some of the Western countries to pay respects to the dead, no matter how well they speak the language. One of the aspects that foreign newcomers need to pay special attention to is how the meaning of nonverbal cues could vary in different cultures such as how they greet each other or how they show approval or disapproval. The term "culture shock" is used to describe the effects of such encounter on some newcomers and the adaptation phase might be quite different from one another. Not understanding and respecting such differences may lead to serious consequences. In the earlier chapter, we have talked a lot about how to communicate and how to improve nonverbal communicative competence. In this chapter, we are going to address the issue of what intercultural communicative competence is and how it is different from the idea of communicative competence before learning some effective tips on how to improve our intercultural communicative competence from the perspective of heart, mind, and skill.

3.1 Communicative Competence & Intercultural Communicative Competence

For effective communication to happen, communicators should know more than syntax, lexis, and phonology. This is especially true when it comes to intercultural communication. Just as communicative competence goes far beyond verbal communication, even though intercultural communicative competence has a lot to do with communicative competence under intercultural context, it is more than that. Before we move on to any specifics, it is especially important to figure out what intercultural communicative competence is and how it is different from communicative competence.

3.1.1 Framework for Communicative Competence

Communicative competence is a term in linguistics which refers to a language user's grammatical knowledge of syntax, morphology, phonology, and the like, as well as social knowledge about how and when to use utterances appropriately. The term was coined by Dell Hymes in 1966, reacting against the perceived inadequacy of Noam Chomsky's (1965) distinction between competence and performance. As there has already been much debate about linguistic competence and communicative competence in the second and foreign language teaching literature, the outcome has always been the consideration of communicative competence as a superior model of language following Hymes' opposition to Chomsky's linguistic competence.

The best-recognized idea of communicative competence was put forward by Canale in 1983. Canale believed that the theoretical framework for communicative competence should at least include four areas of knowledge and skill, which are grammatical competence, sociolinguistic competence, discourse competence, and strategic competence.

According to Canale, grammatical competence is the mastery of the language code itself, which refers directly to the linguistic skills of the communicator. The communicator needs to speak grammatically right for himself or herself to be understood. Canale continues to put forward the idea of sociolinguistic competence, which means the communicator needs to have the ability to adapt to various contexts. Only having the ability to master grammatical forms and meanings is not enough, the communicator also needs to be able to combine those together to achieve unity of text. That is done through cohesion in form and coherence in meaning. The ability to master such a task requires what Canale calls discourse competence. The last competence Canale proposed is strategic competence. Strategic competence is the mastery of verbal and nonverbal communication strategies to compensate for communication breakdowns due to limiting conditions or insufficient competence and to enhance the effectiveness of communication.

3.1.2 Concept of Intercultural Communicative Competence

Among other scholars, Byram (1989) is the one who laid the foundation of intercultural communicative competence. He defined successful intercultural communication as the ability to establish and maintain relationships. Byram believes that the goal of intercultural communication moves from understanding and exchanging information to trying to relate to people from other countries. He put forward some ideas for one to evolve from a competent communicator to a competent intercultural communicator. The first is attitudes, namely to have the curiosity and openness, readiness to suspend disbelief about other cultures and belief about one's own. The second is knowledge, which means to know of social groups including their products and practices in not only one's own country but also the country of other communicators. The third is the skills of interpreting and relating, which mean the abilities to interpret a document or event from another culture and to explain it and relate it to documents from one's own. The fourth is the skills of discovery and interaction, which refer to the ability to get new knowledge of a culture and cultural practices and the abilities to operate knowledge, attitudes and skills under the constraints of real-time communication and interaction. The last one is critical cultural awareness, which means the ability to evaluate critically based on explicit criteria, perspectives, practices and products of one's own as well as other cultures and countries.

For Your Information

Michael Byram and Intercultural Competence

In Europe, the model of intercultural competence developed by Michael Byram, professor of education at University of Durham in England, has been the most influential. Byram claims that intercultural competence consists of five main elements or "savoirs", as he calls them:

- Attitudes (savoir être)
- Knowledge (savoir)
- Skills of interpreting and relating (savoir comprendre)

- Skills of discovery and interaction (savoir apprendre/faire)
- Critical cultural awareness (savoir s'engager)

Most theorists who have entered the discussion of what forms intercultural competence agree with Byram that the concept has to do with attitudes, skills and knowledge, which is also received in this book.

Byram began his career teaching French and German at a secondary school and then involved in adult education in an English comprehensive community school. After being appointed to a post in teacher education at Durham University in 1980, he conducted research into the education of linguistic minorities, foreign language education and student residence abroad, and supervised doctoral students in intercultural studies, language teaching, and comparative education. He has published many books and articles, including *Teaching and Assessing Intercultural Communicative Competence*, *The Common European Framework of Reference*, etc.

3.1.3 Concept of Transcultural Competence

Another scholar named Slimbach (2005) proposed the idea of transcultural competence, which is quite like the idea of intercultural communicative competence and is composed of six categories of competence, which are global awareness, world learning, foreign language proficiency, ethnographic skill, affective development, and perspective consciousness. These six competences further described in great depth the ideas put forward by Byram.

Global awareness is a basic awareness of transnational conditions and systems, ideologies, and institutions, affecting the quality of life of human and non-human populations, along with the choices confronting individuals and nations. World learning is like what Byram refers to as knowledge, which means direct experience with contrasting political histories, family lifestyles, social groups, arts, religions, and cultural orientations based on extensive, immersed interaction within non-English speaking, non-Americanized environments. Foreign language proficiency is the base of interaction that is a threshold-level facility in the verbal and nonverbal communication system used by members of at least one other culture. Ethnographic skill is also important, which is the ability to carefully observe social behavior, manage stress, and establish friendships across cultures, while exploring issues

of global significance, documenting learning, and analyzing data using relevant concepts. Other than interpreting and relating, Slimbach put forward the idea of affective development, which is the ability to demonstrate personal qualities and standards of the heart such as empathy, inquisitiveness, initiative, flexibility, humility, sincerity, gentleness, justice, and joy within specific intercultural contexts in which one is living and learning. Perspective consciousness is just like critical cultural awareness, which is the ability to constantly question the source of one's cultural assumptions and ethical judgments, leading to the habit of seeing things through the minds and hearts of others.

3.1.4 Skills of Multilingual Communicators

In the year 2012, Baker further developed the model of intercultural awareness. Rather than focusing on establishing and maintaining relationships, he emphasized the importance of mediation when miscommunication happens. Baker wrote that the communicator needs to know how to use linguistic and other communicative resources in the negotiation of meanings, roles, and relationships in diverse sociocultural settings of intercultural communication through English.

He continues to put forward some more necessary skills for multilingual communicators. The first thing a successful multilingual communicator should know is the role of accommodation in adapting language to be closer to that of one's interlocutor to aid understanding and solidarity. Negotiation and mediation skills are also essential, particularly between different culturally based frames of reference, which have the potential to cause misunderstanding or miscommunication. The reason why these skills are important is that they enable intercultural communicators to adjust and align themselves to different communicative systems and cooperate in communication.

More to Read

A Study on Intercultural Competence

Half a century has passed since the concept of intercultural competence has been brought up, and research on this topic has flourished both in China and abroad. However, most of these studies are published as papers in academic journals instead of books. The book *A Study on Intercultural Competence* by Dr. Dai Xiaodong has somehow successfully solved the problem.

This book focuses on the following three aspects: building up the boundaries of the concept of intercultural competence, introducing different theoretical perspectives and providing various assessment instruments while presenting the research finding both at home and abroad. The whole book is divided into eight chapters. In the first chapter, the author briefly introduced the three most fundamental questions concerning intercultural competence. In the second chapter, the author presented the development process of research concerning intercultural competence from the 1960s until now. In Chapters Three to Five, the author summarized and reviewed some representative theories or models concerning intercultural competence, covering not only the Western perspective but also the non-Western perspective in Asia, Africa, and the Middle East. In Chapters Six to Seven, the author discussed how to effectively use some evaluating tools to assess intercultural competence. In the last chapter, the author put forward some new questions further while expressing hopes for the research in this field.

3.2 Communicating Under Different Cultural Contexts

We have already learned that quite a few conventional, culture-specific gestures can be used as replacements for words and due to the fact that a few nonverbal signals are universally recognized, these nonverbal signals are suspected by some scholars to be innate. However, a great many of other nonverbal signals are perceived differently from country to country, or even among cultures within a particular country. However, norms for nonverbal communication vary from country to country, and among cultures within a particular country. On the one hand, the expansion of media together with the trend of globalization is leading to more similarities among cultures concerning nonverbal communication. On the other hand, cultural differences are exposed in nonverbal communication in terms of two aspects: How can the same meaning be expressed by different nonverbal signals in

different cultures and how can the same nonverbal signal mean different things in different countries?

3.2.1 Differences in Greetings

There are many ways to greet people around the world. Shaking hands is the most common greeting method and we have learned in detail some of the guidelines toward a successful handshake. But it is not always done the same way. In the United States and Canada, for example, people usually give a strong handshake. It is short but firm. But in Mexico and Egypt, handshakes usually last a little longer and they are usually softer.

Handshaking is not popular everywhere. For example, bowing is the preferred nonverbal greeting over handshaking in Japan. The way the Japanese bow varies based on status, with higher-status people bowing the least. An interesting ritual associated with the bow is the exchange of business cards before bowing when greeting someone in Japan. This exchange allows each person to view the other person's occupation and title first, which supplies useful information to decide who should bow more. Since bowing gives each person an unobstructed view of the other person's shoes, it is very important to have clean shoes that are in good condition, since they play an important part in initial impression formation.

Bowing is the traditional way of greeting in many Northeast Asian countries to show respect as well except in Japan. Even bowing varies among these cultures. In Japan, when you bow, you do not look directly into the other person's eyes. However, in South Korea, it is important to see the other person's face when you bow.

In some cultures, especially in the Western countries, eye contact is interpreted as attentiveness and honesty. Eye contact aversion, however, could be seen as a sign that the other person is being deceptive, bored, or rude. This is exactly the opposite in Hispanic (西班牙的), Asian and Middle Eastern traditional cultures where direct eye contact is thought to be disrespectful or rude. Therefore, avoiding eye contact is considered as a sign of respect. Some Native American cultures believe that people should avoid eye contact with elders, teachers, and other people with high status. As gaze can show intimacy, quite a few cultures have similar rules that women should especially avoid eye contact with men because it can be taken on as a sign of sexual interest.

Case Study: Staring or Not?

Zoe and Robert are a couple from England. When they first came to China, they felt uneasy because people liked staring at them. Some people even quickly walked past them and turned back to look at them. When Zoe caught the third man staring at her, she felt quite offended and stared back at him. The man was scared off and quickly ran away. Why do you think people stared at Zoe? Why is Zoe offended? How could this uncomfortable encounter be improved?

We have learned in the previous session that it is a cultural taboo to engage in eye contact when greeting others in countries like Japan while in some Western countries, it is acceptable or encouraged to look the people in the eye while talking. This rule applies to greetings and other forms of functional communication. Yet staring at strangers is not among them. It is considered rude or ill-mannered to stare at strangers who look different to satisfy one's curiosity in many countries.

Interpreting this case as rudeness is unnecessary and unproductive. The wise response on the part of the person being stared at is simply to ignore it and accept this harmless form of curiosity rather than to misinterpret it. As more and more Westerners are to be seen in a rising number of cities in China, it is only natural that people would not give rise to the same curiosity forever. However, this idea does not change the fact that this kind of staring often embarrasses people and makes them feel self-conscious, which in turn leads to antipathy and misunderstanding on their part. So, Chinese parents and teachers could instruct children from an early age not to stare at people physically different from themselves. This rule applies not only to foreigners but also to people with physical disability or deformity.

Now it is your turn to analyze a case.

Mr. Brown is a teacher from England and has recently arrived in China. He has been recruited by a university. A few days after his arrival he met with one of his students, Wang Li, on campus and praised him for a piece of writing for his course. In response, Wang Li avoided eye contact, looked down at the ground and said nothing back. Mr. Brown was puzzled and unhappy with Wang Li's reaction. If you are Mr. Brown's colleague who knew about the incident, how would you explain this to him? Can you give him any advice in the future?

You can begin with the explanation of the reasons why the student avoided eye contact as the teacher praised him. You can also share your own experience in similar

situations. Then you should continue by expressing your understanding of the reasons why the teacher felt puzzled and unhappy (due to the cultural differences of eye contact). You can end up summarizing the difference of greetings among the East and the West and give the teacher some advice in the future.

3.2.2 Differences in Approval and Disapproval Movements

A head nod is a universal sign of acknowledgment in cultures where the formal bow is no longer used as a greeting method. In these cases, nodding the head up and down essentially serves as an abbreviated bow, which later evolves to signify "yes". In Tonga, raising the eyebrows shows agreement or liking. On the contrary, shaking the head back and forth is an innate and universal head movement to signal "no". This nonverbal signal begins at birth, as a baby shakes its head from side to side to reject its mother's breast and later shake its head to reject being spoon-fed (Pease & Pease, 2004). However, differences in nodding and shaking the head to indicate agreement and disagreement also exist. The Greeks use the upward nod for disagreement; the Iranians and Italians have used the downward nod for agreement for at least three thousand years.

Besides shaking their heads from side to side, the Europeans prefer to wave hand to show "no", the same as the Chinese. People in Mexico and Costa Rica use the gesture of shaking the whole hand from side to side with the index finger extended and the palm outward to mean "no". A similar gesture is used all the way in Japan to indicate negativity. In Bolivia and Honduras, people wave the index finger as a negative sign. In Lebanon, negativity can also be expressed by shaking the index finger side to side. In Bangladesh, the thumbs-up sign is used to show disapproval or rejection. Many countries, including France and several Latin American countries, show approval by the thumbs-up gesture. Nevertheless, in Kenya, the two-thumbs sign means approval. In many parts of the world, people often use handshaking and clapping to show thanks and positive feelings, while they are used to summon a waiter at a restaurant in Spain.

One of the possible reasons for these differences is that different countries may fall into two categories of cultural behavioral patterns: high-contact culture and low-contact culture, which vary significantly in how they express immediacy and closeness. However, it is important to note that these differences are not absolute due to the involuntary and ambiguous nature of nonverbal communication. The meanings of nonverbal cues are always greatly influenced by the specific context where they took place. They can vary between genders within the same cultural group as well.

For Your Information

Introduction to Some South American and African Countries

Tonga is a Polynesian sovereign state and archipelago comprising 169 islands of the southern Pacific Ocean, of which 36 are inhabited. It is surrounded by Fiji, Wallis, and Futuna (France) to the northwest, Samoa to the northeast, Niue to the east, Kermadec (part of New Zealand) to the southwest, and New Caledonia (France) and Vanuatu to the farther west.

Costa Rica, which literally means "Rich Coast", is a country in Central America, bordered by Nicaragua to the north, Panama to the southeast, the Pacific Ocean to the west, the Caribbean Sea to the east, and Ecuador to the south of Cocos Island.

Bolivia is a landlocked country located in western-central South America. It is bordered to the north and east by Brazil, to the southeast by Paraguay, to the south by Argentina, to the southwest by Chile, and to the northwest by Peru. Santa Cruz de la Sierra is the largest city and principal economic and financial center.

Honduras is a republic in Central America. It has at times been referred to as Spanish Honduras to differentiate it from British Honduras, which became modern-day Belize. Honduras is bordered to the west by Guatemala, to the southwest by El Salvador, to the southeast by Nicaragua, to the south by the Pacific Ocean at the Gulf of Fonseca, and to the north by the Gulf of Honduras, a large inlet of the Caribbean Sea.

Lebanon is a sovereign state in Western Asia. It is bordered by Syria to the north and east, and Israel to the south, while Cyprus is west across the Mediterranean Sea. Lebanon's location at the crossroads of the Mediterranean Basin and the Arabian hinterland facilitated its rich history and shaped a cultural identity of religious and ethnic diversity.

Bangladesh is a country in South Asia. It shares land borders with India and Myanmar (Burma). Nepal, Bhutan, and China are located near Bangladesh but do not share a border with it. Bangladesh is the world's eighth most populous country. Dhaka is its capital and largest city.

Case Study: Careful with Counting with Your Fingers

In the movie *Inglorious Basterds* there is a scene that went like this. Some English spies who planned to assassinate Hitler had decided to gather in a pub to further discuss their plan. To avoid being suspected, they pretended as alcoholics who were having a party and playing some games. Unfortunately, a real German officer walked into the pub and somehow suspected these people. The German officer approached the crowd and started to pry against their background by pretending to be a game player. The leader of the crowd, who was an excellent multi-linguistic spy and able to put on a German accent, answered all the questions perfectly, which successfully lifted the officer's suspicion. In the end, the officer decided to leave the pub and the English spy signaled the pub owner for three glasses of beer to send him off. After a glance at the Englishman's gesture, the German officer immediately pulled out the gun and killed the English spy.

What do you think gave the man off? Do you think it could be how he counted three with his fingers?

Although the spy passed the test for accent and cultural background knowledge, it is the sign that he did for three that gave him away. Remember that emblems are gestures that correspond to an agreed-on meaning. When we use our fingers to count, we are using emblematic gestures, but even our way of counting varies among cultures. Take the hand gesture for example. If a man is from the United States or Britain, he is most likely to hold up his index finger and middle finger to indicate the number two. However, if the man is from another European country such as France, Germany, or Greece, he is more likely to hold up his thumb and index finger to indicate two. Nonverbal signs are mostly voluntary and therefore difficult to control with adequate self-monitoring. If you are interested, you can watch the movie and pay attention to how the spy signifies the number three and do a little research on how the Germans would indicate three.

Now, it is your turn to analyze a case.

Wu Min was a first-year student at a university in France. And he was spending time together with his foreign friends in a bar after class. Wu wanted to express thanks to his friends for helping him out with his study by buying a drink for each of his six friends. The bar was very noisy, so Wu went to the bar tender and did the hand gesture for seven to the bar tender. But the bar tender only looked at him with confusion. Wu did the gesture again, but it still did not work. Wu was very frustrated and worried that he was discriminated by the bar tender. If you happen to be standing by the side of Wu and see all of this, how would you explain this to Wu? And how would you help him out?

You can begin by explaining why the bar tender is confused with the differences in counting among different countries. Then you can teach Wu the French way of counting seven. You can extend your advice by showing Wu some other differences in counting if you want to, such as the way to count nine. You can do some research on the Internet if you do not know the sign.

3.2.3 High-Contact Culture & Low-Contact Culture

We have learned how nonverbal cues can affect relationships by expressing interpersonal attitudes and communicating interpersonal closeness through a series of nonverbal actions known as immediacy behavior like touching, open body positions, and eye contact. People in a low-contact culture like Japan tend to stand farther apart, make less eye contact, and touch less during regular interactions when talking to others while people in a high-contact culture are more inclined to stand closer together, engage in more eye contact, touch more often, and speak more loudly. Central and South America, southern Europe, and the Middle East are often classified as high-contact culture regions; in contrast, Asia and northern Europe are viewed as low-contact culture regions.

Classifying cultures as either high- or low-contact inevitably covers up differences. For example, Central and South America are both classified as high-contact, but quite a few scholars state that the observation of people interacting in natural settings suggests that public touching and holding decrease as one moves south from Costa Rica to Panama to Columbia. In addition, as we noted earlier in Chapter 2 when we compare the idea of closeness between Americans and the Chinese, labelling the two cultures as high- or low-contact, we should not forget that there are likely to be important variations within a culture. For example, black Americans tend to establish larger interpersonal distances for conversation than white Americans do, but they also engage in more touch. As we reflect on high- and low-contact cultures, we should also recognize the importance of distinguishing between the frequency of an action and its meaning. Two cultures may display different frequencies of touch, especially in public zones, but it is a separate

question as to whether the meanings attached to those touches are different as well. Communicating intimacy through touch could be done similarly in both cultures even though one culture allows more public touching than the other does.

More to Watch

Cultural Clashes in *Japanese Story*

As the trend of globalization deepens, it is increasingly common for people to engage in political, commercial, or personal contact with foreigners. In the earlier sessions, we have studied some need-to-knows when it comes to intercultural communication. What kind of effects may it have if one person does not address the issue of intercultural communicative competence? The 2003 movie *Japanese Story* may give you some particularly good idea. In the first part of the movie, the female character, who is an American woman, meets the male character, who is a Japanese businessperson for the first time. However, in less than three minutes after picking the man up, the woman commits numerous cultural faux pas, which nearly ruined the business relationship between the two parties. Let us see a few examples to give you some idea.

The first mistake the woman made is to be late for the pickup. The Japanese and Germans are well-known for their punctuality. Lateness on formal occasions could be interpreted as disrespect to the other party, which may lead to negative first impressions. The woman's way of greeting, namely shaking the man's hand, only makes the impression even worse. Why? Remember we have learned before that Japan is what we call a low-contact culture country, which means certain distance needs to be kept during communication to avoid discomfort and show respect. As a result, the Japanese prefer bowing to shaking hands, which is typical in America but too intimate for the Japanese. Since the man already bowed first, it is better to reply with the same greeting manner by bowing back. Another point worth paying attention to is that the woman receives the business card with a single hand before slapping it twice and putting it casually in her pants' pocket. It could well be said that business cards stand for a person's face in business contact that should be put in special business card holders, portfolios, handbags or the inner pockets of suits or jackets for convenience's sake rather than pants' pockets.

Interesting, right? Watch the movie and find out more about the cultural clashes between Japan and America.

3.2.4 Signs Cannot Be Used Casually Abroad

In the earlier text, we have discussed in detail how nonverbal communication signs can vary across different cultures, mainly about how the same thing is represented by different signs in different countries. In fact, as it was mentioned before, the same sign can also mean quite different things in different cultures as well. For example, the sign for five in China with the whole palm facing out is very insulting in Greece. Next, the passage will reveal in detail some common gestures (see Figure 3.1) that may get us into trouble if not used in accordance with its cultural contexts.

The "OK" sign originates from North America to mean strong approval or goodness and it later becomes quite well received in many other cultures as well. However, it is obscene or rude in Russia, Brazil, Türkiye, and the Mediterranean along the lines of saying that someone is a homosexual. Besides, in France and Belgium it means the recipient is a worthless zero. So be careful with it.

If we go to the Philippines, do not tell someone to come here by curling our finger forward and motioning repeatedly unless we want to be arrested. It is considered to be a gesture that can only be used on a dog and it is punishable with jail time if we do it to a person.

Thumbs-up sign means well done. It is also commonly used by hitchhikers in the U.S., but do not use it in Greece, Russia, and Saudi Arabia near West Africa because it will be interpreted as insulting the recipient.

The sign that many people use to note victory or peace in America, or people commonly do for the cameras to show loveliness in China, Japan, and South Korea is the same as the "F" bomb in Great Britain, Australia, Ireland, and New Zealand.

Figure 3.1   Four Common Signs That Cannot Be Used Casually Abroad

Case Study: The "OK" Sign Is Not OK!

Zhang Hong was an overseas student at a University in Belgium. He lived with an elderly couple, who rented their rooms out to students to retain the lively family atmosphere that had existed when their children were at home. One day the elderly couple asked Zhang Hong about how he felt about his life there during dinner. Zhang was pleased with his living conditions and used the gesture "OK" to show his satisfaction as he was chewing some stewed beef in his mouth. To his surprise, the couple turned angry and said, "If you are not satisfied with the life here, you can leave."

Why do you think the couple was angry with Zhang? Was it because he answered the question while chewing food?

The conflict in this case is the different understanding of the gesture "OK"—making a circle with one's thumb and index finger while extending the others. We have learned in the earlier session that this sign means "OK" or "praise" in America. It is also true in China. But to the people of Belgium, this gesture indicates "worth nothing" or "very unsatisfactory". As Zhang Hong did not use verbal messages or other nonverbal cues to complement his message, the couple could only interpret this sign as it was in their own culture. Besides, answering a question with food in the mouth could indicate impatience or contempt. That is why Zhang found himself in such an awkward situation. The "OK" meaning is common to all English-speaking countries and, although its meaning is fast spreading across Europe and Asia, the gesture for "OK" has other origins and meanings in certain places. For overseas travelers, the safest rule to obey is, when in Rome, do as the Romans do. This can help avoid any possible embarrassing circumstances.

Now it is your turn to analyze a case.

Xiao Liang attended the annual boat-rowing competition between Oxford University and Cambridge University. After the competition, he went with his classmates to a bar to celebrate. Maybe because he drank too much, he made the "V" sign with the palm turned inward to other classmates. As a result, the atmosphere became a little tense. If you are Xiao Liang's friend, how can you ease the tension?

You can begin by analyzing the difference in the meaning of the "V" sign in China and England. You can also explain the difference in the way to do the "V" sign. After that, you should probably wake Xiao Liang up and ask him to apologize for the careless mistake. If you are interested, you can look up the history of the "V" sign on the Internet.

For Your Information

A Brief History of the "OK" Sign

The most widely recognized sign for "OK" was popular in the U.S. during the early 19th century. There are many different views about what the initials "OK" stand for. Some believe "OK" stands for "all correct", while others say it means the opposite of "knock-out", that is, K. O. Another popular theory is that it is an abbreviation for "Old Kinderhook", from the birthplace of a 19th-century American president who used the initials as a campaign slogan. There are also people who argue that it is of Greek, American Indian and even African origin. We may never know which theory is the correct one, but the circle stands for the letter "O" in the "OK" signal. As the American-based company Windows, Intel, and Apple as well as other tech giants expand their business with the globalization trend, the American way of doing OK also spreads all over the world. The fact that this symbol is commonly seen in the emoji list of all IME tools and chatting software or apps is a sign of its popularity around the world.

3.3 A Recipe for Successful Intercultural Communication

Language ability is undoubtedly important for successful intercultural communication. However, in most cases, language is not the reason that eventually leads to misunderstanding during intercultural communication. It is how people perceive who they are and how they perceive each other's status that are creating the problems and leading to frustration. Two main ways to build intercultural communicative competence are through experiential learning and reflective practices (Bednarz, 2010). Adapted from the framework of Byram's theory in terms of ways to improve intercultural communicative competence, we need to be equipped with a box of tools: a heart set, a mindset, and a skill set, instead of a list of rules.

It means that we need to foster attitudes that motivate us, discover knowledge that informs us, and develop skills that enable us to achieve successful intercultural communication.

3.3.1 A Heart Set

The heart set is about intercultural sensitivity or awareness. It means to look outside ourselves and be aware of others, their values and customs as well as what our personal action can do to other people. Social science research shows that our values and beliefs about equality may be inconsistent with our behavior. For example, people sometimes use outdated labels such as "savages" or "colored" in cross-cultural encounters that exemplify prejudices. It is not that we do not know they may hurt others; we may be just ironically unaware of it.

1. Concept of Ethnocentrism

The base of intercultural sensitivity or awareness is the ability to avoid ethnocentrism. Ethnocentrism is the inclination to view one's own group as natural and correct, and all others as less so. We tend to think prescriptively that all groups should behave as our own group behaves. In addition, we are naturally proud of our own group and distrustful of others. Obviously, a person who is highly ethnocentric cannot adapt to diverse people and cannot communicate in an interculturally competent manner. Some authorities hold that some degree of ethnocentrism is inevitable, and even functional for the preservation of distinct cultural groups. Competent communicators simply learn to suppress their natural ethnocentric reactions to understand others on their own terms better. Alternatively, it may be possible for individuals to evolve beyond ethnocentrism, to become ethno-relativistic.

2. The Developmental Model of Intercultural Sensitivity (DMIS)

The Developmental Model of Intercultural Sensitivity (Bennett, 1993) is often used in intercultural training and assessment to chart individuals' progress toward ethnorelativism. The model includes six stages:

1) Denial—The individual refuses to acknowledge cultural differences.

2) Defense—The individual begins to see cultural differences and regards them as threats.

3) Minimization—While individuals at this stage do acknowledge cultural differences, they see human universals as more significant than cultural distinctions.

4) Acceptance—The individual begins to accept significant cultural differences first in behavior, and then in values.

5) Adaptation—The individual becomes more adept at intercultural communication by shifting perspectives to the other's cultural worldview.

6) Integration—Individuals at this stage begin to transcend their own native cultures. They define their identities and evaluate their actions in terms of multiple cultural perspectives.

The idea of a heart set is more than just knowing the possible consequences of such cultural differences. It also includes knowing the consequences of one's own behavior. A heart set speaks of an attitude to respect and open our mind to all kinds of contextual similarities and differences, may it be gender, individual or cultural. To foster attitudes that motivate us, we must develop a sense of curiosity about culture. This sense of curiosity may correlate to a high tolerance for uncertainty, which can help us turn potentially frustrating experiences we have into teachable moments.

3.3.2 A Mindset

The mindset refers to the discovery of knowledge that informs us. It means to gain linguistic and cultural knowledge to understand and interact effectively in multilingual or multicultural settings. Discovering knowledge that informs us is another step that can build on our motivation and the knowledge gives room for flexibility and tolerance for the uncertainty, which makes adaptability possible. As we learn more about our cognitive style, or how we learn, we discover that there are differences in how people address and perceive the world, explain events, organize the world, and use rules of logic. Some cultures have a cognitive style that focuses more on tasks, analytic and objective thinking, details and precision, inner direction, and independence, while others focus on relationships and people over tasks and things, concrete and metaphorical thinking, and a group consciousness and harmony.

For example, competent communicators are sensitive to nonverbal communication patterns in other cultures. As the earlier case study shows, one should know the greeting habits of the Japanese before engaging in any communicative contact. We have already learned that some cultures are polychronic where people place little value on demarcating work time as opposed to social time. In polychronic countries like Spain and Mexico, appointments may be scheduled at overlapping periods, making an "orderly" schedule impossible. It is also common to cancel appointments or close

businesses for family obligations. People may also miss appointments or deadlines without offering an apology. There is no need for us to be offended or frustrated. Try to understand and play along. We may find it is not such a dreadful thing to get the job done without sacrificing personal relationships.

Rather than learning a list of rules for cultural variations, it is better to learn more general knowledge in terms of how social norms vary based on cultural values and increase our awareness of the impact of context in which our communication is taking place. By observing cultural behavior of people from the target culture, learners will become aware of the ways in which their own cultural background influences their own behavior and develop a tolerance for behavioral patterns different from their own. Transformative learning takes place at the highest levels and occurs when we meet situations that challenge our accumulated knowledge and our ability to accommodate that knowledge to manage a real-world situation.

3.3.3 A Skill Set

The last step is to develop skills. It is to develop an individual's ability to reach communicative goals during intercultural communication. To learn such skills, people need to develop "tools" for understanding their own and others' way of interacting in order to be able to participate effectively in multilingual or multicultural interactions across a range of languages and cultures. It has many components, like message skill, proper self-disclosure, behavioral flexibility, and interaction management. We have talked about this in how to improve one's communicative skills, which is the first step to begin the journey of the skill learning.

We will develop a foundation for these skills by reading this book, but we can expand those skills to intercultural settings with the motivation and knowledge already described. Contact alone may not be able to increase intercultural skills; there must be more measures deliberately taken. While current research shows that intercultural contact does decrease prejudice, it is not enough to become interculturally competent. The ability to empathize and manage anxiety enhances prejudice reduction, and these two skills have been shown to enhance the overall impact of intercultural contact even more than getting cultural knowledge. There is intercultural training available for those who are interested. If we cannot access training, we may choose to research intercultural training on our own, as there are many books, articles, and manuals written on the subject.

3.3.4 Other Practical Approaches

Reflective practices can also help us process through rewards and challenges associated with developing intercultural communicative competence. As we open ourselves to new experiences, we are likely to have both positive and negative reactions. It can be extremely useful to take note of negative or defensive reactions we have. This can help us find certain triggers that may create barriers to effective intercultural interaction. A more complex method of reflection is called intersectional reflexivity by which we acknowledge intersecting identities, both privileged and disadvantaged, and implicate ourselves in social hierarchies and inequalities (Jones, 2010).

3.4 Culture Shock

Culture shock is an experience we may have when we move to a cultural environment different from our own; it is also the personal disorientation we may feel when experiencing an unfamiliar way of life due to immigration or a visit to a new country, a move between social environments, or simply transition to another type of life. One of the most common causes of culture shock involves individuals being in a foreign environment.

Common problems include information overload, language barrier, generation gap, technology gap, skill interdependence, formulation dependency, homesickness (cultural), infinite regress (homesickness), boredom (job dependency), and response ability (cultural skill set). There is no true way to entirely prevent culture shock, as individuals in any society are personally affected by cultural contrasts differently.

3.4.1 Five Stages of Culture Shock

Anthropologist Kalervo Oberg listed five stages of the culture shock, as shown in Figure 3.2.

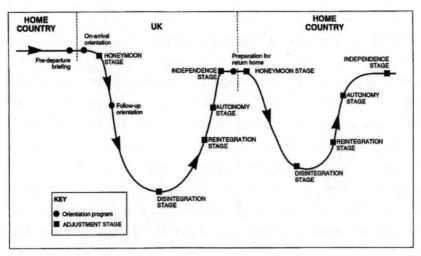

Figure 3.2   W-Curve: Stages of Adjustment Experienced During Orientation (Barker, 1990)

1. Honeymoon Stage

During this period, the differences between the old and new culture are seen in a romantic light. For example, in moving to a new country, an individual might love the new food, the pace of life, and the locals' habits. During the first few weeks, most people are fascinated by the new culture. They associate with nationals who speak their language, and who are polite to the foreigners. Like most honeymoon periods, this stage eventually ends.

2. Disintegration Stage

After some time (usually around 3 months, depending on the individual), differences between the old and new culture become apparent and may create anxiety. Excitement may eventually give way to unpleasant feelings of frustration and anger as one continues to experience unfavorable events that may be perceived as strange and offensive to one's cultural attitude. Language barriers and stark differences in public hygiene, traffic safety, food accessibility and quality may heighten the sense of disconnection from the surroundings.

While being transferred into a different environment puts special pressure on communication skills, there are practical difficulties to overcome, such as circadian rhythm disruption that often leads to insomnia and daylight drowsiness; adaptation of gut flora to different bacteria levels and concentrations in food and water; difficulty in seeking treatment for illness, as medicines may have different names in that culture and the same active ingredients might be hard to recognize.

Still, the most important change in the period is communication: People adjusting to a new culture often feel lonely and homesick because they are not yet used to the new environment and meeting people with whom they are not familiar every day. The language barrier may become a major obstacle in creating new relationships: Special attention must be paid to one's and others' culture-specific body language signs, linguistic faux pas, conversation tone, linguistic nuances and customs, and false friends.

In the case of students studying abroad, some develop additional symptoms of loneliness that ultimately affect their lifestyles as a whole. Due to the strain of living in a different country without parental support, international students often feel anxious and get more pressure while adjusting to new cultures—even more so when the cultural distances are wide, as patterns of logic and speech are different and a special emphasis is put on rhetoric.

3. Reintegration Stage

Some may go through the stage of deculturation while others the acculturation. Deculturation refers to the process of taking away people's original traits. Acculturation is the process of social, psychological, and cultural change that stems from blending between cultures (Sam & Berry, 2010).

There are three basic outcomes of this phase.

Some people find it impossible to accept the foreign culture and to integrate. They isolate themselves from the host country's environment, which they come to perceive as hostile, withdraw into a "ghetto" and see returning to their own culture as the only way out. These "rejectors" also have the greatest problems re-integrating back home after return.

Some people integrate fully and take on all parts of the host culture while losing their original identity. This is called cultural assimilation. They normally remain in the host country forever. This group is sometimes known as "adopters". Approximately 10% of expatriates belong to this group.

Some people manage to adapt to the aspects of the host culture they see as positive while keeping some of their own and creating their unique blend. They have no major problems returning home or relocating elsewhere. This group can be thought to be somewhat cosmopolitan. Approximately 30% of expatriates belong to this group.

Culture shock has many different effects, time spans, and degrees of severity. Many people are handicapped by its presence and do not recognize what is bothering them.

4. Autonomy Stage

Again, after some time (usually 6 to 12 months), one grows accustomed to the new culture and develops routines. One knows what to expect in most situations and no longer feels all that new about the host country. One becomes concerned with basic living again, and things become more "normal". One starts to develop problem-solving skills for dealing with the culture and begins to accept the culture's ways with a positive attitude. The culture begins to make sense, and negative reactions and responses to the culture are reduced.

5. Independence Stage

In the mastery stage, individuals are able to participate fully and comfortably in the host culture. Mastery does not mean total conversion; people often keep many traits from their earlier culture, such as accent and language. It is often referred to as the bicultural stage.

But not everyone goes through all the stages mentioned above and not everyone experiences extreme culture shocks.

For Your Information

Kalervo Oberg (1901—1973), a pioneer in economic and applied anthropology, died on July 11, 1973, in Corvallis, Oregon. Oberg had lived a full and varied life, doing major research on three continents and winning the respect and affection of his students, professional colleagues, and associates in government service.

Kalervo Oberg's formal bibliography is deceptively modest, reflecting the penalty almost always paid by career government anthropologists. The press of daily assignments, and the long reports that must be written, allow scant time for more permanent contributions. Many of his government reports, such as "The Fishermen of Surinam", are in fact major monographs, and plans are now being made to bring together for publication parts of his manuscript materials. Oberg published only when he felt he had something to say. In his bibliography one does not find the "padding", the bits and squibs that are often a part of the promotion ammunition of lengthier bibliographies. An innate modesty made it difficult for Oberg to push forward many of his original ideas. "Culture shock" is a case in point. While living in Rio de Janeiro and explaining Brazilian culture and society to newly arrived American technicians and their families, many of whom had not previously lived abroad, he noticed a common syndrome, a sequence of behavior and attitude: initial exhilaration and excitement with the foreign assignment, quickly turning to depression, disillusionment, harsh criticism of Brazilian ways, and concern with health problems, usually followed by recovery and adaptation to the new conditions of life. These observations led to Oberg's most widely known paper, first given as an informal talk to an American wives' club in Rio de Janeiro. This talk, which remains the definitive statement on culture shock, was reproduced and distributed to American personnel in embassies and technical aid missions in many parts of the world. Only much later did it appear in *The Bobbs-Merrill Reprint Series*, where the year, 1954, is that of the original talk, and not of publication.

Kalervo Oberg's publications on economic anthropology, social organization, law, and above all applied anthropology, should be of interest to students for a long time to come. In his quiet way, Oberg has been an important figure in world anthropology.

3.4.2 Reverse Culture Shock

Reverse culture shock (also known as "re-entry shock" or "own culture shock") may take place—returning to one's home culture after growing accustomed to a new one can produce the same effects as described above. These are results from the psychosomatic and psychological consequences of the readjustment process to the primary culture. The affected person often finds this more surprising and difficult to deal with than the original culture shock. This phenomenon, the reactions that members of the re-entered culture exhibit toward the re-entrant, and the inevitability of the two are encapsulated in the following saying, which is also the title of a book by Thomas Wolfe, *You Can't Go Home Again*.

Reverse culture shock is generally made up of two parts: idealization and expectations. When an extended period of time is spent abroad, we focus on the good from our past, cut out the bad, and create an idealized version of the past. Then, once removed from our familiar setting and placed in a foreign one, we incorrectly assume that our previous world has not changed. We expect things

to remain exactly the same as when we left them. The realization that life back home is now different, that the world has continued without us, and the process of readjusting to these new conditions as well as actualizing our new perceptions about the world with our old way of living causes discomfort and psychological anguish.

3.4.3 Transition Shock

Culture shock is a subcategory of a more universal construct called transition shock, which is a state of loss and disorientation predicated by a change in one's familiar environment that requires adjustment. There are many symptoms of transition shock, including:

- anger;
- boredom;
- compulsive eating/drinking/weight gain;
- desire for home and old friends;
- excessive concern over cleanliness;
- excessive sleep;
- feelings of helplessness and withdrawal;
- getting "stuck" on one thing;
- glazed stare;
- homesickness;
- hostility towards host nationals;
- impulsivity;
- irritability;
- mood swings;
- physiological stress reactions;
- stereotyping host nationals;
- suicidal or fatalistic thoughts;
- withdrawal.

Case Study: A Chinese Medical Doctor's Brief Trip to America

Here are some questions to help you analyze this case:

(1) How many stages of culture shock did Dr. Dong experience?

(2) What symptoms of transition shock did Dr. Dong have?

(3) What can we learn from Dr. Dong's case?

Dr. Dong had a wonderful chance to go to Seattle to present a paper at a professional meeting. He experienced the typical stages of culture shock. He arrived expectant and happy and enjoyed his former days very much. At the medical conference, he felt quite confident in his area of research and was able to perform well in his presentation. But after a few days, he began to feel uncomfortable. His medical English was fine, but the social interaction expectations were different, and he was unsure of the cues and the communication style. He was more and more worried that he was misunderstanding simple English greetings and table talk conventions. When people greeted him with "Hi, how's it going?", he thought they had asked him "Where are you going?" and answered with the name of the conference hall, only to get a quizzical stare from them. At a Western style dinner, a colleague asked, "So how're you enjoying in the States?" He thought he heard, "How are you enjoying your steak?" and answered that he was eating chicken, not beef. That time, his colleague smiled, and patiently repeated the question, with both laughing at the error. Such misunderstandings and miscommunications were minor. But for Dr. Dong, they were the beginning of a sense of cultural confusion. By the end of the meetings, he felt a deep sense of cultural stress and was worn out from having to pay attention to so many new expressions and ways of dealing with things. He felt his handshake was not as firm as Americans', found that people reacted unusually when he modestly insisted his English was not good after they complimented him, didn't know how to accept dinner invitations properly and therefore missed out on going to several lunches, and so on. Eventually, he was so bewildered that he felt the full impact of culture shock.

Dr. Dong has experienced the first two stages of culture shock, i.e., honeymoon stage and disintegration stage. He has the symptoms of transition shock, such as

getting "stuck" on one thing, mood swings, and physiological stress reactions.

Oberg called culture shock the occupational disease of people who have been suddenly transplanted abroad. His use of the word "disease" is a pun, because it implies that it is like an "ailment, with its own symptoms and cure", but also that the root cause is also a feeling of "dis" ease, or unsettled uneasiness.

The "a fish out of water" metaphor is helpful: Only when we are away from our everyday environment, do we suddenly realize how important it is to our comfort or ease of communication. Each unfamiliar new context feels just like the strange air that is a threat to the fish—it surprises or even shocks us. Like Dr. Dong, we feel bewildered, unsure of ourselves, disoriented or even fearful.

Nevertheless the physical difficulties mentioned before Dr. Dong's communicative challenges, or other situational factors, being aware of this need for heightened intercultural awareness can help us note and eventually accept differences, understand the whys and wherefores, and seek to adapt as best as we can. By trial and error, and with a lot of patience with themselves, most people succeed in overcoming culture shock and learn to enjoy their new context. The more we see culture shock as just a normal part of most transitions, the easier it will be.

If you were Dr. Dong, what would you do? By the way, have you ever been abroad and experienced culture shock? What are your solutions to overcome culture shock?

Summary

To avoid being a fluent fool, we need to understand more completely the cultural dimensions of language. A competent communicator is the person who can convey a sense of communication appropriateness and effectiveness in diverse cultural contexts. Developing intercultural competency is no easy task. It goes way beyond linguistic knowledge. It even goes way beyond cultural knowledge. There are plenty of ways to express ourselves besides linguistic competency, as long as we are willing to interact in ways that are ethical and supportive. We should be aware that it takes more than one lesson but continuing efforts and self-monitoring to build up intercultural sensitivity. In order to become a successful intercultural communicator, one needs to have the determination to avoid any type of bias, especially ethnocentrism or stereotype when sending and receiving messages. Besides, one needs to be equipped with the belief that there is no better or worse way of behavior, only appropriate ones and inappropriate ones, especially across different cultures.

Exercises

Questions for Review

1. What's Canale's idea of communicative competence? How is it different from Byram's intercultural competence?

2. Can you summarize the differences between their handshaking manners when people from different countries shake hands with each other?

3. Can you describe the characteristics of high-contact and low-contact cultures and provide at least one example in terms of greeting to demonstrate each category?

4. Can you recall the various stages of DMIS? Can you give one example of typical actions when experiencing each stage?

5. What is cultural shock? Does it mean the same thing as being shocked by some cultural phenomena? What are the typical stages during a cultural shock?

Problems and Application

1. You invited some Arabic friends to your birthday party. When everyone was seated, you started to introduce the dishes in English to your Arabic friends and they were very pleased with the dinner. However, when you were introducing the traditional Chinese cuisine Sweet and Sour Pork Ribs, the Arabic guests suddenly became very upset; they quickly stood up and left the party without bidding farewell to everyone. Why do you think the Arabic guests are offended and how would you make peace with them again?

2. You and your grandmother were invited to visit your sister in America. Everything went well at the beginning, yet only after a few weeks your grandmother wanted to come back to China. However, you still wanted to stay and visit more places in the U.S. As time went on, your grandmother started to show signs of depression and had trouble eating and sleeping, yet you felt just fine. What do you think happened to your grandmother? What would you do to solve the dilemma?

Chapter *4*

Cultural Patterns

Learning Objectives

After learning this chapter, you should be able to:

1. define cultural patterns and three basic components of cultural patterns;

2. compare and contrast three major approaches to studying cultural patterns;

3. illustrate and analyze Hofstede's cultural dimensions.

As we interact with people from all over the world, we will find that there are various differences between our culture and theirs. One of the big differences lies in the food we eat. For example, Americans are used to eating burgers; Italians like lasagna and pizza; the Japanese are fond of sushi and sashimi; Indians prefer curry; and we Chinese are fond of Chinese food.

Each culture is unique and has its own distinctive value system. This system can help people distinguish beauty from ugliness, good from evil, which constitutes the unique cultural pattern of this culture. In this chapter, we will introduce the cultural patterns and three approaches to studying the cultural patterns, including the theory of high-context culture and low-context culture proposed by Edward Hall, the cultural dimension theory proposed by Geert Hofstede, and the theory of five value orientations proposed by Florence Kluckhohn and Fred Strodtbeck.

These theories can help us seek common ground while reserving differences in the process of cross-cultural communication. Even if we do not understand one's cultural background, after mastering the content of this chapter, we can use the knowledge we have learned to make reasonable predictions and interpretations of his or her communicative behavior.

Before we start this chapter, there are some questions for you:

(1) What will you do when you are praised?
(2) Will you try to persuade your leader to accept your opinion when your opinion is different from that of your leader?
(3) When your personal interests conflict with the interests of the whole class, what choice will you make?

4.1 A Brief Introduction to Cultural Patterns

Cultural patterns are shared beliefs, values, and norms that are stable over time and that lead to similar behavior across similar situations (Lustig & Koester, 2007). It is extremely important to identify the differences in cultural patterns which serve as the basis of the development of cultural competence in cross-cultural communication. These cultural patterns enable us to predict a culture and adapt our communication to our prediction accordingly. In other words, they could be seen as the shared mental programs governing people's behavior.

Cultural patterns provide a set of basic standards for guiding thought and action. Of course, some aspects of this mental programming are unique to everyone. As there are no two identical leaves in the world, there are no two persons that are identical in programming even if they are in the same culture. However, in cross-cultural comparison, some mental programs are basically universal. For example, children's dependence on their mothers is one of our common human experiences and shared by people in all cultures.

In addition to those unique or commonly seen mental programs, there are also some mental programs shared only by members of a specific culture. As a result, if people from other cultures want to understand their particular behavior, they need to study them in the context of this specific culture. Only in this way can people communicate and understand each other.

Cultural patterns are, in fact, a by-product of the unconscious experience of daily activities. Most of the core assumptions are programmed early and then endure a continuous enhancement day by day. The Chinese, for example, are taught to appreciate harmony, equality, dedication, integrity, and friendship, while people in America speak highly of the characteristics such as achievement, freedom, personality, and practicality.

Next, we are going to introduce the basic components of cultural patterns: beliefs, values, and norms.

 **4.1.1 Beliefs**

A belief is an idea that people assume to be true about the world. Therefore, beliefs are a set of acquired knowledge, which help cultural members to decide what is logical or illogical, and whether it is correct or not.

Beliefs can range from ideas that are central to a person's sense of self to those that are more peripheral. Central beliefs include the culture's fundamental teachings about what reality is and expectations about how the world works. And there are also beliefs taught by some authorities such as parents, teachers, and so on, from whom we can have a basic knowledge of the world we live in. Peripheral beliefs are about personal judgment and taste. They help everyone form unique ideas and expectations in a larger cultural matrix.

It's difficult to discuss common cultural beliefs because people don't usually realize them. Common cultural beliefs are the basis of assumptions about what the world is like and how it works, so they are not usually noticed. We hope that through

this discussion on cultural beliefs, we will realize that many things we think are reality may not be the reality for people from other cultures. What we think of as an indisputable fact about the world may have a totally different explanation in other cultures.

Here we will take people's different understanding of the Earth's shape as an example. In ancient times, people believed it was a universally accepted fact that the Earth is flat. However, now we all know that this is completely wrong since scientific research has long told us that the Earth is round.

And there are also a lot of other examples. For instance, people in Thailand believe that there are spirits in all kinds of things—whether animate or inanimate. As a result, rural areas are full of spirit houses, where Thais offer sacrifices every day. Chinese people believe the number 4 is unlucky while 8 is a number bringing good luck.

 4.1.2 Values

Cultures differ not only in beliefs but also in values. Values involve what a culture regards as good or bad, right or wrong, fair or unfair, just or unjust, beautiful or ugly, clean or dirty, valuable or worthless, appropriate or inappropriate, and kind or cruel (Rokeach, 2017). Values are seen as the expected characteristics or objectives of a culture; as a result, the values of a culture are not necessarily synonymous with the description of its actual behavior and features. However, values are often used to explain the way people communicate.

Schwartz (1992) made extensive research on the values in 49 countries. According to Schwartz, there are ten types of universal values that can be used as guiding principles or central goals of a culture. We can find these value types in Table 4.1. Besides, Schwartz also proposed that these ten value types can be arranged into two basic dimensions to organize and provide a consistent structure for the relationship between value types. As we can see in Figure 4.1, complementary value types are close to each other, while opposite value types cross each other. For example, a culture that values tradition and conformity may also value security and benevolence, rather than self-direction and stimulation.

In different cultures, the valence and intensity of values are different. Valence refers to people's attitudes (positive or negative) towards the value, and intensity means the degree of importance of the value. For example, in Chinese culture, respecting the elderly has a positive valence and strong intensity. However, in the eyes of many Americans, the contrary is indeed true. Therefore, when communicating with others, never judge others using our own values. Only when we learn to study their values within the framework of their culture can our research be truly objective and fair.

Table 4.1   Schwartz's Value Types

Value Types	Characteristics	Representative Values
Power	Social status and prestige, control or dominance over people and resources	Social power, wealth, authority
Achievement	Personal success through demonstrating competence according to social standards	Successful, capable, ambitious, influential
Hedonism	Pleasure or sensuous gratification for oneself	Pleasure, enjoying life
Stimulation	Excitement, novelty, and challenge in life	Daring, a varied life, an exciting life
Self-direction	Independence in thought and action choosing, creating, and exploring	Creativity, freedom, curiosity, independence, ability to choose one's own goals
Universalism	Understanding, appreciation, tolerance, and protection for the welfare of all people and nature	Social justice, a world at peace, broad mind, equality, wisdom, unity with nature, a world of beauty, protecting the environment
Benevolence	Preservation and enhancement of the welfare of people with whom one is in frequent personal contact	Helpful, forgiving, honest, loyal, true friendship
Tradition	Respect, commitment, and acceptance of the customs and ideas that one's culture and religion impose on the self	Accepting one's portion in life, devout, respect for tradition, humble, moderate
Conformity	Restraint of actions, inclinations, and impulses that are likely to upset or harm others and violate social expectations or norms	Obedience, self-discipline, politeness, honoring parents and elders
Security	Safety, harmony, and stability of society, relationships, and the self	Family security, national security, social order, reciprocation of favors

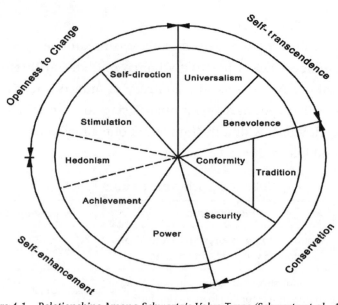

Figure 4.1   Relationships Among Schwartz's Value Types (Schwartz et al., 1997)

It is important to note that with the changing of cultures, the values of the culture will also change accordingly. Let's take "women's rights movement" as an example. As we all know, it has dramatically altered the social organizations and the value systems in the United States. With more and more women getting their college degrees nowadays, great changes have taken place in the workplace and classrooms in the United States in the last twenty years. Besides, it's a very common phenomenon that young people in some traditional countries wear Levi's and listen to Western pop music. Although we face the dynamic nature of culture and the corresponding value systems, the deep structure of a culture remains unchanged regardless of the seemingly change of the culture. No matter how influential American culture nowadays is all around the world, most countries would unquestionably resist the complete takeover of their core values by American cultural values, since the core value of a country is closely related with its cultural identity. Therefore, the study of cultural patterns and values is a very interesting topic worthy of special attention.

 **4.1.3 Norms**

Cultural norms are behavioral standards that a society adopts as a whole and follows when interacting with one another. Norms are the rules that a group uses for appropriate and inappropriate values, beliefs, attitudes, and behavior. These rules may be explicit or implicit. They are different according to each culture.

For example, a common group norm amongst academics is that dress is casual (with the underlying implication that what goes on in the mind is more important than what goes on in the body). Similarly, we rarely see programmers in suits all day long, which is considered to be the dress code of insurance sales or stockbrokers.

Failure to stick to the rules can result in severe punishments, the most feared of which is exclusion from the group. A common rule is that the norms must frequently be displayed; neutrality is seldom an option.

Norms are often transmitted by nonverbal behavior. For example, when people act outside the norms, others might give them dirty looks. Norms may also be transmitted through stories, rituals, and role-model behavior.

Cultural norms are further broken down by sociologists into four subcategories, including folkways, mores, taboos, and laws.

Folkways, sometimes known as conventions or customs, are standards of behavior that are socially approved but not morally significant. Breaking a folkway is a less-criticized offense because folkways are not considered as morally consequential as taboos. An example of breaking a folkway is when a person attempts to shake another person's hand during a first meeting and does not see the gesture returned. While the action is a bit offensive, it is not reprehensible enough to warrant feelings of disgust toward that person.

Mores are norms of morality and norms that define the standards of moral behavior within a culture. A common example is the unacceptability to some people that a couple gives birth to a child out of wedlock.

Taboos refer to what a culture absolutely forbids. Generally speaking, the members of a society judge one another when a person breaks a cultural norm. This is especially true when people behave in a manner that violates a taboo, which is a norm that is so strongly upheld that breaching it results in extreme judgment and shaming from others. Examples include drug addiction, prostitution, incest, and bestiality.

Lastly, laws are norms that are clearly defined and upheld by a culture's governing body. Virtually all taboos, like child abuse, are enacted into law, although not all mores are. For example, wearing a bikini to church may be offensive, but it is not against the law.

To sum up, beliefs, values, and norms are three important components of cultural patterns, which are relatively stable over a long period and considered to be the reason why people in the same cultural group behave similarly.

4.2 High-Context & Low-Context Cultures

In the previous section, we have introduced the concept of cultural patterns and their basic components—beliefs, values, and norms. Then how to study the cultural patterns? From this section, we will introduce three major approaches to studying cultural patterns. The first approach was proposed by Edward Hall (1976), who divided culture into two dimensions: high-context culture and low-context culture.

High-context culture and low-context culture are terms used in different cultures based on how explicit the messages exchanged are and how much the context means in certain situations. These concepts were first introduced by the anthropologist Edward Hall in his book *Beyond Culture* which was published in 1976. Hall believes that in the high-context culture, the communication information implies more information than the actual spoken part, while in the low-context culture, the information has a clear meaning, and there is nothing behind it.

4.2.1 High-Context Culture

Edward Hall is the first person to discuss and define high-context culture and low-context culture, which are used to describe the communication style of a culture. High-context culture refers to the culture in which the communication rules are mainly transmitted through the use of context elements, and are not clearly expressed. This forms a direct contrast with low-context culture. In a low-context culture, information is mainly transmitted through language and the rules are clear. High-context culture has many assumptions about the commonality of communication, opinions, and knowledge. In this culture, there is more quiet understanding of what is happening and less talk about it, because ultimately, we should be "understood". Examples of high-context cultures are China, France, Brazil, Greece, and Japan.

Members of high-context cultures usually have a close relationship for a long time. Because of the interaction among the members over years, they are very clear about the rules, thinking modes, and behavior of the community, so the rules don't have to be explicit. This makes it difficult for those who do not understand the hidden rules of communication to live and communicate in a high-context culture.

In short, the characteristics of high-context culture are listed as follows:

- Less explicit communication.

- More internalized understanding of what is communicated.

- Long-term relationships.

- Strong boundaries between who is accepted as belonging and who is considered an "outsider".

- Knowledge is situational and relational.

- Decisions and activities focus on personal face-to-face relationships.

4.2.2 Low-Context Culture

On the other hand, Hall describes low-context culture as a kind of culture that communicates information in a direct way, which mainly depends on words. Low-context culture does not rely on contextual factors to convey information. People communicate in a more direct and explicit way. This is in sharp contrast to the high-context culture, which to a large extent relies on the implied information and contextual clues to convey the information. In the low-context culture, issues are fully elaborated in communication. Information is much more specific. People pay great attention to what they say. Examples of low-context cultures are the United Kingdom, the United States, Australia, Germany, and Switzerland.

Members of low-context cultures have many short-lasting relationships. It's important to follow the procedures and objectives when completing any transaction. Cultural rules and norms need to be made clear so that people unfamiliar with the culture know what to expect. Communication should be precise and straightforward, and words should be used to convey the whole message effectively.

In short, the characteristics of low-context culture are summarized as follows:

- Rule-oriented: People play by external rules.

- More knowledge is codified, public, external, and accessible.

- Sequencing, separation—of time, space, activities, or relationships.

- More interpersonal connections of shorter duration.

- Knowledge is more often transferable.

- Task-centered: Decisions and activities focus on what needs to be done, and the division of responsibilities.

4.2.3 Differences Between High-Context Culture & Low-Context Culture

In a high-context culture, the way of saying is more important than the content of saying. Since in a high-context culture, a lot of things are left unsaid, the explanation of which depends on the context at that time and the whole culture. In a low-context culture, in order to be fully understood, communicators must use words very clearly.

Remember, every culture has its high and low sides. Usually, a situation contains an internal high-context core and an external low-context ring.

For example, a PTA (Parent Teacher Association) is usually regarded as a low-context situation: Any parent can attend; the date and the content of the meeting are all explicit information. As a result, everyone is expected to be very clear about how to attend the meeting.

However, if it is a small town, all the parents in the PTA are very familiar with each other. They may have some unspoken agreements on the running of PTA. Other parents from outside may have difficulty in understanding these unwritten rules. Under such a condition, the subgroup becomes high context, although the PTA as a whole is low context.

In Table 4.2, the differences between high-context culture and low-context culture are illustrated.

Table 4.2　Differences Between High-Context Culture & Low-Context Culture (Hall, 1976)

	High-Context Culture	**Low-Context Culture**
Information	◆ Context is very important, and most of the information is hidden in the context.	◆ Most of the information is vested in an explicit manner.
Relationship	◆ The relationship is stable and slowly established, based on mutual trust. ◆ Clear boundaries distinguish people inside and outside social groups or circles. ◆ The execution of tasks depends on the relationship between people and attention is paid to the process. ◆ A person's identity is determined by the group to which he or she belongs.	◆ The relationship is short-lived. ◆ Many people are allowed to enter a certain social circle since the boundaries are ambiguous. ◆ Tasks are performed by following predetermined procedures, and focusing on the ultimate goal. ◆ A person's identity is established by himself or herself according to his or her achievements.

(Continued)

	High-Context Culture	Low-Context Culture
Interaction	◆ Widely use gesture elements (such as tone, facial expression, eye contact, body language, etc.) in conversation. ◆ The communication of information is implicit and to a large extent depends on context rather than actual words. ◆ Communication is lengthy, indirect, and revolves around the main points. ◆ Communication is regarded as an art, a means of establishing and nurturing interpersonal relationships. ◆ Disagreements or conflicts are regarded as personal, so conflicts must be avoided or resolved as quickly as possible.	◆ Conversation involves the use of verbal factors rather than nonverbal factors. ◆ Information is clearly conveyed in an accurate and understandable form. It depends on the actual word, not the context. ◆ Communication is direct, concise, and to the point. ◆ Communication is considered as a means of exchanging ideas, information and facts. ◆ Disagreements are not personal, but differences in opinions that do not affect personal relationships. Instead, both sides focus on developing a reasonable solution.
Personal Space	◆ Personal space is not so important. Instead, people are used to standing together, and sharing the same space.	◆ Privacy is regarded to be very important. Therefore, everyone has his or her own private space, which is strictly defined.
Learning	◆ Deductive thinking. ◆ Use multiple sources or information when acquiring knowledge. ◆ Knowledge is obtained from clues in a specific situation. ◆ Learning and problem solving are regarded as group tasks. ◆ Pay attention to the quality and accuracy of the acquired knowledge.	◆ Inductive thinking. ◆ Only a single source of information is used to develop knowledge. ◆ The knowledge gained depends on personal perception. ◆ Learning and problem solving are regarded as personal tasks. ◆ Pay attention to the speed and efficiency of knowledge acquisition.
Examples	◆ Russian ◆ South Korean ◆ Hungarian ◆ Italian ◆ Japanese	◆ Scandinavian ◆ Dutch ◆ Australian ◆ German ◆ English

If we travel a lot, we may find that people in different places have different levels of expression when using language. In low-context cultures, people are often asked to express their meanings straightforwardly, instead of making rounds and beating around the bush. People in low-context cultures pay more attention to self-expression, statement of personal views, and the ability to persuade others. The United States is such a low-context cultural country. In addition, Canada, Israel, and most modern European countries belong to such culture.

In countries with high-context cultures, people are taught to speak tactfully and not too directly from an early age. Such groups include Koreans, Maori in New Zealand, and the Japanese. In these societies, it is more important to maintain social harmony and prevent conflicts with others. Therefore, people will speak more tactfully and act more cautiously. They often express their meaning through more subtle behavioral information or contextual cues such as facial expressions and tone of voice.

From the way people handle criticism and objections, we can get a glimpse of the impact of this cultural difference on communication behavior. In a low-context culture, the boss may openly and severely reprimand an irresponsible subordinate, using him as an example to warn others. The boss may reveal the mistakes of the subordinates without any consideration. At the same time, he will directly say what he wants the other party to correct and what the consequences will be if the other party fails to meet his expectations.

However, in a high-context culture, the boss may take into account the face of his subordinate instead of reprimanding him in public. On the contrary, the boss will criticize his subordinate in private and choose some tactful language to express the meaning of criticism. He won't directly tell his subordinate what he has done wrong, but will guide him to find his own mistakes by going around the circle. For example, an employee is often late. In a high-context culture, the boss will not directly criticize him for being late. On the contrary, the boss may constantly emphasize the sense of responsibility among colleagues, and it is shameful to be a laggard in the team. At this time, the subordinate should be able to understand what the boss wants to express through his tone of voice, body movements, and facial expressions.

When a person with a low-context cultural background enters a high-context culture, the possibility of him being misunderstood is greatly increased. To illustrate this point, let's assume a situation like this. You want to invite two friends to have a cup of coffee in a very popular bookstore café tomorrow evening. Tina, a friend from a low-context cultural background, said to you, "No, I have to study tomorrow evening, but thank you for your invitation." And another friend from a high-context cultural background, Lee, told you, "That's great," but then you would be surprised to find that he did not come to the café as scheduled.

How do you account for this behavioral difference? People who grow up in a high-context culture have a hard time saying no to others. Even if they really want to refuse something, they will tactfully say it for fear of offending others. People from the same cultural background as Lee may immediately understand his meaning through his voice intonation and facial expressions. He actually doesn't really want to drink coffee. But if you live in a low-context culture, you would think that he agrees without directly rejecting it, so you would mistakenly think that he is willing to go with you.

4.2.4 China—A Country in a High-Context Culture

High-context cultural communication requires communicators to understand more than the explicit language, but also to figure out more illocutionary meanings. Both sides of the communication must be highly sensitive to the information that the environment can convey. Therefore, it is more suitable for the communication participants who share homogeneous culture, common social background, similar customs and habits, and similar thinking modes. China is a typical country advocating high-context culture. In the process of growing up, people have gradually acquired the skills of gauging people's mind and understanding tacitly, which will be brought into full play in their future communication. As a typical example of high-context culture communication, this kind of culture has its specific historical origin.

From the perspective of historical evolution, people from high-context cultures have lived in a fixed place for a long time, and their life rhythm is in order. Over time, social changes are slow and small, people's life experience and interpersonal networks are very simple. In this kind of society, people always make the same response to the environment, and communication behavior has become a fixed pattern (Zhao & Zeng, 2009). China had been a feudal society for more than 2,000 years. Although the country has experienced division and war in the long history, it has finally returned to unification. In such a united country with a long history, people have a relatively stable living environment. Over time, a relatively homogeneous mode of thinking and communication has been formed, and a large amount of information has become people's consensus, which can be widely recognized without saying it.

From the perspective of cultural origin, *The Analects of Confucius*, more than 2,000 years ago, had some admonitions, such as "The gentleman is slow in speech but quick in action" and "He that talks much errs much". It is a principle rooted in everyone's heart who has been educated in Confucianism. It's also an extremely unwise choice to tell the whole story without thinking twice. In Lao-Tzu's *Tao Te Ching*, the first sentence is "Tao that can be described is not universal and eternal

Tao; Name that can be named is not universal and eternal Name", which tells people that the truth is unspeakable. And "He who knows doesn't speak; he who speaks doesn't know" is a straightforward expression of the concept of speaking less and thinking more. Since the Han Dynasty, Confucianism has occupied the dominant position of the Chinese culture. And since the Sui and Tang Dynasties, Confucianism, Buddhism, and Taoism have been the mainstay of the Chinese culture. Confucianism which preaches "being not communicative" , Taoism which advocates "those that can only be sensed, but cannot be explained in words", and Buddhism which emphasizes "the power of understanding", have jointly influenced people's communication patterns and habits, and implicitly promoted people's language expression to be more and more implicit.

From the perspective of complexity and artistry of language, Chinese is one of the most profound and difficult languages in the world, with variable sounds and complicated grammar. The ancient written language is concise in writing. It pays attention to the refinement of the words and emphasizes the use of allusions and rhymes. The complex language system and implicit cultural gene give birth to the implicit euphemism of Chinese. For example, to express the meaning of "death", there are many different expressions. All kinds of euphemisms are aimed at avoiding taboo and seeking elegance, which have been widely used for thousands of years and have become a common language habit. Chinese people believe that language is an art; we don't need to say too much, just like the "blank" in traditional Chinese painting, which emphasizes the beauty of space and artistic conception.

4.2.5 America—A Country in a Low-Context Culture

Compared with Chinese culture, American history and culture basically do not have the natural conditions to form a high-context culture. The history of the United States is short (from the War of Independence to the present), while that of China's feudal society alone is more than 2,000 years. In addition, China, especially in the period of feudal dynasties, has been in a relatively integrated state. However, this is not the case in American society. Most Americans are Europeans who immigrated from the old world, slaves who were traded from Africa and other places, and local indigenous people. With the development of society, the flow of population is quick, and people's living conditions are relatively diverse. Due to the different migration times and reasons, people almost have no chance to get along and live for a long time in the same social environment. Moreover, in the early stage of the formation of American culture, people's backgrounds were diverse, and there were no unified constraints on people's languages and behavior.

After the basic framework and characteristics were formed, American culture is mainly influenced by the values of English culture and Christian belief. It advocates freedom, independence, and individual struggle both in action and in thought. Such a society emphasizes equality and is individual-oriented rather than group-oriented. People put more emphasis on the independence and freedom of personality, and advocate the realization of self-worth. They don't rely so much on groups and society like people in a high-context culture, and they typically emphasize the equal relationship between family members and social members. The low-context culture formed thereby makes Americans tend to be self-centered in communication, with simple and direct language expression. The characteristics of the communication between them are direct language expression, straightforward language style, and less consideration of other's face and feelings.

In cross-cultural communication, we should pay attention to the influence of the different characteristics on cross-cultural communication, and actively face the communication problems caused by cultural differences in context. Through the study of high context and low context, when we communicate with different groups, we can better understand people's different communication priorities and behavior, and comprehensively understand the communication modes and differences in different context cultures. The research on the causes of different communication cultures is also helpful to understand the differences between Chinese and American cultures, so as to enhance our cross-cultural awareness, improve our ability of mutual understanding and prediction in cross-cultural communication, and guide our cross-cultural practice from a deeper level.

Case Study: Monsooned (Peace, 2018)

Read the following passage and try to analyze it by answering these questions:

   (1) Did Abhinav agree to the initial timeline requested by Rebecca?
   (2) What might Rebecca be thinking about Abhinav?
   (3) What might Abhinav be thinking about Rebecca?
   (4) How will this incident affect their future interactions?

Rebecca works with United Technologies, a Chicago-based company. She is

talking on the phone to Abhinav, a manager of one of United Technologies vendors for customer service outsourcing, and he is from India.

> **Rebecca:** We really need to get all of the customer service representatives trained on our new process in the next two weeks. Can you get this done?
>
> **Abhinav:** That timeline is pretty aggressive. Do you think it's possible?
>
> **Rebecca:** I think it will require some creativity and hard work, but I think we can get it done with two or three days to spare.
>
> **Abhinav:** OK.
>
> **Rebecca:** Now that our business is settled, how is everything else?
>
> **Abhinav:** All's well, although the heavy monsoons this year are causing a lot of delays getting around the city.
>
> [Two weeks later…]
>
> **Abhinav:** We've pulled all of our resources and I'm happy to say that 60% of the customer service representatives are now trained in the new process. The remaining 40% will complete the training in the next two weeks.
>
> **Rebecca:** Only 60%? I thought we agreed that they all would be trained by now!
>
> **Abhinav:** Yes. The monsoon is now over so the rest of the training should go quickly.
>
> **Rebecca:** This training is critical to our results. Please get it done as soon as possible.
>
> **Abhinav:** I am certain that it will be done in the next two weeks.

After the first conversation, Abhinav felt that he had made it clear to Rebecca that the training would not be completed within the time she asked. Rebecca, on the other hand, felt that Abhinav had made it clear that he would finish the task before the deadline. What caused the failure of communication between them?

As a matter of fact, this is an example of the miscommunication caused by different ways of communication. Abhinav, who comes from a high-context culture, relies heavily on context to convey meaning. In this case, he hinted that the schedule was too tight and that the monsoon would cause delays. If Rebecca was an Indian, she would clearly understand the real meaning of Abhinav and would not expect to complete the training on time.

However, Rebecca comes from a low-context culture, in which the understanding of the utterances depends largely on the literal meaning of the words she utters. From her point of view, Abhinav agrees on the schedule when he answers "OK". If Abhinav is an American, he will know that he is still expected to finish the task on time.

Both Rebecca and Abhinav need to work hard to understand this cultural difference. Rebecca should not misjudge Abhinav as "irresponsible" and "unreliable"; similarly, Abhinav should also be careful not to regard Rebecca as "rude" and "inconsiderate".

Now, it's your turn to analyze another case.

A Chinese lady in the United States was going to take a plane for her vacation. She hoped her American friend would drive her to the airport. But she was embarrassed to speak out her real wish, and the other party, influenced by the direct way of expression, was not good at getting the implied meaning of the expression. So the result could only be counterproductive. Here was their conversation.

Chinese Lady: I'm going to New York City this weekend.

American Friend: Great! I wish I could go with you. How long will you stay there?

Chinese Lady: [I hope she can offer to drive me to the airport.] Three days.

American Friend: [If she wants me to send her, she will say it.] I wish you have a good time!

Chinese Lady: [If she is really willing to drive me to the airport, she will take the initiative to say it. She didn't take the initiative to say it. It seems that she doesn't want to send me. Obviously, she is not a real friend.] Thank you. Bye!

What caused the misunderstanding between the Chinese lady and her American friend?

For Your Information

Edward Hall and High-Context & Low-Context Cultures

Edward Twitchell Hall, Jr. (1914–2009) was an American anthropologist and cross-cultural researcher. He is remembered for developing the concept of proxemics and exploring cultural and social cohesion, and describing how people behave and react in different types of culturally defined personal space.

From 1933 to 1937, Hall lived and worked with the Navajo and the Hopi on Native American reservations in northeastern Arizona, the subject of his autobiographical *West of the Thirties*. He received his Ph.D. from Columbia University in 1942 and continued with field work and direct experience throughout Europe, the Middle East, and Asia. During the 1950s, he worked for

the United States State Department, at the Foreign Service Institute, teaching intercultural communication skills to foreign service personnel. He developed the concept of "high-context culture" and "low-context culture", and wrote several popular practical books on dealing with cross-cultural issues. He is considered a founding father of intercultural communication in this academic area of study.

4.3 Cultural Dimensions Theory

Cultural dimensions theory is a framework for cross-cultural communication, developed by Geert Hofstede (1984). It describes the effects of a society's culture on the values of its members, and how these values relate to behavior, using a structure derived from factor analysis (Blessing & Lawrence, 2014).

In 1965, Hofstede established the Personnel Research Department of IBM Europe. From 1967 to 1973, he conducted a large-scale survey on the differences in national values among the global subsidiaries of the multinational company. He compared the answers of 117,000 IBM employees in different countries. He first focused on the 40 largest countries and then expanded the study to 50 countries and three regions. This theory is the first quantifiable theory that can be used to explain the differences between different cultures.

This first attempt identified the systematic differences of national culture in four main dimensions: masculinity, power distance, individualism and uncertainty avoidance. As Hofstede explains on his academic website, these dimensions relate to four anthropological problem areas that different national societies handle differently: the emotional implications of having been born as a girl or as a boy, ways of coping with inequality, ways of coping with uncertainty, and the relationship of the individual with his or her primary group (Hofstede & Hofstede, 2005). In 1984, he published *Culture's Consequences*, which combines the statistical analysis of researches and his personal experience.

In 1991, Michael Harris Bond and his colleagues carried out a study among students in 23 countries. The results of this research enable Hofstede to add a new dimension to his model—Long-Term Orientation (LTO). Thus, the five dimensions of Hofstede's cultural values are formally formed. The details are shown in Figure 4.2.

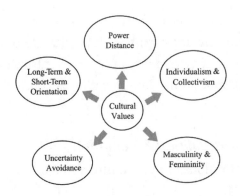

Figure 4.2   Five Dimensions of Cultural Values

Hofstede's contribution has established a major tradition of research in cross-cultural psychology, which has also been used for reference by many researchers and consultants in the field of international business and communication. This theory has been widely used in many fields, especially in international management, cross-cultural psychology, and intercultural communication. It has inspired some other major cross-cultural values research and contributed a lot to the study of other aspects of culture.

4.3.1 Masculinity & Femininity

1. Definitions of Masculinity & Femininity

The masculinity index, proposed by sociologist Geert Hofstede, measures the degree to which stereotypically masculine and feminine traits prevail in a culture.

According to Hofstede (1984), masculinity stands for a society in which social gender roles are clearly distinct: Men are supposed to be assertive, tough, and focused on material success; women are supposed to be more modest, tender, and concerned with the quality of life. Femininity stands for a society in which social gender roles overlap: Both men and women are supposed to be modest, tender, and concerned with the quality of life.

Japan is the most masculine nation in the world; Sweden is the most feminine nation. Other masculine cultures include the United States, Mexico, the German-speaking world, the United Kingdom, Ireland, and Italy. The Netherlands, South Korea, the Middle East, Spain, Portugal, Thailand, and West Africa all have feminine cultures.

However, this cultural feature has a little relationship with gender roles (for

example, Germany is regarded as a masculine nation, but the gender empowerment of Germany is high; similarly, most Muslim countries are considered to be feminine cultures, but the gender empowerments of these countries are generally low). Like Hofstede's other ratings, masculinity/feminization is considered to be deeply rooted in the cultural mindset.

2. Characteristics of Masculinity & Femininity

According to the definitions of masculinity and femininity, the characteristics of them are listed in Table 4.3.

Table 4.3　Characteristics of Masculinity & Femininity (Hofstede, 1984)

	Masculinity	Femininity
Social Norms	Self-oriented	Relationship-oriented
	Material success is important	Quality of life is important
	Live to work	Work to live
Economics and Politics	Focus on economic growth	Focus on environment protection
	Solve conflicts through force	Solve conflicts through negotiation
Religion	Very important in daily life	Not so important in daily life
	Only men can work as priests	Both men and women can work as priests
Work	Fewer women in management	More women in management
	Larger wage gap between male and female workers	Smaller wage gap between male and female workers
	Pay attention to higher payment	Pay attention to fewer working hours
Family and Education	Traditional family structure	Flexible family structure
	Girls can cry, but boys are not allowed; boys fight, but girls don't have to	Both boys and girls can cry; neither of them fight
	Failing is a serious disaster	Failing is only a minor accident

From the table above, we can see clearly the differences between masculine and feminine cultures. Firstly, in the aspect of social norms, people in masculine cultures are mostly self-oriented. For them, money and things are important, and they live in order to work. However, people in feminine cultures, who are mainly relationship-oriented, are greatly different. They put more stress on the quality of life and people, and they work in order to live. The quality of life is highly appreciated, as is shown by the belief that "Life is short and we need to experience and taste it slowly and carefully", which is tremendously different from the belief of a masculine culture that "Life is transitory and we need to make more achievements at high speed". Therefore, this dimension is often renamed as "quantity of life vs. quality of life" by many researchers.

Secondly, in the aspect of economics and politics, people in masculine cultures tend to put a high priority on economic growth, and when things are in conflict, they always try to solve them through force. In contrast, people in feminine cultures put high priority on environmental protection, and they always try to solve conflicts through negotiation.

Thirdly, in the aspect of religion, it is regarded as something very important in life in masculine cultures, and only men can be priests. Things turn out quite differently in feminine cultures. People there generally think religion not so important in life, and both men and women can work as priests.

Fourthly, in the aspect of work, in masculine cultures, we can see fewer women in management. Besides, there is a larger gender wage gap compared with that in feminine cultures. Also, it is very common for employees in masculine cultures to work overtime to obtain higher payment while in feminine cultures, they prefer fewer working hours.

Last but not least, in the aspect of family and education, they are also quite different. In masculine cultures, the traditional family structure is very common; it is a common belief that only girls can cry and it is boys' responsibility to fight; failing is seen as a disaster. While in feminine cultures, the family structure is quite flexible; both boys and girls can cry and no one has the obligation to fight; failing is only a minor accident.

4.3.2 High Power Distance & Low Power Distance

1. Definitions of High Power Distance & Low Power Distance

Power distance refers to the strength of a social hierarchy. It measures the degree to which people at a lower level accept the fact that social status or power is unevenly distributed in society. Psychologists and sociologists often use this dimension. Researchers found that people at the bottom of the social hierarchy tend to choose a system of equal distribution of power, while people at the top of the social hierarchy like things as they are because those with vested interests don't want

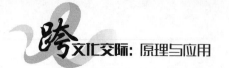

to lose their interests at all.

To put it another way, power distance is a term used to explain how people in a particular culture perceive the power relationship between people—the superior vs. the subordinate, including the extent to which people who are not in power accept the spread of power inequality.

In a culture with high power distance, individuals are very respectful to the authority and generally accept the unequal power distribution. In a culture with low power distance, individuals tend to question the authority and are willing to participate in decision making.

Specifically, how a person views the power relationship will affect his or her performance as a manager or employee in business negotiation. It may be counterproductive to use high power distance management on people who are used to the management style of low power distance and vice versa.

Table 4.4 shows the Power Distance Index (PDI) of some countries. If the index is higher than 70, it is considered as high; if the index is lower than 40, it is considered as low. For example, the index of Austria is 11, which is regarded to be a low score; while the index of China is 80, which shows that China is a country of high power distance.

Table 4.4   Power Distance Index

Countries	PDI	Countries	PDI
Malaysia	104	United States	40
Guatemala	95	Australia	36
Panama	95	Germany	35
Philippines	94	United Kingdom	35
Mexico	81	Switzerland	34
Venezuela	81	Finland	33
China	80	Norway	31
Egypt	80	Sweden	31
Iraq	80	New Zealand	22
Saudi Arabia	80	Austria	11

Many things can bring power to people, such as money, valuable resources, education, profession, age, popularity, talent, intelligence, and experience. In the United States, people have the concept of equality; that is, all people are created equal, and no group or individual can have privileges. This is a characteristic of typical low power distance cultures. The United States, Canada, Israel, New Zealand, Denmark, Austria and other countries all belong to this kind of culture. People living in this cultural background are educated from an early age to be born equal. Although some people are born with certain advantages, such as wealth and reputation, they are not supposed to be superior to others. However, this does not mean that people living in this kind of society will definitely be treated equally; they just have the concept of equality more than others.

In high power distance cultures, power is hierarchical. Certain groups such as aristocrats or ruling parties have more power than ordinary civilians. People living in this cultural background have been told from an early age that some are born noble, so they have more power, and respect for power is more meaningful than respect for equality. Mexico, Brazil, India, Singapore, and the Philippines are countries under this cultural influence.

2. Characteristics of High Power Distance & Low Power Distance

According to the definitions of high power distance and low power distance, the characteristics of them are listed in Table 4.5.

Table 4.5　Characteristics of High Power Distance & Low Power Distance (Hofstede, 1984)

	High Power Distance	Low Power Distance
Social Norms	Those in power enjoy privileges	All people enjoy equal rights
	Inequality is seen as the norm; everyone has his or her specific position in the society	Inequality should be minimized; everyone is seen as equal with each other
	Show high respect for authority	Show high respect for individuality
Politics	Autocratic government	Democratic government
	Little discussion	Much discussion
Work	The superiors have absolute authority	The superiors expect to discuss with subordinates
	Large wage gap from top to bottom	Small wage gap from top to bottom
Education	Teacher-centered	Student-centered
	Students are expected to treat teachers with respect, even out of school	Students share equal relationship with teachers

Power distance affects many aspects of our communication behavior. For example, people in societies with low power distance usually transcend social status to develop friendships and romantic relationships. But on the contrary, in a society with high power distance, people are more inclined to look for friendships and romantic relationships under the same social status, and emphasize a marriage between families of equal social rank.

In a family, we can also see different behavior for people from different cultures. In cultures with low power distance, children are treated as equals. They learn to be independent and have to do their own stuff when they are very young. Besides, children are allowed to contradict their parents since they learn to say no very early. On the other hand, in cultures with high power distance, children are expected and educated to be obedient to their parents. Independent behavior of children is not encouraged. Younger ones are always being taken care of by older ones and are expected to yield to them. Authority continues to play a role in children's life, even if they are adults.

At school, we can also find some differences between these two cultures. In cultures with low power distance, teachers and students are treated as equals to each other. The educational process is student-centered. Teachers have no responsibility for students' study. Students are expected to find their own way of study. Most importantly, students can express disagreement in front of the teachers. While in cultures with high power distance, it turns out quite differently. Teachers are treated with respect, even outside school. The educational process is teacher-centered. Teachers plan intellectual paths for students to follow. Students can speak up only when they are invited to.

Another impact it has on us involves our perception of authority. Societies with high power distance emphasize obedience and respect to authority. People are educated from childhood to unconditionally obey their parents and teachers. On the contrary, children in societies with low power distance are taught from an early age to bravely challenge authority. In this culture, it is not surprising to ask why to parents and teachers.

This kind of cultural difference is especially common in the communication style of employer-employee relationship. Employees in societies with low power distance value the right to freedom more, and at the same time they hope to get more decision-making opportunities, especially when it comes to their own work. These employees may reflect their opinions through labor unions or employee satisfaction surveys. But in a society with high power distance, employees are often accustomed to the status quo at work and rarely put forward opinions. On the contrary, they want their bosses to give orders directly, so they only need to follow the orders.

Power distance could be used in many ways in social research, among which, one of the examples is to compare the inequality of income. In some countries, the power distance in this aspect is low. This means that the gap between the richest and the poorest in society is small. Austria is just a typical example of low power distance, while Saudi Arabia is a country of high power distance. On the other hand, power distance could also be used in psychology, in which it could be used to judge the workplace. If a CEO's hourly income is 500 times that of an ordinary employee, then the power distance in this workplace is very high.

Understanding different psychological concepts can help psychologists better understand interpersonal relationships. Besides, it could also help to deal with problems among employees. The commanding of the definition and characteristics of power distance is good progress in the research or practice of organizational psychology and industrial psychology.

4.3.3 Collectivism & Individualism

1. Definitions of Collectivism & Individualism

Individualism and collectivism describe the relationship between individuals and the group they belong to. This dimension involves what a culture values in terms of personal or group achievement. Therefore, collective culture is also called "we" culture, and individual culture is also called "me" culture.

Collectivism and individualism are both principles, practices, cultural models, and political theories. They are usually seen as contrasting with each other. Collectivism puts group cohesion above individual pursuit. It believes that long-term relationship is very important because it promotes the realization of group objectives. On the other hand, individualism emphasizes human independence as well as freedom.

In terms of collectivism, we find that people in a collectivist society integrate into strong and cohesive groups from birth, usually extended families (with uncles, aunts, and grandparents), and they continue to protect them in exchange for unquestionable loyalty.

It is easy for people in a collectivist society to sacrifice their personal interests for the sake of the progress of the whole society. In fact, a person who is deeply

influenced by collectivism will even feel embarrassed if he or she is singled out for praise alone. A study about decision making showed that people with a higher level of collectivism tend to rely more on the members of in-groups, and they are less likely to betray their group (Rebecca & Volker, 2013). Collectivism is a common cultural pattern in traditional communities such as Africa, Asia, and Latin America. It is contrary to the individualism which is common in Western Europe, North America, New Zealand, and Australia (Triandis, 2001).

Besides, collectivism is also a political theory related to communism, because it proposes that power should be placed in the hands of all citizens, rather than in the hands of only a few people. Therefore, it is beneficial to build a system conducive to the realization of common objectives.

To sum up, the culture of high collectivism considers the group as the most important unit. Some features are:

- showing a high degree of loyalty to the group;
- group orientation;
- shame culture;
- making decisions on the basis of group interests;
- "we" mentality;
- emphasizing the sense of belonging.

Individualism is the opposite of collectivism. In terms of individualism, we find that the connection between individuals in society is loose: People have to take care of themselves and their immediate family members. For example, Germany can be considered as an individualist with a relatively high score on the Hofstede scale (67 points), while Guatemala is a country with strong collectivism (the score on the Hofstede scale is 6 points).

In Germany, people emphasize individual achievement and individual rights. The Germans expect each other to meet their needs. The work of the group is important, but everyone has the right to express his or her own opinions. In a country like Germany, the relationship between people is often looser than that in a collectivist country, where people have a large family.

The study about decision making also showed that people with a higher level of individualism tend to be more rational than people with a higher level of collectivism (Rebecca & Volker, 2013). A society with individualistic culture regards people as autonomous and gives priority to uniqueness. Individualism contradicts the view of collectivism which emphasizes interdependence and tradition.

Accordingly, a highly individualistic culture considers the individual as the most important unit. Some features are:

- people only caring for themselves and their nuclear families;
- self-orientation;
- guilt culture;
- making decisions based on personal needs;
- "me" mentality;
- emphasizing personal initiative and accomplishment.

2. Characteristics of Collectivism & Individualism

According to the definitions of collectivism and individualism, the characteristics of them are listed in Table 4.6.

Table 4.6   Characteristics of Collectivism & Individualism

	Collectivism	Individualism
Education	Education brings social acceptance	Education brings self-respect
Family	Children are expected to stay with their parents	Children take care of themselves by 20–22
	Privacy is not so important	Privacy is very important
	More fixed social networks	More social mobility
Work	Cooperation rather than competition is emphasized	Competition is encouraged
	The subjugation of the individual to a group	Independence takes precedence over dependence
Festival	Festivals are for family members to get together	Stress the importance of the ecstasy of an individual

In the aspect of education, in collectivist cultures, the role of education is social acceptance. A diploma is a great honor not only to the holder but also, or more importantly, to his or her group. But in individualist cultures, one's self-respect that comes with the diploma is more important than social acceptance.

In the aspect of family, in collectivist cultures, people care more about the relationship of relatives. It is really a common phenomenon in collectivist cultures that "four generations live under one roof". The children are expected to stay with their parents. But in individualist cultures, children usually move out of their parents' house. And parents in individualist cultures usually live by themselves rather than with their children. Besides, in collectivist cultures, it is really a very common phenomenon for parents to look up children' diary by keeping them in

the dark. However, in individualist cultures, this is obviously not allowed. Instead, parents will respect their children. When the young go into their own bedrooms, without their permission, even their parents cannot enter either. And in collectivist cultures, people enjoy more fixed social networks while in individualist cultures, more social mobility is seen.

In the aspect of work, in collectivist cultures, cooperation rather than competition is emphasized, and it is believed that group goals are more important than personal goals. In contrast, in individualistic cultures, the individual is the most important element in any social setting. Independence takes precedence over dependence and individual achievement is stressed. Personal goals override group goals and competition is encouraged.

In the end, the differences between collectivism and individualism are also reflected in the festivals. Here let's take the typical collectivist country China and traditional individualist country America as an example. Traditional Chinese festivals mainly include Tomb-Sweeping Day, Dragon-Boat Festival, Mid-Autumn Festival, Spring Festival, etc. They are mainly the festivals for family members to get together. In contrast, American traditional festivals mainly include Valentine's Day, Halloween, Mother's Day, Father's Day, Christmas, etc. Most of the American festivals stress the importance of the ecstasy of an individual.

Although these two approaches have obvious advantages, none of them is perfect. Individualism encourages creativity and personal excellence, but it can also lead to conflicts and refusal to cooperate. Employees may be reluctant to follow predefined norms and rules, which may affect the team and the entire group. Some people may even use immoral means to achieve their own goals.

Organizations using collectivist methods may also encounter these problems, but to a lesser extent. On the negative side, due to the neglect of employees' personal efforts, they may be less motivated to work and achieve the best performance. In addition, this method may damage creativity and innovation ability. If one employee comes up with a good idea, but the rest of the team disagrees, he may feel frustrated and give up trying to be creative and do things better.

The ideal situation is to find a balance between collectivism and individualism. In fact, collectivism and individualism are not mutually exclusive. For instance, projects could be assigned to groups that will cooperate to achieve the desired results. Employees can still make individual assessments on basis of their performance and their respective contribution to the project.

4.3.4 Uncertainty Avoidance

1. Definition of Uncertainty Avoidance

Uncertainty avoidance refers to the lack of tolerance for ambiguity and uncertainty and the need for formal rules and high-level organizational structure. The index measures the extent of tolerance of uncertainty as well as ambiguity. This dimension mainly considers how to deal with unexpected events and unknown situations. Does culture hold expectations for rigid and clear behavior, or does it enjoy uncertainty and ambiguity? Different cultures have different degrees of fear of unknown and uncertain things. Therefore, in this respect, we can find two different forms: high uncertainty avoidance and low uncertainty avoidance.

The high uncertainty avoidance index indicates that the tolerance of uncertainty and risk-taking behavior is low. In this culture, people always try to minimize the unknown through strict regulations and rules. They fear failure, resist change, pursue a sense of security in life and work, and are eager to follow the code of conduct in their interactions with others. China, Greece, Spain, Russia, Japan, and France are all countries with a high uncertainty avoidance index.

The low uncertainty avoidance index indicates that the tolerance of uncertainty and risk-taking behavior is high. The unknown is easier to be accepted publicly, and rules and regulations are also looser. Low uncertainty avoidance culture is more likely to accept uncertainty and ambiguity. People in cultures with a low uncertainty avoidance index are able to deal with the stress and anxiety caused by uncertainty. Therefore, they can better tolerate different opinions. They are more active, more flexible, and more relaxed in social situations. Denmark, Ireland, Finland, Sweden, Norway, the Netherlands, the United Kingdom, the United States, and the Philippines are all countries with a low degree of uncertainty avoidance.

2. Characteristics of Uncertainty Avoidance

Uncertainty avoidance will have great influence in our lives. Table 4.7 shows its characteristics.

Table 4.7   Characteristics of Uncertainty Avoidance

	High Uncertainty Avoidance	**Low Uncertainty Avoidance**
Social Norms	Reduce the level of ambiguity and uncertainty	Exhibit greater flexibility
	Desire clear behavioral rules	Tolerate deviant behavior and different opinions

(Continued)

	High Uncertainty Avoidance	Low Uncertainty Avoidance
Work	Formal organizational structures are desired	Less formal organizational structures
	Employees always show higher loyalty to their bosses	Employees usually show lower loyalty to their bosses
Politics	Little interest in politics	Very interested in politics
	Protests are repressed	Protests are accepted as tool for change
	Specific and more laws and regulations	General and fewer laws and regulations
Education	Teachers are viewed as having all the answers	Teachers are not necessarily viewed as knowing all
	Learning is structured	Learning is open-minded

In the aspect of social norms, in low uncertainty avoidance culture, people have a strong willingness to live day by day and generally they have a low level of stress. While in high uncertainty avoidance culture, since people have greater anxiety about the future, they usually have a high level of stress. Besides, in low uncertainty avoidance culture, people are more risk-taking, and they always hope for success. While in high uncertainty avoidance culture, people are less risk-taking and they are fearful of failure. As a result, we can find that people in high uncertainty avoidance culture are more reluctant to change. What's more, in low uncertainty avoidance culture, differences are tolerated while in high uncertainty avoidance culture, differences will always be seen as threats.

In the aspect of work, in low uncertainty avoidance culture, generally speaking, less formal organizational structures are desired and initiative of subordinates is encouraged. Employees usually show lower loyalty to their bosses because they would never expect a job for life. On the contrary, in high uncertainty avoidance culture, formal organizational structures are desired and initiative of subordinates is discouraged. Employees always show higher loyalty to their bosses since they hold that if they keep their nose clean, they could keep their job for life.

In politics, citizens in cultures with low uncertainty avoidance tend to be very interested in politics as it serves as a tool for change. Protests are accepted as another tool for change. On the other side of the spectrum, citizens in cultures with high uncertainty avoidance tend to have low interest in politics and protests are repressed. This is because political unrest would bring about changes which the majority would not be comfortable with.

In the aspect of education, in cultures with low uncertainty avoidance, teachers are not necessarily viewed as knowing all and learning is open-minded with less focus on facts. In cultures with high uncertainty avoidance, teachers are viewed as having all the answers and learning is structured.

Just as mentioned above, China, a member of high uncertainty avoidance group, pursues stability. The Chinese prefer to try their best to arrange everything well to narrow the instability. As a result, they hold a view that "look before you leap" and know how to plan ahead so as to maximize the use of resources. In contrast, America is a young country. Since American conquests of the American continent, the Americans are described as a pioneer, an explorer, moving out of wilderness and obscuration. The early immigrants made their way along with axe and rifle. They built their own civilization starting from the very beginning. The unknown field for them means not only challenges but also great opportunities. Due to this historical origin, there is no doubt for Americans to display low uncertainty avoidance inclination.

4.3.5 Long-Term Orientation & Short-Term Orientation

1. Definitions of Long-Term Orientation & Short-Term Orientation

Long-term orientation is Hofstede's fifth dimension, which is added after the original four dimensions to try to distinguish the differences between Eastern thinking and Western thinking.

As Hofstede & Hofstede (2005: 207) notes, "Long-term orientation stands for the fostering of virtues oriented towards future rewards, in particular perseverance and thrift. Its opposite pole, short-term orientation, stands for the fostering of virtues related to the past and present, in particular, respect for tradition, preservation of 'face' and fulfilling social obligations."

In other words, long-term orientation is to face the future and seek future returns through thrift and perseverance. Short-term orientation aims at the past and the present by fulfilling social obligations, respecting tradition, and seeking immediate rewards. Put simply, people in some cultures seek quick returns, while people from other backgrounds prefer to postpone gratification and pursue long-term objectives. In a culture that advocates long-term orientation, people consider a lot about what may happen in the future and try to prepare for the good and bad in the future. They attach importance to persistence, thrift, patience, shame, and humility. However, people in a short-term orientation culture pay more attention to what is happening now and what happened in the past. They are deeply aware of

consumption, efficiency, quickness, respect for tradition, effectiveness, stability, and personal steadiness; they always pay attention to saving face for themselves and others; and reciprocity is a high virtue.

China, South Korea, Japan, India, and Brazil score the highest on this dimension while the Philippines, Pakistan, Canada, Nigeria, Great Britain, and America score the lowest on this dimension.

Here we will take Americans as an example. Since America is a typical country with a strong short-term orientation, American companies generally measure performance on a short-term basis, and profit and loss statements are released quarterly. This also motivates individuals to strive to achieve rapid results in the workplace.

2. Characteristics of Short-Term Orientation & Long-Term Orientation

The characteristics of short-term orientation and long-term orientation are shown in Table 4.8.

Table 4.8   Characteristics of Long-Term Orientation & Short-Term Orientation (Hofstede, 1984)

	Long-Term Orientation	Short-Term Orientation
Work	Emphasis on persistence	Emphasis on quick results
	Focus on personal adaptability	Focus on personal stability
Face	Face is not so important compared with ultimate rewards	Protecting the "face" of self and others
Money	Thrift, saving	Spending
Attitude towards tradition	Adapt tradition when conditions change	Prefer to maintain time-honored traditions and norms

From the table above, we can find obvious differences between long-term orientation and short-term orientation. Long-term-oriented societies focus on the future and long-term results, and people in long-term-orientated cultures are willing to pursue slow results through perseverance and persistence. While short-term-oriented cultures focus on the present; for them, efforts should produce quick results. Or simply speaking, members of some cultures look for quick payoffs, while people from different backgrounds are willing to defer gratification in pursuit of long-range goals.

For people from long-term-oriented societies, face is not so important compared with ultimate rewards; while for people from short-term-oriented societies, it's quite important for them to protect the face of self and others.

Long-term-oriented cultures usually tend to save and invest, while people in short-term-oriented cultures are constantly under social pressure towards spending, so they usually do not tend to save or invest.

Normative societies, which score high on this dimension, show more respect for circumstances and are able to adapt tradition when conditions change. Those cultures which score low in this aspect, on the other hand, prefer to maintain time-honored traditions and norms while viewing societal change with suspicion. What's more, people in long-term-oriented cultures usually concern more with personal adaptiveness and they are willing to subordinate themselves for one specific purpose. However, people in short-term-oriented cultures concern more with social and status obligations, and they value more on personal stability.

Case Study: Status and Age

Read the following passage and try to analyze it by answering these questions:
(1) What do you think caused the conflict?
(2) What would you do to resolve the conflict if you were the general manager?

The general manager of a data-processing company came across difficulty in dealing with a conflict between a young, ambitious Canadian man and his colleague, an elderly Chinese woman. She recently became uncooperative and made it clear to her manager that she was not willing to go to Congress with the young man to discuss a new product with legislators.

When the manager asked her about the reason, the woman did not give a clear explanation. And the young man also had no idea what had happened. Besides, the young Canadian was quite annoyed by the Chinese woman's refusal to share data with him, which meant he couldn't make a statement to the legislators because she had all the important data.

The manager asked the woman for several times but he got no answer. So he decided to change the approach. As the company's manager, he began to express his ideas about the meeting with legislators. He made an unemotional explanation. In that atmosphere, she began to feel like she wanted to explain. She disclosed that she felt that as an older person, which means to be a more senior staff, in her opinion, she should not be sent to discuss with legislators with a young colleague

who would be responsible to introduce the materials she had developed. In her opinion, that would affect her status and prestige.

There are two cultural factors causing this contradiction: different attitudes towards status and age, and different ways of expression. People's understanding of power varies with cultural background. According to Hofstede's research, people in low power distance countries emphasize personal ability, and the equality of rights and relations between people, while high power distance countries, such as China, Japan, and Thailand, emphasize status, experience, age, and qualifications. Therefore, in the eyes of this young Canadian, he and this lady are equal partners; there is no difference in status, and he has the ability to participate in the project and make a final report. However, in the eyes of this Chinese lady, it is a disgrace for her to go to Congress with a young man considering her age, qualification, and dedication in her work, and let the other person make a report.

In addition, the different ways of expression between the two parties also lead to the deepening of the contradiction. According to Hall's theory, Canada belongs to low-context culture, and China belongs to high-context culture. Therefore, when her Canadian colleague directly asked her the reason, the Chinese lady did not express her own ideas. When the manager changed the way and talked about her difficulties in a roundabout way, she expressed her concerns in this context.

Now, it's your turn to analyze another case.

A British general manager came to Thailand to take office. At the beginning of his tenure, he did not expect that the small problem of what kind of car to use to work caused him a lot of trouble.

The British general manager refused to ride in his predecessor's car after arriving in Thailand. The Thai finance manager asked the general manager what type of Mercedes he wanted. Unexpectedly, the general manager only asked for a Suzuki or Mini, or any car that was easy to commute in the heavy traffic of Bangkok.

Three weeks later, the general manager called the finance manager to ask when his car would be in place. The Thai has repeatedly emphasized: "We can buy you a new Mercedes-Benz tomorrow, but Suzuki will take more time." The general manager rejected the proposal to buy a new Mercedes-Benz and asked the purchasing department to speed up the process of purchasing a small car. Four weeks later, the general manager asked again about the purchase of the car. The purchasing department replied that they decided to order a Mercedes-Benz because it took a long time to buy a small car.

The general manager's patience has been exhausted. At the management meeting, he raised the question and asked for an explanation. The Thai management team explained shyly that they did not want to ride a bicycle to work.

Here are two questions that may be helpful:

- Why is it difficult for the general manager to get a Suzuki or Mini?
- Why do the management team say that they don't want to go to work by bike?

For Your Information

Geert Hofstede and Cultural Dimension Theory

Geert Hofstede (1928–2020) was a Dutch social psychologist, IBM employee, and professor emeritus of Organizational Anthropology and International Management at Maastricht University in the Netherlands, well known for his pioneering research on cross-cultural groups and organizations.

He is best known for developing one of the earliest and most popular frameworks for measuring cultural dimensions in a global perspective. Here he described national cultures along five dimensions: masculinity, power distance, individualism, uncertainty avoidance, and long-term orientation. He was known for his books *Culture's Consequences* and *Cultures and Organizations: Software of the Mind*, co-authored with his son Gert Jan Hofstede.

At IBM International, working as a management trainer and manager of personnel research, Hofstede founded and managed the Personnel Research Department. This was his transition from the field of engineering into psychology. He played an active role in the introduction and application of employee opinion surveys in over 70 national subsidiaries of IBM around the world. He traveled across Europe and the Middle East to interview people and conduct surveys regarding people's behavior in large organizations and how they collaborated. He collected large amounts of data, but was unable to conduct a significant amount of research due to the pressures of his daily job. When he took a two-year sabbatical leave from IBM in 1971, he delved deeper into the data he had collected from his job, and discovered that though there were significant differences between cultures in other organizations, they got the same ranking of answers by country. At the time, the results of the IBM's surveys, with over 100,000 questionnaires, were one of the largest cross-national databases in existence.

> Between 1973 and 1979, he worked on the data, and analyzed it in a variety of ways. He used existing literature in psychology, sociology, political science, and anthropology to relate his findings in a larger scope of study. In 1980, he published his book *Culture's Consequences*, where the results of his analysis were presented.

4.4 Values Orientation Theory

The third approach that studies the cultural patterns is the values orientation theory proposed by Kluckhohn and Strodtbeck (1961). Florence Kluckhohn and Fred Strodtbeck, both of whom are American anthropologists, made a theoretical analysis of the concept of values. They provided us with a taxonomy to analyze cultural patterns. After studying hundreds of cultures, Kluckhohn and Strodtbeck concluded that people would always turn to their culture for answers. Besides, Florence's husband Clyde Kluckhohn also did a lot of work in the study of cultural values. He believed that human beings had common biological characteristics, which form the basis of cultural development. People usually feel that their cultural beliefs and practices are normal and natural, while others' cultural beliefs and practices are strange, abnormal, or inferior.

Florence Kluckhohn and Fred Strodtbeck put forward a theory to put these principles into practice. The theory is based on the following three basic assumptions:

(1) Any nation in any era must provide solutions to some common human problems.

(2) The solutions to these problems are not unlimited or arbitrary.

(3) Each value orientation exists in all societies and individuals, but each society and individual have different preferences for value orientation.

They believe that the preferred solutions to these common human problems in a given society reflect the values of that society. Therefore, the measurement of the preferred solutions will indicate the values embraced by the society. They put forward five basic problems that need to be solved in every society:

(1) What is the basic nature of people? (Human-Nature Orientation)

(2) What is the appropriate relationship between man and nature? (Man-

Nature Orientation)

(3) How should we best think about time? (Time Orientation)

(4) What is the best mode of activity? (Activity Orientation)

(5) What is the best form of social organization? (Relational Orientation)

Each orientation mentioned above is a common problem that all human beings and society will face. Obviously, the values orientation theory of Kluckhohn and Strodtbeck laid the foundation for us to study the differences between different cultures. Putting all the directions together, we make Table 4.9 as follows.

Table 4.9　Values Orientation Proposed by Kluckhohn and Strodtbeck (Samovar, 2019)

	Values		
Human-Nature Orientation	evil	mixture of evil and good	good
Man-Nature Orientation	subordinate to nature	harmony with nature	dominant over nature
Time Orientation	past-oriented	present-oriented	future-oriented
Activity Orientation	being	becoming	doing
Relational Orientation	hierarchical	collateral	individual

From the table above, three possible answers could be seen for the five questions, which also show people's different values on the same question in different cultures.

4.4.1 Human-Nature Orientation

Human-nature orientation involves the inherent characteristics of human nature. Kluckhohn and Strodtbeck believed that when answering the question of human-nature orientation, two aspects should be considered: first, whether human nature is good, evil, or a mixture of good and evil; second, whether human nature is changeable. Besides, they further proposed that the "mixed" can not only mean "a mixture of good and evil", but also mean "neither good nor evil". Therefore, in answering the question of human nature, we can have eight ways to solve the problem:

(1) Human nature is evil but changeable.

(2) Human nature is evil but immutable.

(3) Human nature is mixed but changeable.

(4) Human nature is mixed but immutable.

(5) Human nature is neither evil nor good but changeable.

(6) Human nature is neither evil nor good but immutable.

(7) Human nature is good but changeable.

(8) Human nature is good but immutable.

People in different cultures have different views on human nature. Westerners, influenced by Christianity, advocate the theory of original sin and think human nature is evil, while the Chinese, influenced by Confucianism, think human nature is good. American culture has a more complicated view of human nature. Americans do not simply think that human nature is good or evil, but that human nature is a mixture of good and evil. They also believe that the good and evil part of human nature may change after birth. It reflects the changeable belief of human nature. On the contrary, some societies take a single view of human nature. For example, in China, Confucianism dominates, and the most basic theoretical basis of Confucianism is that men are born good. Mencius believes that the fundamental difference between man and other animals is that human nature is good. There is no need to doubt human goodness, just as water flows down. The first sentence in the *Three-Character Classic*, a popular song for teaching children in ancient China, is also "Man's nature at birth is good. People are born about the same, but habits make them differ." In other words, human nature is good. Moreover, this nature is similar and universal. It is only because of the changes in living habits and environment that different behavior is formed, which leads to the deviation from "good". Therefore, although in the Spring and Autumn Period and the Warring States Period, there was a dispute between the good and the evil of human nature, today's Chinese mainstream culture still holds the view that human nature is inherently good. When analyzing a specific culture, we should not arbitrarily impose a certain orientation on everyone in that culture.

4.4.2 Man-Nature Orientation

According to the values orientation theory of Kluckhohn and Strodtbeck, there are three kinds of potential relations between man and nature, namely, conquering nature, living in harmony with nature, and subordinating to nature.

The Confucian view of human nature interprets the relationship between man and nature from the perspective of "the heaven and man as one". It holds that "the heaven and man as one" is not only the necessity of human nature but also the goal that man should pursue, showing the idea that "Man is an integral part of nature". Mencius pointed out that people should be obedient to nature and walk in accordance with the natural law.

However, humanism in the West advocates the use of reason and emphasizes the will to transform the environment in life, encouraging people to conquer nature and enjoy the material life of this world. This orientation holds the view that all natural forces can and should be utilized and conquered.

In addition to the above two orientations, some cultures believe that the relationship between man and nature is man's subordination to nature. For example, with regard to the Southeast Asian tsunami incident, some Southeast Asians attributed the incident to fate, thinking that the tsunami was an arrangement from heaven. Although grief, there is nothing to complain about. Some people in Southeast Asia believed that the coming of this natural disaster is the result of human beings' offending against nature, and it is the retribution that humans deserve. Americans reacted completely differently. They believed that this is the result of human beings' inaccurate predictions and insufficient preparation for possible disasters. If human beings can design more accurate scientific instruments or prepare for possible disasters in advance, disasters can be completely avoided.

4.4.3 Time Orientation

Time orientation can be divided into three types: One is past orientation, emphasizing tradition and respecting history; the second is present orientation, usually focusing on short-term and immediate returns; the third is future orientation, stressing long-term development and change.

Past orientation mainly exists in the culture that attaches great importance to tradition. People in past-oriented cultures usually assume that life follows a track predestined by tradition or God's will. They worship ancestors and emphasize close family relationships. Chinese people attach great importance to the past. They worship their ancestors, respect the elderly and teachers, and value age and experience, because all of these are related to the past. Past orientation has always influenced Chinese people's behavior and their way of thinking. When people do things, they usually have to consider whether anyone did it in the past, what successful experiences can be learned from, and what lessons should be drawn from

failures. Therefore, following the rules has become a social norm.

People from present-oriented cultures are less concerned about what happened in the past and what may happen in the future. People think that only the present moment is the most important. They tend to seize the day and hardly plan for tomorrow. People who are present-oriented tend to focus only on the short-term and immediate returns. The traditional Islamic culture belongs to the present-oriented culture. They believe that the future belongs to Allah and is beyond the control of mortals. Anyone who tries to predict the future is mentally abnormal, because only Allah knows about the future, and it is too presumptuous for ordinary people to talk about the future. Therefore, Arabs are not willing to predict the future. Compared with other cultures, people in these cultures are more random in their attitude towards time. This kind of indifference to time often makes Westerners misunderstand it as a sign of laziness and inefficiency.

The future-oriented culture attaches great importance to change. In a future-oriented society, change is usually considered necessary and beneficial, while the past is outdated and should be abandoned. Kluckhohn, Strodtbeck, and Hall all believe that this time orientation exists in American society. In the United States, new products and packaging emerge one after another, because they think that only in this way can they attract customers.

4.4.4 Activity Orientation

There are three orientations of human activities, namely doing, being, and becoming. American society is one that emphasizes action ("doing"), and people must constantly do things in order to be meaningful and create value. Americans work hard and want to get promotions, salary increases, and other ways of recognition for their achievements. At the same time, they also pay attention to the types of activities, which must be quantifiable so that they can be seen and touched. When evaluating a person, Americans always ask "What has he done?" or "What has he accomplished?" If a person sits and thinks, he will be regarded to have done nothing, because thinking cannot be quantified or measured.

The orientation of "being" is just opposite to that of "doing". Patience is seen as one of the virtues, not as a sign of idleness. Chinese culture belongs to the orientation of "being", which advocates coping with all motions by remaining motionless and coping with shifting events by sticking to a fundamental principle.

The "becoming" orientation emphasizes who we are rather than what we have done. The center of human activities is to strive to become a more complete self in the process of self-development. Zen monks, for example, are one of the best examples. In order to perfect themselves, they spend their whole life in contemplation and meditation.

4.4.5 Relational Orientation

Kluckhohn and Strodtbeck proposed that there are three orientations in dealing with the relationship between human beings: individual orientation, hierarchical orientation, and collateral orientation.

Individual orientation is characterized by individual autonomy, and individuals are regarded as unique and independent. In this orientation, individual goals are more important than group objectives.

Hierarchical orientation focuses on the group, and group goals are thought to be the most important. In hierarchical countries, groups are divided into different levels, and the status of each group remains stable and does not change over time. Hierarchical societies tend to practice aristocracy. Aristocracy in many European countries is an example of this orientation.

Collateral orientation also pays attention to groups, but it is not groups with time continuity, but groups in which members have the closest relationship with each other. In fact, this orientation only considers people's group memberships rather than specific people. For example, Chinese people are accustomed to seeing themselves as a member of a group. When personal interests conflict with group interests, individuals should sacrifice their own interests to protect group interests. The Americans are just the opposite. They think that everyone is an independent individual and should be responsible for himself. Therefore, young Americans live away from home by the age of 18. Even if their school or workplace is close to their parents' home, they will find another house and live independently.

Using values orientation theory to distinguish culture can help us understand many of the cultural differences observed in our daily life, and make a reasonable explanation for some "anomalies". People of different nationalities and countries have quite different ideas on these five major issues, and these different ideas will significantly affect their attitude and behavior towards life and work.

文化交际：原理与应用

Case Study: Value Differences in Chinese and Western Luxury Wine Advertising

Read the following passage and try to analyze it by answering the question:

Why do China and the West adopt different publicity strategies in luxury wine advertising?

There are great differences between China and the West in the way of advertising luxury wine. The advertisements of various brands in China show the pride brought by the long history of wine culture. For example, the brand name of "National Pits 1573" indicates that the brand originated in the Wanli Period of the Ming Dynasty, which has a history of more than 400 years. In the advertisement, after comparing with the history of phonograph, photography, and other inventions, "National Pits 1573" emphasizes to enable consumers to "taste the history" for 437 years. Similarly, "Daoguang Twenty-five" also emphasizes a century-old model of wine making craftsmanship in its advertisement. The slogan "crossing history, inheriting civilization" in the advertisement of Shuijingfang also highlights its 600 years of long history and 600 years of high quality. In addition, traditional Chinese cultural elements and symbols are also widely used in Chinese wine advertisements. Take Shuijingfang as an example. Traditional symbols with strong symbolic significance such as Peking Opera figures, Chinese ink paintings, classical poems, etc. are used in advertisements.

Compared with Chinese wine advertisements, Western wine advertisements choose different ways of publicity. For example, in the advertisements of Remy Martin, we can often see parties held by a large group of people. The slogan of the advertisement is "living for the moment and enjoying your life". In addition, the slogan of Chivas, "This is Chivas life", emphasizes the current enjoyment and quality of life that the brand brings to consumers. Another example is Hennessy's slogan: "To me, the past is black and white, but the future is always colorful."

Chinese luxury wine advertisements often emphasize the long cultural heritage of the brand and respect the inheritance of history. Compared with Chinese wine advertisements, Western wine advertisements pay little attention to the past, but focus on the present and the future. Although these Western luxury wine brands also have a history of more than 100 years, they do not emphasize the long history of the brands in the advertisements, but place more emphasis on the present quality and the future unlimited possibilities. It can be seen from Western wine advertisements that Westerners do not pay much attention to the past. On the contrary, they are full of strong visions for the future.

The reason why China and the West adopt different publicity strategies in luxury wine advertising is closely related to their differences in time orientation. China belongs to the past-oriented culture. People in this culture worship their ancestors, respect others, emphasize experience, tradition, and history. This orientation is naturally reflected in their advertising behavior. In contrast, most Western countries belong to the present-oriented or future-oriented culture, so Westerners generally believe that only the present is the most important, and they don't pay much attention to what has happened in the past. In addition, they focus on the future, emphasizing long-term development and change.

Now, it's your turn to analyze a case. Proverbs are the concentrated embodiment of wisdom in people's daily life, from which we can see the cultural orientation of a nation. Collect relevant proverbs and analyze the differences between Chinese and Western values from Chinese and English proverbs.

For Your Information

Kluckhohn & Strodtbeck and Values Orientation Theory

Florence Kluckhohn and Fred Strodtbeck are American anthropologists who put forward cultural theories. Florence Kluckhohn participated in a team of about 30 experts formed by the U.S. military during the Pacific War to study the value and morale of different cultures. Through the analysis of the psychology and value of the Japanese nation, the research group proposed to the U.S. government not to abolish the Japanese emperor. U.S. government thus revised the declaration of unconditional surrender in accordance with their suggestions. Soon after World War II, Harvard University strengthened its support for the study of cultural value dimensions, and together with Rockefeller Foundation, it funded Kluckhohn and others to carry out a large-scale study on five different cultural communities in an area of 40 square miles of Texas, U.S. One of the main results of this research is Kluckhohn & Strodtbeck's five value orientation models, which were published in the book *Variations in Value Orientations* (1961).

Summary

In this chapter, we mainly introduce the cultural patterns and the three main components: beliefs, values, and norms. On this basis, we discuss three major approaches to studying the cultural patterns, i.e., Edward Hall's high-context and low-context cultural taxonomy, Hofstede's cultural dimensions theory, and Kluckhohn and Strodtbeck's values orientation theory. And one thing we should always bear in mind is that no matter to which culture we belong, only when we can thoroughly understand the diversities of different cultures and learn to respect others' culture can we cooperate with others well.

Exercises

Questions for Review

1. Can you explain the three components of cultural patterns?

2. What are the five dimensions of cultural values?

3. What are the differences between high power distance culture and low power distance culture?

Problems and Application

Read the following dialog between Mr. Jones (an American manager) and Mr. Sugimoto (a Japanese worker), and try to answer the following questions:

Mr. Jones: Mr. Sugimoto, I noticed that you did a good job on the assembly line. I hope other workers could learn from you.

Mr. Sugimoto: It is unnecessary to praise me. I'm just doing my job. [He's uneasy and hopes other Japanese workers do not notice their conversation.]

Mr. Jones: I believe you are the most industrious, outstanding, and dedicated employee in our company.

Mr. Sugimoto: [He blushes and nods a few times and continues to work.]

Mr. Jones: Mr. Sugimoto, are you going to say "thank you" or just keep silent?

Mr. Sugimoto: Mr. Jones, sorry, can I have five minutes off?

Mr. Jones: Of course. [He is angry and watches Sugimoto to leave.] [I can't believe how impolite these Japanese workers are. They just keep silent and seem to have trouble in accepting compliments gracefully and never respond to your compliment.]

1. Why was the conversation between Mr. Jones and Mr. Sugimoto not so pleasant?

2. Why did they react so differently towards praising in public?

3. If you were Mr. Sugimoto, would you accept praise from Mr. Jones in the workplace?

4. If you were Mr. Jones, how would you deal with the situation more appropriately?

Chapter *5*

Intercultural Communication in Various Social Contexts

Learning Objectives

After learning this chapter, you should be able to:

1. understand the concept of face;

2. know how people's views on family and friendship differ across cultures;

3. know how Hofstede's cultural dimensions affect what happens in a classroom;

4. know the main factors influencing international communication in business;

5. know the principles and rules people should obey in international communication.

As we all know, communication always happens in all kinds of contexts. Social context, also called social environment, refers to the settings surrounding individuals, including the culture they live in and groups they interact with. Social context influences customs, traditions, and other socially acceptable standards. These social environments help to direct how people relate to one another, how family members live and communicate with each other, and how companies interact with their staff.

Before we start this chapter, there are some questions for you:

(1) How is your relationship with your parents? If your point of view is different from theirs, what will you do to let them accept your point of view?

(2) When your company is preparing to enter the international market, what are the first issues you need to consider? Can a successful domestic company guarantee the same success abroad?

5.1 Family and Friends

5.1.1 Brief Introduction to Relationship

All cultures have relationships that connect the people in that culture. Simply defined, relationships are how we deal with others in our everyday life. Like communication, relationships are ever changing. In addition, relationships are reciprocal when the parties in the relationship can meet each other's needs. According to Schutz (1958), these needs are inclusion, control, and affection. Inclusion means the sense of belonging. Control refers to the ability to be in charge of our own life and to influence others around us. Affection is our desire to love and be loved. How we fulfill these needs varies depending on the culture in which we live. For example, the degree of self-disclosure in relationships differs from culture to culture. Self-disclosure is a process of passing on information about ourselves to someone else—whether we intend to or not. The details can range from our favorite food or TV shows to religious beliefs, and big turning points in our private life. In the United States, people use self-disclosure as a means of developing relationships— to feel included, to control, and to give and gain affection. In Chinese culture, self-disclosure is more conservative. Self-centered speech would be considered boastful and pretentious. The Chinese seem to prefer talking about external matters, like world events. Self-disclosure is a gift shared only with the most intimate relatives and friends.

In all kinds of relationships, the most important ones are those of family and friends. Although there are certain general concepts in relationships across cultures, each culture puts its own special mark on how these concepts are "played out" in day-to-day communication.

5.1.2 Family Relationships

Family relationships vary from country to country. Families have a variety of forms: single-parent families, step-families, extended families, and so on. Within each family structure, the rules, themes, decision making, ways of dealing with conflict, degree of support for one another, boundaries, roles, and the closeness of family members may differ, and each affects communication within that family. In the United States, extended families usually do not live together. In Latin America, members of the extended family often live together. Family roles in the United States are not as strictly defined as in other cultures. For example, the family roles in Argentina are strictly defined. The mother raises the children, takes care of the household, and shows respect to her husband.

In collectivist cultures, such as China, Japan, South Korea, and Latin America, a family consists of numerous members—grandparents, uncles, aunts, cousins—living closely together. Thus, children grow up defining themselves as members of this large group. In fact, they define themselves in relation to this collectivist "we" of family rather than as an individual "I". Lifelong loyalty is owed to this group. Since harmony is a major value, "speaking one's mind" is not encouraged. The word "no" is seldom used. Rather, "We will think about it" or "You may be right" are used. Also, the word "yes" does not necessarily mean agreement. "Yes" often means that the speaker was heard, as in "Yes, I understand you."

The obligation to the family in collectivist cultures is financial. Resources are shared. If a member of a collectivist family does not have a job, the others in the family support the unemployed member. Yet, the obligation is not just financial. Ritual obligations are also owed to the family. All occasions, such as birth, deaths, marriages, are very important and the celebrations must be attended by all family members.

One final important concept in collectivist cultures is face. Face describes the

proper relationship between a person and his or her social environment. "Losing face" is synonymous with humiliation. Because of the collectivist "we" of the family, if one individual in the family loses face, all members lose face. One loses face if he or she fails to meet the essential requirements placed on him or her by society. In addition to losing face, one can "give face" which means to give prestige and honor by the way one acts toward another.

The Western family, which is individualistic, differs greatly from the Eastern family. Western family emphasizes "I" rather than "we" and it is this difference that makes all the other differences. A Western family member is much more likely to speak his or her mind and disagree with his or her parents. The individual decides, for the most part, which college to attend, which profession to choose, and who to marry. Obligations to the family are looser, both financially and in terms of rituals. Parents focus on helping their children to become independent.

5.1.3 Friendships

Intercultural friendship varies in a number of ways: Who can be a friend, how long the friendship lasts, how many friends, and how long a relationship exists before it can be considered a friendship. Western Europeans feel that close friends can be developed within a few months. Asian Americans, African Americans, and Latinos take about a year to develop a friendship that they would consider close. African American friends can criticize one another, often quite loudly, whereas Western European friends do not consider this behavior appropriate. Each group emphasizes a slightly different aspect of the important characteristics of friendship. African Americans emphasize respect and acceptance; Asian Americans emphasize a positive, caring exchange of ideas; and Anglo Americans emphasize recognition of the individuals' needs.

In addition, Anglo American friendships are often compartmentalized. For example, an Anglo American might have friends with whom he or she plays tennis, friends with whom he or she studies, friends with whom he or she goes to the movies, and so on. In other words, friends are for specific purposes. European Americans tend to classify others into what they can do rather than who they are. Thais are not that kind. In Thailand, a friend is chosen for the person as a whole. A Thai would not choose a friend whose values, beliefs, or lifestyles are different from his or her own.

People in the United States tend to be quite mobile, moving from job to job, location to location. As they move, they make new friends. However, friendship does not usually last after one has moved to a different area. In other words, friendships are often transient. In Asian cultures, a friend is for a lifetime. Once we are friends, we remain so, regardless of the distance between us or the time that has passed since we last met. It is not uncommon in the United States for people to lose track of the people who were in their wedding party. Such an event will not occur in Asian countries.

Case Study: **American Friendship**

Read the following passage and try to analyze it by answering the question:

What are the differences between the two's views of friendship in this case?

Steve and Yaser first met in their chemistry class in an American university. Yaser was an international student from Jordan. He wanted to learn more about American culture and hoped that he and Steve could become good friends. At first, Steve seemed very friendly. He always greeted Yaser warmly before class. Sometimes he offered to study with Yaser. He even invited Yaser to have lunch with him. But after the semester was over, Steve seemed more distant. The two former classmates did not see each other very often in school. One day Yaser decided to call Steve. Steve did not seem very interested in talking to him. Yaser was hurt by Steve's change of attitude. "Steve said we were friends," Yaser complained, "and I thought friends were friends forever." Yaser was a little confused.

As a foreigner, Yaser does not understand the way Americans view friendship. Americans use the word "friend" in a very general way. They may call both casual acquaintances and close companions "friends". These friendships are based on common interests. When the shared activity ends, the friendship may disappear. Now as Steve and Yaser are no longer classmates, their friendship has changed. In some cultures, friendship means a strong lifelong bond between two people. In these cultures, friendships develop slowly, since they are built to last. American society is one of rapid changes. Studies show that one out of five American families move every year. American friendships develop quickly, and they may change just as quickly. People from the United States may at first seem friendly. They often chat with strangers. But American friendliness is not always an offer of true friendship. After an experience like Yaser's, people who have been in this country for only a few months

may consider Americans to be fickle. Learning how Americans view friendship can help non-Americans avoid misunderstandings. It can also help them make friends in the American way.

Now it's your turn to think about how two people from different cultures become friends. List all the things that you think can help to build up friendship and discuss with your partner to see if there are any differences between your ideas.

5.2 Education

5.2.1 Relationship Between Education and Culture

Educational institutions can develop the abilities of the individuals and create socially important ideals that could construct the future of society. The educational system meets people's needs in getting knowledge throughout life as well as the needs of society in the social adaptation of young people to use their skills for the development of the economy. Education passes on the knowledge and values that are part of a culture. Good education can even help bridge the gap between past differences in cultures and allow people to come together in a new, shared understanding of the world. The needs of the society, whether religious, social, cultural or psychological, all are fulfilled by education. The valuable cultural heritage, which has accumulated a vast store of human knowledge and experience, is transmitted to the coming generations through education. In the process of education, history is being studied which is the main and basic record of culture, hence it cannot be denied that it is being nourished by education. Learning and education are the most effective when they connect with people's culture background and seem relevant to their past experiences. Similarly, the purposeful and suitable education helps in the strength and spread of culture.

While no culture is better or worse for education, culture can affect how people learn and what knowledge they place value on. Cultural background affects attitudes, beliefs, and values about education, which include ideas about how classes ought to be conducted, how students and teachers ought to interact, and what types of relationships are appropriate for students and teachers. As we have seen, cultural differences affect relationships in the educational environment. They may result in differences in learning styles. So understanding cultural differences can help us communicate more effectively with our classmates when we have the chance to study abroad or interact with foreign students in our own country.

5.2.2 Cultural Dimensions in an Educational Context

In the previous chapter, we have learned Hofstede's cultural dimensions. Now we are going to talk about how these cultural dimensions affect what happens in a classroom. The first is collectivism and individualism. In terms of classroom behavior, this dimension suggests that in collectivist cultures students expect to speak up in class only when called on personally by the teacher. Formal harmony is important and neither a teacher nor any student should ever be made to lose face. For example, Vietnamese students are always taught to be respectful of their teacher and never to criticize. On the other hand, in individualistic cultures, students expect to speak up in class in response to a general invitation by the teacher. In addition, confrontation is not necessarily avoided; conflicts can be brought into openly; and the face-consciousness is weak. That's why native American children learn better in an environment that is noncompetitive and cooperative.

In a collectivist culture, harmony with the group is emphasized rather than the individual. Because of the culture emphasizing cooperation, Mexican children allow others to share their homework or answers. This shows group solidarity, helpfulness, and generosity, which are important characteristics of their collectivist culture. However, the U.S. educational system emphasizes competition and the individual. If an American student shares his or her homework, he or she is seen as dishonest, perhaps even a cheater!

A second dimension is power distance. In societies with low power distance, the educational process is student-centered. The students initiate communication, outline their own paths to learning, and even contradict the teacher. In societies with high power distance, the educational process is teacher-centered. The teacher initiates all communication, outlines the paths of learning that students should follow, and is never publicly criticized or contradicted. The emphasis is on the personal "wisdom" of the teacher. In societies with low power distance, the emphasis is on objective "truth" that can be obtained by any competent person. In Asian societies, the teacher is given much respect. There is a high power distance between the teacher and the student. A Chinese or Vietnamese student would not consider arguing with a teacher. The role of Asian students is to accept and respect the wisdom of the teacher.

The teacher presents information and the students accept it without question. Asking questions is seen as a challenge to the teacher's authority or an admission of the students' ignorance.

In the United States, where the power distance is low, students are encouraged to challenge the teacher and one another. The teacher encourages students to discuss and debate issues, learn how to solve problems, and create their own answers to the questions. In general, Americans prefer to learn through personal discovery and problem solving.

Uncertainty avoidance is the third dimension. In a society with weak uncertainty avoidance, students feel comfortable in unstructured learning situations like vague objectives, no timetable, and broad assignments. And they are rewarded for innovative approaches to problem solving. Teachers are allowed to say "I don't know", interpret intellectual disagreement as stimulating, and seek parents' ideas.

In societies with strong uncertainty avoidance, students feel comfortable in structured learning situations, such as precise objectives, strict timetable, detailed assignments, and are rewarded for accuracy in problem solving. Teachers are expected to have all the answers, interpret intellectual disagreement as personal disloyalty, and consider themselves experts who do not need parents' ideas. Students prefer clear instructions, avoid conflict, and dislike competition. Examples of the countries with strong uncertainty are France, Chile, Spain, Portugal, Japan, Peru, and Argentina. By comparison, the United States, Great Britain, Denmark, Ireland, and India are characterized by weak uncertainty avoidance. Students in these countries are competitive, need fewer instructions, and see conflict as stimulating.

The fourth dimension is masculinity and femininity. In terms of the classroom, we can again make some assumptions about behavior, depending on whether a culture is feminine or masculine. In feminine societies, teachers avoid openly praising students because academic achievements are less important than successful interpersonal relationships, and cooperation among students is fostered. Teachers use average students as the "norm". A student's failure in school is a relatively minor event. The system rewards students' social adaptations. In masculine societies, teachers openly praise good students because academic achievement is highly regarded and competition is fostered. Teachers use the best students as the "norm". Academic failure is a severe blow to the self-image. The system rewards academic performance. A masculine culture values assertiveness and competitiveness. Examples of high masculinity countries include Japan, Mexico, Ireland, Austria, Switzerland, Great Britain, and Germany. High feminine countries include Chile, Portugal, Thailand, Sweden, Norway, the Netherlands, Denmark, and Finland.

These countries place a high value on interpersonal relationships, compassion, and nurturing.

Case Study: Are Our Kids Tough Enough? Chinese School

Please analyze this case with power distance and individualism and collectivism of Hofstede's cultural dimensions.

"In a sleepy Hampshire village, battle lines are being drawn. Five Chinese teachers have come to shake up the British education system. British pupils are falling behind in the international race. The Chinese teachers have come to prove that even a high-achieving school has a lot to learn. It's an unforgiving regime based on high-pressure learning and ruthless competition. And after four weeks, the students in the Chinese school will be tested against their British counterparts. Will the long days and strict discipline produce superior students, or will the clash of two cultures create chaos in the classroom?"

This is the opening line of a documentary produced by BBC in 2015 *Are Our Kids Tough Enough? Chinese School*. In the documentary, five top Chinese teachers spent a month with students at the Bohunt School in Liphook in Hampshire, England. China's tough education system produces strong results in subjects like math and science, capturing the interest of educators in the U.S. and Europe where some feel the child-centered approach does not do enough to teach the basics.

Li Aiyun, one of the teachers featured in the documentary, described the classroom in Britain as "chaotic". "When I assigned them to do some work in the classroom, some of the students were eating and some were even putting on their makeup when I walked in," she said.

Miss Yang's science lesson and Mr. Zou's math lesson are essentially lectures. They stand in the front writing the theory on the board, while the students (are supposed to) take notes and learn. This may be OK in China, where education is based on authority and respect is given to the teacher, but less so in a British comprehensive school, where autonomy and questioning are encouraged.

Rosie Lunskey, a 15-year-old participant of the Bohunt School experiment, described to BBC journalists how she clashed with the Chinese teachers: "Acting like robots was the right way to go. I'm used to speaking my mind in class, being

bold, giving ideas, often working in groups to advance my skills and improve my knowledge. But in the experiment, the only thing I felt like I was learning was how to copy notes really fast and listen to the teacher lecture us."

Classes quickly descended into chaos, and respect went out of the window. "They've got this discipline that probably works in China because everyone does what the teachers say, but it doesn't work here because no one really cares," says Rosie. "Everyone just finds it hilarious."

The program has generated debate across both China and the U.K., with many suggesting teenagers should be taught with firmer rules and regulation.

We can approach the problems in this case through two cultural dimensions. Firstly, power distance. We can see that autonomy and questioning are encouraged in British schools. The power distance is low, and students are encouraged to challenge the teacher. Students prefer to learn through personal discovery and problem solving rather than through memorizing facts presented to them by an authority figure. So when a Chinese teacher stands in the front writing the theory on the board, asking the students to take notes and learn, they feel boring.

Secondly, individualism and collectivism. In collectivist cultures, students expect to speak up in class only when called on personally by the teacher. So the Chinese teacher regards the classroom in Britain as "chaotic" when students talk or eat without permission. We also find that students do not care much about teachers' criticism. That is because in individualistic cultures, confrontation is not necessarily avoided; conflicts can be brought into openly; and the face-consciousness is weak.

Now it's your turn to continue analyzing the documentary with the rest three cultural dimensions.

5.3 Economics and Business

5.3.1 Three Main Factors Influencing International Communication in Business

As we know, different cultures have different ways of business negotiation. This process involves many factors, among which the most influential ones are language, interpersonal relationship, and persuasive style. Let's discuss them one by one.

The first is language. Language plays an important role in intercultural communication. In a business environment, our language differences can cause major economic and personal problems. Compared with people from the East who like to beat around the bush when they speak, the way of communication in the West is often more direct. Therefore, Americans sometimes think that people who use indirect communication are deceptive or untrustworthy. However, Americans are often considered insensitive or rude by people from the East as a result of their direct way of communication.

Nevertheless, besides the language itself, the style of communication can also cause problems. Brazilians often talk without any pause, while Americans prefer to pause for a little while between utterances. If we talk to people from a culture with many verbal overlays, such as Brazilians, we may need to be more assertive. If we talk to people from a culture with many language pauses, we may need to pause more so that others could have a chance to speak. The Japanese even have pauses lasting much longer compared with Americans. The result is that Americans often have to wait for such a long time that in the end, they have to start talking again since the silence makes them feel so uncomfortable and embarrassed. However, as a matter of fact, the Japanese keep silent just to show respect for others. When they think it's time for them to speak, Americans have already begun to speak again. Finally, the conversation between a Japanese and an American is likely to end with the Japanese's silence and American's non-stop talking.

The second is interpersonal relationship. Different cultures have different rhythms of business transaction. This is partly due to the way people from different cultural backgrounds develop and maintain relationships. For example, at the beginning of the negotiation, German business managers may ask many questions about technical details; Scandinavians want to get down to the business directly; Italian managers prefer to socialize and cultivate good relations before talking about business. And if we are in Spain or Mexico, it may take a few days at the beginning of a negotiation, since a good relationship is the foundation of business cooperation. Therefore, it is obvious that in some countries, interpersonal relationship is seen as a key factor in cross-cultural negotiations.

The third is persuasive style. Reasoning is extremely important in business negotiation. However, not every culture has the same way of reasoning. Different cultures differ in their understanding of persuasive and reasonable shreds of evidence.

European Americans equal facts with evidence. As we can see, many of the

detective stories on TV emphasize facts: clues at the scenes of the crimes, witnesses' testimony, and other relevant scientific data. These facts enable investigators to understand not only the behavior of the individuals involved in the crime but also their motives.

For some cultures, facts are not so acceptable. For Muslims, stories or fables, are regarded as the most powerful forms of evidence. In the cultures affected by Confucianism, metaphors, as well as analogies, are accepted as evidence. In African culture, testimony is not as powerful a form of evidence as it is in the American legal system. Some African cultures even regard that a witness' words should not be accepted as a useful testimony.

5.3.2 Important Tips on Doing Business Internationally

Once we have established a nationwide business, the next step may be to sell our products all over the world. That is to say, we have to globalize our business, because globalization means new markets, new opportunities, and new sources of revenue, all of which can be a great help to our business.

However, international expansion cannot be achieved overnight. Such initiatives require a lot of research and planning. Nowadays, most enterprises, especially those in the digital field, are trying to use technology to make the world a global village. This could mean recruiting overseas employees, serving overseas customers, and working with companies around the world. Here are five very important tips to help us do business internationally.

The first one is to be patient: When doing business abroad, it is vital to understand and appreciate cultural differences. We have adapted to the rapid development of today's digital commerce, but when doing business overseas, we need to spend extra time to win the trust and understand the habits of other people we work with. As a result, patience is a kind of quality that should be attached great importance to.

The second one is to socialize and enjoy: One of the best ways to win the trust and learn about foreign cultures is to spend time with our foreign colleagues. In this way, we can not only open new doors by meeting a lot of strange people but also establish a reputation in the new community. By participating in various social activities, such as wine tasting, club activities, and so on, we can learn a lot about foreign culture. More importantly, it's a great way to develop a close relationship with our partners.

The third one is to respect others' customs and try something new: When we meet new friends, it's always a good way to show our respect by understanding other's culture and trying something that is shared by our new partners. It can be anything from the food we like to an unforgettable trip. Sharing is always a happy thing. In the process of sharing and being shared, we can not only have a closer relationship with our business partners but also enjoy ourselves and learn something new.

The fourth one is to reciprocate: As the old saying goes, "Friendship cannot stand always on one side." Therefore, it's wise to invite our foreign colleagues to our hometown and show them the unique charm of our culture. Giving them more opportunities to understand our culture will not only help the two parties to work more efficiently in cross-cultural communication but also create a more equal and mutual-trust cooperative relationship.

The fifth one is to keep in touch: It's easier to start a business than to keep it. In the same way, it's easy to meet a new partner, but it's not easy to maintain a long-term good relationship with a partner. This requires us to maintain regular contact with our partners. With the development of science and technology, cross-cultural communication has become more and more convenient, and many communication tools are provided. Meanwhile, the cost has been continuously reduced. Keep good daily contact with our potential partners. When there is a need for cooperation, we will be included in their business cooperation consideration list in the first place.

Case Study: Law or Relationship, Which Is More Important When Doing Business?

Read the following passage and try to analyze it by answering these questions:

(1) Why did the two sides have such conflicts?
(2) How can you solve the conflicts between the Japanese Sugar Company and the Australian Sugar Exchange?

In 1974, the Japanese Sugar Company signed a long-term contract with the Australian Sugar Exchange. According to the contract, the Australian side should provide sugar to the Japanese side at a fixed price and transaction volume. Later, the international sugar prices plummeted, and the Japanese Sugar Company ran into deficits. From July 1976 to November 1977, the Japanese Sugar Company

repeatedly asked the Australia side to lower the price of sugar. At the same time, the Japanese Sugar Company rejected Australian sugar for three consecutive months. In the sugar dispute, the Japanese side believed that as a long-term partner, Australia should help when the Japanese side was in crisis, while the Australian side believed that the Japanese side made trouble out of nothing.

The reason for such a dispute actually has a close relationship with the cultures of both sides. The Japanese attach importance to human interest and the establishment of harmonious interpersonal relationships in transaction negotiations. In the sugar dispute, the Japanese side believed that as a regular customer of the Australian side, the two sides had established a firm and close cooperative relationship, and the friendship between the two sides was obviously more important than the established contract. However, the Australian side believed that the contract was sacred and reasonable. In their view, the law was much more important than any relationship and could never be easily changed. To solve the conflicts between the two sides, it's important to have a clear knowledge of the culture of the other party, and find a solution to the problem within the bottom line acceptable to both parties.

Suppose your company needs to purchase a set of professional equipment, and you are appointed as the representative to negotiate with the Japanese, American, and Italian companies to determine the most suitable equipment. Try to summarize the different negotiation strategies that will be employed in the process of negotiating with them.

5.4 Principles and Rules of Intercultural Communication

In our interaction with others, we try to make sure whether we are being fairly treated. Everyone has a way to judge the concept of fairness in these exchanges. And it is a common belief that "I helped you, and you should help me in return." The sociological term for this kind of exchange is called "reciprocity". The main function of reciprocity is to teach people the principle of cooperation. It is very important for cross-cultural interaction because once a favor is given, the success or failure to return the favor can determine the quality of the subsequent interactions with our partners. The key to reciprocity is to maintain a balance between expectation and behavior, which is difficult to reconcile in cross-cultural communication. Therefore, in the process of intercultural communication, we have to follow four principles: mutuality, nonjudgmentalism, honesty, and respect.

Mutuality means that we must try our best to find a common understanding in cross-cultural contact. We should bear in our mind that the experiences we share with others are not guided by our cultural background, nor by their cultural background. When we communicate with people from another culture, we should actively seek some mutual ground in order to have a real exchange of ideas. We should be willing to consider those ideas that may be inconsistent with our own culture or moral values. If either party requires the interaction to be completely carried out in accordance with his or her customs, he or she is in fact creating obstacles for successful cross-cultural communication. As a matter of fact, China, as the largest developing country in the world, has long put forward this principle in its relations with other countries. Time proves everything! China's prosperity today is closely related to the adoption of this principle at that time. This principle not only helps to solve the conflicts between countries but also has great significance in dealing with other problems in cross-cultural communication.

Nonjudgmentalism typifies the concept of open-mindedness. We not only should be willing to express ourselves openly, but also consider the expressions of others without judgment. This means that we should be willing to recognize and appreciate different views, from which we can have a good understanding of another culture. When we get to understand that all cultures have their own values and beliefs, we begin to really recognize and appreciate these differences without making value judgments. In fact, this principle is very useful in our daily communication with others. Violating this principle at will may result in very serious consequences. As we all know, *Pride and Prejudice* is a famous novel by Jane Austen. In the novel, it is because of Darcy's arrogance and Elizabeth's prejudice that the two lovers narrowly miss each other. Finally, after a series of events, the couple got rid of their prejudgment and lived happily together. From this story, we can see the importance of never judging others before we know them.

Honesty is our confidence in the commitment of others. The general rule of intercultural communication is that a person's commitment should be consistent with what he or she delivers. To be honest, we have to understand our cultural biases and know how these biases affect our communication with others. In another word, we should be honest with ourselves before we start to be honest with others. We ought to discuss things as they are, not as we think they should be. Honesty also

requires that the information is real and that the sender is able to communicate it in an effective way. As a country with an ancient civilization, China has long put honesty in an important position. Many big families choose honesty as their family motto, which is passed down from generation to generation. In China, we could meet many people whose names are composed of the Chinese character "信", which means honesty in English.

Respecting others means that we try to protect their basic human rights. It requires our correct understanding of the needs of others. A polite communicator will always consider how the information will affect the other party and how to respond respectfully to the information provided. There is an old Chinese saying, "Do not do to others what you would not have them do to you," which means that when we communicate with others, the first thing we need to take into consideration is understanding and respecting. Only when we fully respect others can we have a good start in our communication.

Case Study: Why Does He Always Answer Beyond the Question?

Read the following passage and try to analyze it by answering these questions:

(1) Why didn't the Chinese employee give a clear and definite answer?
(2) What stereotype did the Chinese employee form towards Americans?
(3) How can Mr. Jia effectively solve the awkward situation?

An American human resource (HR) manager of Philips Lighting talked to a potential Chinese employee. The HR manager wanted to know the employee's career development plan and the position he wanted to get in the company in the future. However, the Chinese employee did not directly answer this question. Instead, he only talked about the company's future development direction, promotion system in the company, and his current position. He talked a lot but did not give a clear and direct answer to the question. The manager was confused and annoyed because the same situation had happened several times. Later, the manager complained to another HR manager, Mr. Jia: "I just want to make clear his career plan for the next five years and his target position, but why can't I get the answer I want?" The Chinese employee also made a complaint to Mr. Jia: "Why is he so aggressive?" As a HR manager of a multinational company, Mr. Jia knew that different ways of communication might lead to misunderstanding. So, he tried to explain to both sides, but it was not easy to reduce the barriers between them.

One party in the case is an American and the other is a Chinese. One of the main reasons for such a bad result is that there is a huge difference between China and the United States in the way of interpersonal communication, especially in the way of answering questions, but the two parties are not aware of this. This cultural difference is reflected in the fact that Chinese culture focuses on maintaining a harmonious interpersonal communication environment for groups, while American culture focuses on creating an interpersonal communication environment that emphasizes individuality.

If the Chinese employee answered the HR manager's question directly, it would violate the Chinese people's psychological habit of being modest and tactful, since a direct response may expose his ambition and arrogance. Modesty could give him a way back. Even if he can't get the ideal position or realize his plan in the end, he won't lose face and be laughed at. The Chinese employee may have a grand blueprint for the future, but his cultural background advocates the restraint of emotions. Therefore, when he answered the questions of the American HR manager, he did not directly express his own ideas. Instead, he talked about a lot of things related to the future development of the company. In his opinion, his approach is completely in line with social norms. He also believes that closely connecting his own future with the future of the company is conducive to maintaining the harmony of the organization. This is quite normal in the eyes of the Chinese. On the other hand, straightforwardly speaking out one's salary or position goal will be regarded as an ambitious expression.

Besides, Chinese people often judge a person by what he has done rather than by what he has said. No matter how magnificently he portrays his ideals and ambitions, if he can't realize them in the end, all of these would only turn out to be the laughing stock of others. Americans have always been very straightforward. When the American HR manager asked the employee about his plans for development in the next five years, that is, what kind of position he would like to take at Philips, it can be seen that Americans pay attention to the development of individuals in the enterprise. This may have a lot to do with the individualism that the United States has always advocated. They attach great importance to independence and openness and have a weak sense of hierarchy and identity. They think that it is natural and justifiable to pursue personal interests. American culture advocates bold and direct expression of ideas.

In this case, the HR manager believes that it is not inappropriate to speak out one's expectations and requirements straightforwardly. On the contrary, it is considered as a sign of sincerity and confidence, which is conducive to the success of employees. In contrast, the Chinese employee is accustomed to euphemistic expressions, and it would be impolite and abrupt to say directly about his requirements. So he is also very dissatisfied with the straightforwardness of the HR manager.

Now, it's your turn to analyze a case. You can do it by answering these questions:

- Why did Wang Lan feel that her American classmates were hostile and unfriendly to her?
- What principles should you follow in your interaction with people from different cultures?

Chinese student Wang Lan went to study in the United States. When she went to the United States, she found that the teacher dressed casually and often sat on the desk during class. Teachers seldom taught by themselves but asked students to discuss and made presentations. Her American classmates did not respect their teachers as much as Chinese students. They not only called their teachers by their first names, but even argued with their teachers. Wang Lan was very uncomfortable with the teachers' teaching methods. When it was her turn to give a presentation, she often felt very embarrassed because the teachers and her classmates always stared at her. During the discussion, her American classmates often asked questions and even argued with her. This made her feel that her American classmates were hostile and unfriendly to her.

Summary

In this chapter, we talked about how intercultural communication happens in various social contexts. Any culture has relationships that connect the people in that culture. We will always find that intercultural communication differs across cultures, no matter when we deal with family and friend relationships, engage in educational activities at schools and universities, or do business with others. Although there are certain general concepts in relationships across cultures, each culture puts its own special mark on how these concepts are "played out" in day-to-day communication.

Exercises

Questions for Review

1. What is social context?

2. What is relationship?

3. What does "face" mean in Chinese culture?

4. How do Hofstede's cultural dimensions affect what happens in a classroom?

5. What are the main factors that influence cross-cultural communication?

6. What are the four principles we need to follow in cross-cultural communication?

Problems and Application

Read the following passage and answer the questions: What do you think about the documentary and Chinese education system? Do your ideas change after you read the passage? What attitude should you hold when you read media reports?

Are Our Kids Tough Enough: A Documentary or a Reality Show?

After the second episode of *Are Our Kids Tough Enough? Chinese School*, a BBC documentary series on Chinese teaching methods in a British class aired, it sparked even more debate in Chinese media and on the Chinese Internet than last week.

As greater conflict was shown between the five Chinese teachers and the British teens in the second episode, more and more Chinese netizens began to question the authenticity and reliability of the documentary.

Meanwhile, Chinese media tried to dig into the making of the documentary. They interviewed some of the teachers and students in the documentary, education experts in both China and abroad, and even the staff of the BBC.

Does BBC Exaggerate the Contrasts in the Classroom?

According to an interview with Li Aiyun, a Chinese teacher in the documentary from Nanjing Foreign Language School, by *Nanjing Morning Post*, the real situation in the classroom was much better than what audiences saw in the documentary.

"In fact, the British teens are very cute with their own advantages and characteristics. We set up a friendly relationship during that month. I know nothing about the final version of the documentary after their editing and rearrangement.

What I want to say is that our relationship is really good," Li said.

She also admitted that both the teachers and students were not accustomed to each other at the very beginning, and it was a little bit disorderly in the classroom.

"But what audiences see in the documentary is the most disorderly moment. They (BBC) chose the most disorderly part from all the disorderly moments," she added.

Wu Yun, a mathematics teacher in Shanghai Experimental School who was twice involved in a teaching-exchange project in Britain, told the Shanghai based news website that the BBC documentary may exaggerate or even sensationalize the real situation.

"I taught British kids for one month in 2014 and 2015. My students are really disciplined. It's totally different from what we see in the documentary. As far as I'm concerned, the BBC might have sensationalized the real situation to make a dramatic contrast," Wu said.

Many Chinese netizens agree with Wu's view, and think that the BBC made a reality show with a dramatic plot, instead of a documentary. A Chinese Weibo user, nicknamed Minitu, wrote in her comment, "With the background of a different culture, teaching those British students in a Chinese way for just one month was not the right way to examine a teaching method, but a good subject for an entertaining reality show." The comment was widely praised on Weibo.

Who Defines the "Chinese Teaching Method"?

The "Chinese teaching method" in the documentary featured a 12-hour teaching system and more than 50 students in one classroom. Many complained that this was not an accurate reflection of teaching in China. Even the Chinese teachers in the documentary were not satisfied.

Li Aiyun told Chinese journalists that she and Zou Hailian, the mathematics teacher in the documentary, tried to negotiate with BBC crews and told them about the real situation in Chinese schools they worked for.

"In Nanjing Foreign Language School, students leave the school at about 4 p.m. But the British side insisted that in the traditional Chinese teaching system, there should be an evening study course," she said.

Many Chinese netizens also criticized that the teaching method in the documentary seems out of date. Some said that Chinese schools, especially schools in big coastal cities, are very different from ten years ago.

"In my city, the atmosphere of key schools is really relaxed. Our teachers encourage us to have our own ideas and often play jokes with us. They never say 'parents are always correct' and allow us to use our own mugs in the classroom. Maybe the teachers in the documentary are old-fashioned? Or maybe they just teach in a BBC style Chinese method," some said.

Another comment also achieved wide agreement. It wrote that if the "Chinese teaching method" in the documentary was defined by the BBC, it could be a sign of British decline.

Chapter 6

Cultural Bias

Learning Objectives

After learning this chapter, you should be able to:

1. understand the concepts of stereotype, prejudice, discrimination, and racism;

2. identify different types of stereotypes, prejudice, and racism;

3. identify and employ strategies to tackle with stereotypes, prejudice, and racism;

4. view and analyze racial tension through sociological lens.

Everyone has different beliefs, experiences, abilities, appearances and so on. However, certain people and groups are more likely to experience stereotypes, prejudice, and discrimination. Where do stereotypes come from? What's prejudice? Why do people like to hold stereotypes and prejudice towards others? What's the relationship among stereotype, prejudice, and discrimination? When facing problems and crisis caused by them, how should one react? To answer all of these questions, we have to know the concepts of stereotype, prejudice, discrimination, and racism.

Stereotypes, prejudice, and discrimination create physical and emotional distance between members of different social groups. Mild forms of bias can lead to awkward and uncomfortable interactions, intentional or unconscious avoidance, and interactions lacking warmth or civility. More extreme forms of bias can lead to tension and conflict, hostility, harassment, or aggression. Thus, it's of great importance for us to understand these terms well. In this chapter, we will approach intercultural communication from the perspective of social psychology where stereotype and prejudice are important concepts for us to learn. When bearing stereotype and prejudice in mind, we may cause some misunderstandings or lead to ineffective intercultural communication. Here, we will focus on some basic knowledge about stereotype, prejudice, and racism, and discuss the causes of these cultural biases and their effects in intercultural communication.

6.1 Stereotype

"Birds of a feather flock together." When people have no enough time to know others, they usually divide them into groups and think each group has the similar characteristics. For example, in our daily life, we are not strangers to such statement as "Boys are always good at math, while girls language." This statement, in fact, does not hold true for everyone. It has something to do with what we are interested in this section—stereotype.

6.1.1 Definition of Stereotype

What is a stereotype? To understand different examples of stereotypes, we should first define what a stereotype is. Any time we group people by their races and make a judgment about them without knowing them, it is an example of a stereotype.

In our daily life, it's obvious that American people do hold certain stereotypes on Asians. They think Asians are nerds or Kung Fu masters and like to speak loud in public. However, is it necessarily true that all Asians are loud? Is it true that all Asians are nerds or Kung Fu masters or fighters? Of course, the answer is negative. But Americans take Asians as a group and come to a conclusion based on a prior assumption, or in other words, their impressions are based on a few individuals in this group. Hence, to put it simply, stereotypes are characteristics imposed upon groups of people because of their race, nationality, sexual orientation, etc., also known as implicit biases.

These characteristics tend to be oversimplifications of the groups involved. Stereotypic people tend to label something or somebody formulaically. They may think, for example, that all African Americans like to eat chicken; Jews are smart in making money but somewhat mean; people from East Asia are poor in English and lack of humor; blonde equals to beauty; etc. Hence, stereotypes can be harmful even if they seem positive.

6.1.2 Three Major Types of Stereotypes

Almost every culture or race has stereotypes. However, stereotypes are not just centered on different races and backgrounds. Gender stereotypes and sexual orientation stereotypes also exist.

One of the more common stereotype examples is stereotypes surrounding race. For example, saying that all blacks are good at sports is a stereotype, because it's grouping the race together to indicate that everyone of that race is a good athlete.

There are also some common stereotypes of men and women. For example, women aren't as smart as men; women can't do a job as good as men; girls are not good at sports; men are messy and unclean; men who spend too much time on the computer or reading are geeks; etc.

There are three basic kinds of gender stereotypes. The first type relates to personality traits. For example, women are often expected to be passive and submissive, while men are usually expected to be self-confident and aggressive. And the second relates to people's domestic behavior. For example, caring for children is often considered best done by women, while household repairs are often considered best done by men. Third, it relates to people's occupations. For example, women are expected to take such jobs as nurses, teachers, while men CEOs, doctors, lawyers.

Sexual orientation stereotypes are also common. These stereotypes occur when people have negative views on gays, lesbians, bisexual, and transgender individuals. Sexual orientation stereotypes suggest that any feminine man is a gay and any masculine woman is a lesbian. Those who have gay stereotypes may also believe that homosexuality is immoral, wrong, and an abomination.

6.1.3 Two Dimensions of Stereotypes

There are two dimensions of stereotypes. In other words, stereotypes can also exist when cultures or countries are taken as a whole and different groups of individuals are considered as a whole. Stereotype examples of the first one include the premises that:

- All people who live in England have bad teeth.
- Italian or French people are the best lovers.
- All blacks outside of the United States are poor.
- All Asians are good at math; they like to eat rice and drive slowly.
- All Irish people are drunks and eat potatoes.

Stereotypes can also group individuals. Skaters, Goths and gangsters are a few examples. Most of this kind of stereotyping is taking place in schools. For example:

- Girls are only concerned about physical appearance.
- All blonds are unintelligent.
- Punks wearing spikes, chains, are a menace to society and are always getting in trouble.
- All librarians are women who are old, wear glasses, tie a high bun, and have a perpetual frown on their face.

6.1.4 Characteristics of Stereotypes

To some people, stereotype can be a confusing concept. So what are the characteristics of stereotypes?

First, stereotypes are universal. Whatever ethnic group we come from or whether we are a man or a woman, stereotypes exist.

Second, stereotypes can be individual or social. Stereotypes can become social when they are shared by large numbers of people within social groups.

Third, stereotypes can be negative or positive. For example, when some people think about black people, several negative words will come up in their mind. And people usually think doctors as wise and intelligent.

Last but not least, stereotypes can become a self-fulfilling prophecy, the tendency to see behavior that we expect to see. For example, if we expect that heads of corporations are tall, slender, white males, we don't see the disabled, women, and people of color in that group.

6.1.5 Causes of Stereotypes

Why do we have stereotypes? To begin with, categorizing things and people is a very natural and adaptive thing to do—imagine shopping in a supermarket with no categorization. It makes life easier to navigate given the enormous number of stimuli our brains take in each day and over our lifetime.

There's another reason why we like to group things and people. Social identity theory, conducted by the British social psychologist Henri Tajfel and his colleagues in the early 1970s, was developed from a series of studies to explain how individuals create and define their place in society. In social identity theory (as shown in Figure 6.1), Tajfel (1978) explains how being part of a group gives us a sense of worth, identity, strength, security, and a strong sense of "us". Unfortunately, the existence of an "us" means that there tends to be a "them" and this is when stereotypes are being formed and individuals are becoming polarized against other groups—those that aren't like their own. To add to this challenge, when we feel under threat—such as when a merger or acquisition is on the horizon or a new leadership team starts to drive through significant change in the organization—our brains try to protect us. "Bigging up" our own group and denigrating other groups make us feel better about "us" and put responsibility on "them".

The central hypothesis of social identity theory is that group members of an in-group will seek to find negative aspects of an out-group, thus enhancing their self-image. For example, in order to increase one's self-image, he or she will enhance the status of the group to which he or she belongs. He or she would probably assume that his or her hometown is the best place in the world. And, he or she can also increase his or her self-image by discriminating and holding prejudice views against the out-group (the group he or she doesn't belong to). For example, people from

other places are lazy or have a bunch of thieves.

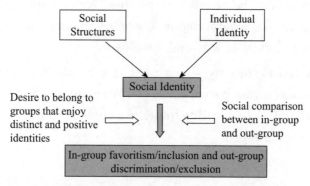

Figure 6.1   Major Concepts of Tajfel's Social Identity Theory

When we stereotype, we often make errors in the interpretation of others' behavior. We also make assumptions about how these people will behave and we make judgments about that behavior.

6.1.6 Influences of Stereotypes

Stereotypes are harmful as they impede intercultural communication from several aspects. For one thing, they cause us to assume that a widely held belief of any group or an individual is true when it may not. A classic psychology study in the 1970s had two groups of undergraduates read stories about a woman. The stories were identical, except that one had the sentence "Betty is a lesbian." One week later, the group who had read that "Betty is a lesbian" were much more likely to recall having read that Betty never dated men than the other group. In fact, the story that both groups had read stated that Betty dated men occasionally. The group's stereotype of a lesbian influenced what they recalled.

For another, stereotyping others may cause false interpretations of an individual's behavior. People tend to make assumptions about how others will behave and then make judgments about their behavior. For example, in the act of failing a test, ethnic stereotypes may lead us to attribute such failure to laziness if the student is black but to low ability if the student is white.

In the end, it is important to point out that we all have stereotypes. It is a part of human interaction—a way we categorize data in order to communicate. However, we need to be aware of and move beyond our stereotypes to communicate with each individual as an individual, not as a group member.

6.1.7 Tips on Reducing Stereotypes

Here are four tips to help people avoid stereotyping people in real-life scenarios. To begin with, one may try his or her best to widen his or her source of information instead of focusing on only one medium to know other people. People can read more books and reports, watch TV programs, listen to the radio, etc. Moreover, an individual may make direct contact with others to see them with his or her own eyes and make his or her own observation. Third, one can get himself or herself exposed to educational lectures to know specific topics and increase his or her awareness in this aspect. Last, one may travel to some places to know the local people.

For Your Information

An Introduction to Henri Tajfel

Henri Tajfel, (1919–1982), Polish-born British social psychologist, best known for his concept of social identity, a central idea in what became known as social identity theory. He is remembered in Europe for the effort he gave to establish a European style of social psychology, one that recognized the social, political, and historical context within which social behavior takes place.

Born into a Jewish family in Poland, Tajfel was a student at the Sorbonne in France when Germany invaded Poland in September, 1939. As a fluent French speaker, he served in the French army, and then was captured by the invading German forces in 1940. He spent the rest of the conflict as a prisoner of war. His survival depended on his assuming a French identity and concealing his Polish Jewish descent.

All of Tajfel's immediate family and most of his friends in Poland were killed in the Holocaust. After the war, he spent six years helping to rehabilitate war victims and refugees and to repatriate or resettle them in other countries. Those events affected him deeply and provided him with important intellectual signposts for his later research and writing on discrimination against minorities and on how identity was shaped by nationality and ethnic group membership. Regarding his own wartime experience, he observed that, had his Polish Jewish identity been revealed, his fate would have been determined by his social category.

Tajfel married in 1948 and moved to England in 1951. As an undergraduate student at Birkbeck College, University of London, he won a scholarship for an essay on prejudice. He graduated in 1954, worked as a research assistant at the University of Durham, and later became a lecturer in social psychology at the University of Oxford. In 1967, he was appointed to a chair in social psychology at Bristol University, a post that he held until his death. Bristol soon became a European center for research in social psychology.

Tajfel drew widely on theory and examples from history, literature, sociology, politics, and economics in elaborating his ideas. He went to considerable lengths to link social identity theory to large-scale social structures and to ideology. Unlike many theorists in social psychology, Tajfel made a deliberate connection between collective movements and political action.

Although Tajfel conducted experimental research and encouraged others to do the same, his goals were more ambitious, and he was explicitly opposed to reductionism in social psychological theory. He was mindful of the scope and magnitude of North American social psychology and what it had achieved in defining the discipline in the 20th century. However, he was convinced that a European perspective could offer something different and valuable. He argued that North American social psychologists were mostly reductionist, even myopic, in their pursuit of psychological laws that applied primarily to individuals rather than to groups. In contrast, Europe's political history and wars created a need for theoretical constructs that were embedded in social groups.

Case Study: A Plot in *Green Book*

In the movie *Green Book* released in 2019, Tony Lip, a bouncer in 1962, is hired to drive pianist Don Shirley on a tour through the Deep South in the days when African Americans were forced to find alternate accommodations and services due to segregation laws below the Mason-Dixon Line relying on a guide called *The Negro Motorist Green Book*.

Here is one of the plots in the movie. Why do they use the brochure *Green Books* (short for *The Negro Motorist Green Book*)?

Use the following questions for an in-depth thinking.

(1) Tony is a white guy and Dr. Shirley a black. Does their behavior deviate from people's cognition of white and black people?

(2) Why did Dr. Shirley never eat fried chicken before?

(3) What do they use the brochure green paper for during their journey?

(4) In your opinion, what does the movie try to express with the name *Green Book*?

(When seeing the Kentucky Fried Chicken sign, Lip sits up, excited.)

> **Lip:** Kentucky Fried Chicken...in Kentucky! When's that ever gonna happen?!

(The Cadillac pulls into the parking lot. Lip looks over the seat back.)

> **Lip:** Hey, you want some?

Dr. Shirley: I'm fine. Thank you, Tony.

(They're back on the road, a bucket of Kentucky Fried Chicken in the front seat next to Lip. He wolfs down a chicken leg as he drives.)

> **Lip:** I think this is the best Kentucky Fried Chicken I have ever had. But I guess it's fresher down here, right?

(Dr. Shirley shrugs.)

Dr. Shirley: I don't think I've ever met anyone with your appetite.

> **Lip:** No, I've bought the bucket so you could have some.

Dr. Shirley: I've never had fried chicken in my life.

> **Lip:** Who (are) you bullshitting? You people love the fried chicken, the grits, the colored greens... I love it, too. The Negro cooks used to make it all time when I was in the army.

Dr. Shirley: You have a very narrow assessment of me, Tony.

> **Lip:** (Pleased) Yeah, right? I'm good.

Dr. Shirley: No, you're not good; you're bad. I'm saying, just because other Negros enjoy certain types of music, it doesn't mean I have to. Nor do we all have to eat the same kind of food.

(Lip looks at Shirley in the mirror.)

> **Lip:** Whoa, wait a minute. If you said all guineas like pizza and spaghetti and meatballs, I'm not gonna get insulted.

Dr. Shirley: You're missing the point. For you to make the assumption that...

Lip: Hey, you want some or not? (Lip holds up the bucket.)

Dr. Shirley: No.

(Lip takes another big, juicy bite.)

Lip: Tell me that don't (doesn't) smell good?

Dr. Shirley: It smells okay. I prefer not to get grease on my blanket.

Lip: Oooh, I'm gonna get grease on my blankie— Come on, have a piece. It ain't gonna kill ya. Come on. Take it easy.

(Lip takes a piece of chicken, (and) holds it out to Shirley.)

Lip: Just grab it and eat it!

Dr. Shirley: No.

Lip: Take it. I'm gonna throw it in the back.

Dr. Shirley: Don't you dare!

Lip: Then you better take it.

Dr. Shirley: How? Do you have plates? Or utensils?

Lip: Bah fongool! Eat it with your hands; that's how you're supposed to.

Dr. Shirley: I can't do that.

Lip: Eat it. Come on. Take it. Take it...

(Shirley reluctantly takes the chicken.)

Dr. Shirley: I can't do this, Tony.

Lip: Eat the goddamn thing. Jesus.

(Shirley takes a bite. Lip can see he's enjoying it.)

Lip: What, no good?

Dr. Shirley: Just seems so... so unsanitary.

Lip: Who gives a shit?! Just relax and enjoy it. You know my father used to say, whatever you do, do it a hundred percent. When you work, work; when you laugh, laugh; when you eat, eat like it's your last meal.

(Shirley is clearly enjoying the chicken.)

Lip: You want another piece? Here, have a breast! (Lip hands Shirley a leg.)

Dr. Shirley: What do we do about the bones?

Lip: We do this. (Lip throws his bones out the window.)

(After a beat, Shirley rolls down his window and does the same. They smile at one another for the first time. Then Lip finishes his Coke and tosses the cup put on the window. As Shirley loses his smile, the Caddy is backing up in the breakdown lane. It stops next to the discarded cup; Lip's door opens and he picks it up.)

For the first question, their behavior does deviate from people's cognition of white and black people. In the movie, Tony is a white Italian who has lost his job in a bar and is unemployed at home. He even needs to mortgage his watch and compete with others to eat hamburgers to supplement his family. But even so, he still maintains his superiority as a white man. But he was forced to become a driver and bodyguard for Shirley, a black pianist. He works lowly, behaves rudely and philistinely, speaks slang, and likes to intimidate and warn others with his fists. Tony is full of the uninhibited and unruly characters of the typical black community culture, which is quite different from the stereotype of white people.

The prototype of Donald Shirley is a real piano master. Throughout the 1950s and 1960s, Donald was the most famous piano musician in the United States. In the movie, Donald always holds his head high even when he faces racial discrimination and provocation. He has money and reputation. He is in and out of the upper class. Even the president's brother has to be courteous to him. Except for the color of his skin, we could hardly see any stereotyped black image in him.

The difference in the intellectual levels of the two men and flipped stereotypes create situational irony, such as when the viewers laugh at comical scenes where Dr. Shirley helps the hopelessly illiterate Tony write love letters to his wife. These scenes, added with Tony's idle chit-chat and the backgrounds of rolling countryside, create a light atmosphere, which is very pleasant to watch.

As for the second question, one of the stereotypes about black people is that they like fried chicken and watermelon. At that time, slavery was still practiced in the United States, and the kinds of food available to blacks were limited. Pork was the most widely used one, while chicken was relatively cheap. White people did not eat chicken wings, chicken gizzards, chicken necks, and other parts, so black people could get chicken from slave owners.

In addition, considering the high calorie demand, they would fry the chicken with lard. Fried chicken naturally became the daily diet of black slaves. "Soul cuisine" was used to refer to the catering culture of black people in the south, which has a similar etymological background with "soul music". The word "soul" implies the miserable black history. The reason why "soul" was used is that black people could only cook

meals with the limited ingredients they got, and then use their own souls to make up for the inadequacies. Thus, Dr. Shirley was certainly not confident about his black identity.

For the third question, at that time, the use of public facilities by blacks was restricted, such as hotels, restaurants, hair salons, toilets and so on. On their journey south, because of Dr. Shirley's black identity, they need the *Green Book* as a guide, to make their journey comfortable and safe.

As for the last question, the outstanding feature of the *Green Book* is that it hides satire in the two people's humorous and warm interaction. However, humor does not drown the theme. The dialog and interaction between the two people is a collision of values on the surface, but it also conveys the idea that the shaping of values comes from their respective classes and ethnic backgrounds. Therefore, the *Green Book* is a masterpiece against racial discrimination.

Green Book presents jaw-droppingly shocking racism, where as simple an act as going into a bar could result in harsh beatings and unjustified police arrests. These scenes are often matched with dark nights, dirty alleyways, creating a feeling of uncertainty and opening the eyes of the audience as they feel as if they themselves are the subject of this ridiculous racism.

However, these harsh scenes are responsible for changing Tony's backward view of African Americans, while also changing our views as the audience of the movie. Beyond a doubt, *Green Book* has the eccentric ability to touch the audience's emotions and morals: It presents a startling look at a real story of the injustices that people of color have to experience and how even Tony, who previously threw away the cups which were used by African Americans, can change into a man who would protect and care for African Americans.

In addition to eliminating discrimination, *Green Book* also conveys the outlook on life, which is the identity of self. Although the pianist Shirley always maintains his dignity, he is still not accepted by the white world, let alone understood by the black compatriots. He was lonely, living alone in his castle. Tony's friendship opened his heart. At the end of the movie, on Christmas Eve, he finally bravely knocks on Tony's door.

Although the movie is about racial discrimination and class differences, behind the black and white, we see the praise of human nature and the courage to change ourselves.

For Your Information

Background Information on *Green Book*

Green Book, in full *The Negro Motorist Green Book, The Negro Travelers' Green Book*, or *The Travelers' Green Book*, a travel guide published (1936–1967) during the segregation era in the United States identified businesses that would accept African American customers. Compiled by Victor Hugo Green (1892–1960), a black postman who lived in the Harlem section of New York City, *Green Book* listed a variety of businesses—from restaurants and hotels to beauty salons and drugstores—that were necessary to make travel comfortable and safe for African Americans in the period before the passage of Civil Rights Act of 1964. The movie *Green Book* released in 2019 echoes on such a special historical period.

Figure 6.2   Cover of The Negro Travelers' Green Book

It's the year 1962. Colored with soft pistachio greens and mellow yellows, *Green Book* presents the story of the real-life relationship between Tony Lip and Dr. Shirley as they travel alongside each other in a cramped car across the southern States. However, beneath the light, roadtrip-like atmosphere of the movie, *Green Book* spotlights the stereotypes, racism, injustice, and prejudice in the U.S. merely 60 years ago. Renowned comedy director Peter Farrelly creates a masterpiece, breaking one stereotype after another.

Based on his father's true story, screenplay writer Nick Vallelonga spins the unlikely tale of how those with different ethnic backgrounds, Italian and African American, can become great friends over time. What makes *Green Book* so unique and unforgettable is how the stereotypes of the white man and black man are switched: Hollywood movies typically feature the African American as less educated and the white man as the wealthy and privileged, while *Green*

Book is the complete opposite. Here we follow the story of the sly, uneducated and ever-talking Italian hitman, Tony, as he is employed as a driver by intellectual piano expert Dr. Shirley. Director Farrelly elegantly uses the contrast in the atmosphere between different scenes to shock the audience as they realize just how unpredictable, demoralizing, and unfair life could be to people of color.

More to Read

Persistent Racial Stereotypes in Movies and Television Shows

Campaigns such as OscarsSoWhite have raised awareness about the need for more racial diversity in Hollywood, but diversity isn't the industry's only problem—the way that people of color are persistently stereotyped on screen remains a major concern.

Too often, actors from minority groups who land roles in movies and TV shows are asked to play stock characters, including maids, thugs, and sidekicks with no lives of their own. These racial stereotypes of various ethnicities, from Arabs to Asians, continue to persist.

(1) Arab Stereotypes in Movies and Television Shows

Americans of Arab and Middle Eastern descents have long faced stereotypes in Hollywood. In classic cinema, Arabs were often depicted as belly dancers, harem girls, and oil sheiks. Old stereotypes about Arabs continue to upset the Middle Eastern community in the U.S.

A Coca-Cola commercial that aired during the 2013 Super Bowl featured Arabs riding on camels through the desert in hopes of beating rival groups to a bottle of giant Coke. This led Arab American advocacy groups to accuse the ad of stereotyping Arabs as camel jockeys.

In addition to this stereotype, Arabs have been depicted as anti-American villains well before the 9/11 terrorist attacks. The 1994 movie *True Lies* featured Arabs as terrorists, leading to protests of the movie by Arab groups nationwide at the time.

Movies such as Disney's 1992 hit *Aladdin* also faced protests from Arab groups who said the movie depicted Middle Easterners as barbaric and backward.

(2) Native American Stereotypes in Hollywood

Indigenous peoples are a diverse racial group with a range of customs and cultural experiences. In Hollywood, however, they are typically subject to sweeping generalizations.

When they aren't being depicted as silent, stoic types in movies and television shows, they're seen as bloodthirsty warriors who are violent toward white people. When indigenous peoples are characterized more favorably, it's still through a stereotypical lens, such as medicine men who guide white people through difficulties.

Indigenous women are also depicted one-dimensionally—as beautiful maidens, princesses, or squaws. These narrow Hollywood stereotypes have made indigenous women vulnerable to sexual harassment and sexual assault in real life, feminist groups argue.

(3) Black Stereotypes in Hollywood

Black people face both positive and negative stereotypes in Hollywood. When black people are portrayed as good on the silver screen, it's usually as a "Magical Negro" type like Michael Clarke Duncan's character in *The Green Mile*. Such characters are typically wise black men with no concerns of their own or desire to improve their status in life. Instead, these characters function to help white characters overcome adversity.

The mammy and black best friend stereotypes are similar to the "Magical Negro". Mammies traditionally took care of white families, valuing the lives of their white employers (or owners during enslavement) more than their own. The number of television programs and movies featuring black women as selfless maids perpetuates this stereotype.

While the black best friends aren't maids or nannies, they mostly function to help their white friends, normally the protagonists of the show, transcend difficult circumstances. These stereotypes are arguably as positive as it gets for black characters in Hollywood.

When black people aren't playing second fiddle to white people as maids, best friends, and "Magical Negroes", they're depicted as thugs, victims of racial violence, or women with attitude problems.

(4) Hispanic Stereotypes in Hollywood

Latinos may be the largest minority group in the United States, but Hollywood has consistently portrayed Hispanics very narrowly. Viewers of

American television shows and movies, for example, are far more likely to see Latinos play maids and gardeners than lawyers and doctors.

Furthermore, Hispanic men and women have both been sexualized in Hollywood. Latino men have long been stereotyped as "Latin Lovers", while Latinos have been characterized as exotic, sensual vamps.

Both the male and female versions of the "Latin Lovers" are framed as having fiery temperaments. When these stereotypes aren't at play, Hispanics are portrayed as recent immigrants, gang-bangers, and criminals.

(5) Asian American Stereotypes in Movies and Television Shows

Like Latinos and Arab Americans, Asian Americans have been frequently portrayed as foreigners in Hollywood movies and television shows. Though Asian Americans have lived in the U.S. for generations, there is no shortage of Asians speaking broken English and practicing "mysterious" customs on both the small and big screens. In addition, stereotypes of Asian Americans are gender-specific.

Asian women are often portrayed as "dragon ladies", domineering women who are sexually attractive but bad news for the white men who fall for them. In war movies, Asian women are most often portrayed as prostitutes or other sex workers. Asian American men, meanwhile, are consistently depicted as geeks (people who are skilled with computers), math whizzes (people who are dazzlingly skilled in any field), techies (people who are expert in or enthusiastic about technology, especially computers), and a host of other characters viewed as non-masculine. About the only time Asian men are portrayed as physically threatening is when they're depicted as martial artists. But Asian actors say the Kung Fu stereotype has hurt them also. That's because after it rose in popularity, all Asian actors were expected to follow in Bruce Lee's footsteps. (Nittle, 2002)

6.2 **Prejudice**

As we all know, *Pride and Prejudice* is one of the most well-known works by Jane Austen. In this classic piece of literature, the ever-satiric Jane Austen brings us a love story that is critical of the 19th-century English society and reminds us not to take first impressions too seriously. In this book, women are thought of as objects and wives. However, Darcy did not consider Elizabeth's elder sister Jane as a possible wife for his friend Bingley at first because of her low social status. This is typically a social class prejudice. And it leads to the topic: prejudice.

6.2.1 Definition of Prejudice

Prejudice can have a strong influence on how people behave and interact with others, particularly with those who are different from them. When our opinions are based solely on the generalizations we've made about members of a certain group of people without any form of real-life interaction with them, we're essentially prejudging them. We assume that we know everything about them without getting to know them in person, just as Elizabeth and other people thought Mr. Darcy as a proud and arrogant person in their first impression. So, to put it simply, prejudice is a baseless and usually negative attitude towards members of a group.

Common features of prejudice include negative feelings, stereotyped beliefs, and a tendency to discriminate against members of the group. While specific definitions of prejudice given by social scientists often differ, most agree that it involves prejudgments that are usually negative about members of a group.

Prejudice forms the breeding ground for all kinds of discrimination that plays out in real life. Throughout history, prejudice has caused some of humankind's worst atrocities against one another—war, torture, murder, human rights violation, and despotism.

In the movie *Schindler's List*, the Nazi's extreme prejudice against the Jewish people in World War II influenced them to force the Jews to wear the Star of David. This widespread persecution escalated to the point where the Nazis began engaging in mass "ethnic cleansing", which involved the imprisonment of their victims in concentration camps and the merciless execution of thousands of them in gas chambers.

6.2.2 Seven Types of Prejudice

Broadly speaking, there are seven types of prejudice based on dominant factors such as religion, race, gender, age, socioeconomic status, nationality, and sexual orientation; they are gender prejudice, ethnic prejudice, prejudice on immigrants, age prejudice, sexual orientation prejudice, class prejudice, and disability prejudice.

1. Gender Prejudice

Gender prejudice, or sexism, is the belief that members of one gender are inferior to another. Sexism in a society is most commonly applied against women and girls. It functions to maintain male domination, through ideological and material practices of individuals, collectives, and institutions that oppress women and girls on the basis of sex or gender.

Such oppression usually takes the forms of economic exploitation and social domination. Sexist behavior, conditions, and attitudes perpetuate stereotypes of social roles based on one's biological sex. Women and men are opposite, with widely different and complementary roles. Women are relegated to the domestic realm of nurturance and emotions and, therefore, according to that reasoning, cannot be good leaders in business, politics, and academia. Although women are seen as naturally fit for domestic work and are superb at being caretakers, their roles are devalued or not valued at all when compared with men's work (Masequesmay, 2022).

Here's another example. Saudi Arabia may have just considered allowing women the right to drive but Nigeria is one of the worst places for a woman to be a driver. There is an unspoken consensus among Nigerians that women cannot aptly handle the wheel and as such, the average woman has to convince those around her that she is capable of driving.

When she navigates the road or is stuck in traffic like every other person is prone to, she will most likely hear a few slurs or other forms of verbal abuse, even when she is completely within her rights on the road. It is so bad that within most family units, the man is seen as the driver, and when the woman offers to fill the role, her attempts are often laughed off with a few insensitive jokes (Akande, 2018).

2. Ethnic Prejudice

Ethnic prejudice is also referred to as racial prejudice, or racism. There are many examples of racial prejudice in today's society. For starters, when the owner of a large company chooses not to employ those of a certain race or ethnicity because he believes they are in some way inferior to others, he is discriminating based upon a specific kind of prejudice called racism.

This also includes profiling, which happens when a person of color is, for example, pulled over based on his skin color, instead of an actual suspicion of a committed crime. In 2017, something similar happened in one of the Starbucks stores. The store manager refused to serve a customer and kicked him out just because he was black. In such a case, the store manager did not take the time to get to know individuals in this minority group, and was prejudging them as inferior based on generalizations and stereotypes.

3. Prejudice on Immigrants

"Human beings have always been group beings," says Rupert Brown, a social psychologist at the University of Sussex in Brighton, U.K. Prejudice can be directed against any group by any other. But immigrants, and even more so refugees and asylum seekers, may be especially vulnerable because of their tenuous place in a larger society. "You don't really belong anywhere; by definition you're stateless, you're fleeing from some place of torture or persecution," Brown says. "And yet you're not a citizen of the country in which you're now living, either." (Couzin-frankel, 2017)

Stereotypes on immigrants, refugees, and Gypsy populations are linked with racial prejudice as well as the attitudes towards immigrants, refugees, and nomadic populations, which can also form the basis of legislation that discriminates against these groups. The underlying belief is that these people "are not from here", and are thus viewed as "the other" and inferior.

This particular kind of attitude, the fear of foreigners, is called xenophobia. For example, at the turn of the 20th century in the U.S., prejudice was held against the most recent immigrant groups who arrived to their shores. And unfortunately, this xenophobic attitude towards new immigrant groups from Asia, Latin America, war-torn countries in the Middle East still exists today. In Europe, the Roma, also known as "Gypsies" or "travelers", remains one of the most persecuted minority groups.

Here is another example. When the Japanese attacked Pearl Harbor on December 7, 1941, the U.S. public viewed Americans of Japanese descent suspiciously. Although many Japanese Americans had never stepped foot in Japan and knew only of the country from their parents and grandparents, the notion spread that the Nisei (second-generation Japanese Americans) were more loyal to the Japanese empire than to their birthplace. Acting with this idea in mind, the federal government decided to round up more than 110,000 Japanese Americans and place them in internment camps for fear that they would team up with Japan to plot additional attacks against the United States. No evidence suggested that Japanese Americans would commit treason against the U.S. and join forces with Japan. Without trial or due process, the Nisei were stripped of their civil liberties and forced into detention camps. This is a case of racial prejudice on immigrants leading to institutional racism.

4. Age Prejudice

Age prejudice is also called ageism. It is the stereotyping and discrimination against individuals or groups on the basis of their age. It can mean assuming someone is uneducated or unintelligent or ignorant because of their age, assuming someone is below us because of their age, or blaming negative social changes on a specific age group or groups. It can take many forms, including prejudicial attitudes, discriminatory practices or institutional policies and practices that perpetuate stereotypical beliefs. When an elder-care facility refuses to install Internet technology because of the belief that older people don't have the energy or ability to learn web navigation, the belief is that those above a certain age aren't qualified for Internet technology, thus they don't need to get access to it. They are acting upon ageism. If an older employee is given a role which demands using of advanced technology, people generally start questioning whether he or she is suitable for this job even without assessing his or her level of skill (Abbas, 2022). That's also ageism.

According to a Canadian study on ageism published May, 2019 in *Aging Research Reviews*, ageism is now thought to be the most common form of prejudice and sadly the full impact of this kind of prejudice against the elderly is not completely recognized. The study was launched by two nursing professors from the University of Alberta, Gail Low and Donna M. Wilson. They examined questionnaires used by researchers all over the world. The reality is that one in five Canadian seniors over the age of 65 are still working at their jobs. More than a third of Canadian seniors are active in volunteer work. Only about 20% of hospitalized patients are seniors and only about 3% of Canadian seniors are chronically ill and in long-term care in nursing homes. Yet, according to the results, 48%–91% of all seniors had experienced ageism and 50%–98% of younger people admitted to having discriminatory feelings and prejudicial behavior against seniors.

5. Sexual Orientation Prejudice

Sexual orientation prejudice is also referred to as homophobia. In other words, prejudging people because of their sexual orientation is called homophobia, and it's often based on the stereotype that all LGBT (lesbian, gay, bisexual or transgender) people are in a certain way inferior.

6. Class Prejudice

Class prejudice is also called classism. Classism is the belief or attitude that those of a certain economic class are inferior to people from another class.

Examples of social class prejudices can be found in *To Kill a Mockingbird*, a novel written by American author Harper Lee, published in 1960. The small town of Maycomb is stratified, and there is a clear social hierarchy in the community. Certain families are considered lower or higher than others based on various factors like education, profession, and family history.

In the novel, Scout demonstrates social class prejudice towards Walter Cunningham Jr. when he joins them for lunch. Scout embarrasses Walter by rudely commenting on his eating habits, and Calpurnia chastises her in the kitchen. Scout displays social class prejudice by telling Calpurnia, "He [Walter] ain't company, Cal, he's just a Cunningham." Scout knows that Walter comes from a poor family and dismisses his feelings because he is considered lower class.

The most prevalent example of social class prejudice comes from Aunt Alexandra when she refuses to allow Scout to play with Walter Cunningham Jr. Aunt Alexandra believes that Scout and Jem are too good to be associating with a poor child like Walter and prohibits her niece from playing with Walter. Aunt Alexandra displays her social class prejudice by referring to Walter as "trash" (Khan, 2022).

7. Disability Prejudice

Disability prejudice is also referred to as ableism, which refers to the belief that those with physical or mental disabilities or handicaps are inferior to able-bodied people. Discrimination against the disabled is born of this belief and involves limiting the rights of disabled individuals to basic things that able-bodied people take for granted, such as adequate housing, health care, employment, and education.

6.2.3 Causes of Prejudice

There are four contemporary theories to explain the causes for prejudice.

1. The Out-Group Homogeneity Effect

The Out-Group Homogeneity Effect is the perception that members of an out-group are more similar or homogeneous than members of the in-group. In sociology and social psychology, an in-group is a social group in which a person psychologically identifies as being a member. By contrast, an out-group is a social group with which an individual does not identify. Social psychologists Quattrone and Jones conducted a study demonstrating this with students from the

rival schools of Princeton University and Rutgers University. Students at each school were shown videos of other students from each school choosing a type of music to listen to for an auditory perception study. Then the participants were asked to guess what percentage of the videotaped students' classmates would choose the same. Participants predicted a much greater similarity between out-group members (the rival school) than between members of their in-group. This means that people would assume more similarities between out-group members, thus more likely to form generalized views towards others.

2. The Realistic Conflict Theory

The Realistic Conflict Theory states that competition between limited resources leads to increased negative prejudice and discrimination. This can be seen even when the resource is insignificant. In the Robber's Cave experiment, negative prejudice and hostility were created between two summer camps after sports competitions for small prizes. The hostility was lessened after the two competing camps were forced to cooperate on tasks to achieve a common goal.

3. The Integrated Threat Theory

The Integrated Threat Theory (ITT) was developed by Walter G. Stephan. It draws from and builds upon several other psychological explanations of prejudice and in-group/out-group behavior such as the Realistic Conflict Theory. ITT suggests that out-group prejudice and discrimination are caused when individuals perceive an out-group to be threatening in some way. ITT defines four threats: realistic threats, symbolic threats, intergroup anxiety, and negative stereotypes. Realistic threats are tangible, such as competition for a natural resource or a threat to income. Symbolic threats arise from a perceived difference in cultural values between groups or a perceived imbalance of power. For example, an in-group perceives an out-group's religion as incompatible. Intergroup anxiety is a feeling of uneasiness experienced in the presence of an out-group or out-group member, which constitutes a threat because interactions with other groups cause negative feelings, such as a threat to comfortable interactions. Negative stereotypes are similar threats in that individuals anticipate negative behavior from out-group members in line with the perceived stereotypes. ITT differs from other threat theories by including intergroup anxiety and negative stereotypes as threat types.

4. The Social Dominance Theory

The Social Dominance Theory states that society can be viewed as group-based hierarchies. In competition for scarce resources such as housing or employment, dominant groups create prejudiced "legitimizing myths" to provide moral and intellectual justification for their dominant position over other groups and validate their claim over the limited resources. Legitimizing myths, such as discriminatory hiring practices or biased merit norms, work to maintain these prejudiced hierarchies.

6.2.4 Influences of Prejudice

Effects of prejudice include the following five aspects: difficulties in performing tasks, exclusion, internalization; difficulties in integrating into groups and tendency to perform discrimination.

1. Difficulties in Performing Tasks

Researchers at the University of Toronto Scarborough studied individuals' reactions to negative stereotyping, and found that after being placed in a situation where people were victims of prejudice, many people found it hard to concentrate. Since an individual's ability to turn his or her full attention to a task is impaired, a victim of prejudice might be placed at a disadvantage in academic environments. So victims of prejudice may have difficulty in focusing on tasks and making clear decisions, an effect which can linger after the incident.

2. Exclusion

Prejudice excludes people in many ways. For example, an employer might be prejudiced against a certain ethnic group, say, blacks, and would therefore be less likely to accept job applications from members of that group and would look more favorably on candidates from another ethnicity.

3. Internalization

Over a period of time, a victim of constant prejudice might begin to believe that he or she deserves the abuse or problems he or she has encountered, and that prejudiced individuals are right to treat him or her in such a way. An individual who believes negative comments about his or her own group is suffering from self-stigma. This belief can, in turn, lead to further problems, as the individual is likely to suffer from poor self-esteem and may even fall into depression. For example, if teachers think that African American students are not so smart as white students,

those students may think that is true, not trying to work harder and becoming less confident or feeling depressed.

4. Difficulties in Integrating into Groups

If an individual begins to believe his or her own behavior or beliefs are wrong as a result of prejudice, this can cause conflict with others in his or her own group. For example, a Christian who encounters negative attitudes towards his or her religion may begin to question the Christian way of life within his or her church and immediate family.

5. Tendency to Perform Discrimination

Prejudice often ends in discrimination. In essence, prejudice is a feeling. And the act of discrimination is the end result. This is due to the major difference between prejudice and discrimination. Prejudice refers to the idea or opinion without factual backing or evidence, and discrimination refers to biased treatment based on someone's race, gender, religion, sexual orientation, socioeconomic background, or other characteristics. With prejudice holding in mind, people often tend to present their prejudicial thoughts in their actions by performing discrimination actions.

For Your Information

Schindler's List

Schindler's List is a remarkable work of fiction based on the true story of German industrialist and war profiteer, Oskar Schindler, who, confronted with the horror of the extermination camps, gambled his life and fortune to rescue 1,300 Jews from the gas chambers during the World War II. In this milestone of Holocaust literature, working with the actual testimony of Schindler's Jews, Thomas Keneally, the author, used the actual testimony of the Schindlerjuden —Schindler's Jews—to brilliantly portray the courage and cunning of a good man in the midst of unspeakable evil.

Steven Spielberg, director of *Jurassic Park*, made this story into a movie. The movie opens in September of 1939 in Krakow, Poland, with the Jewish community under increasing pressure from the Nazis. Into this tumult comes Oskar Schindler, a Nazi businessman interested in obtaining Jewish backing for a factory he wishes to build. He makes contact with Itzhak Stern, an accountant, to arrange financial matters. For a while, there is no interest and nothing happens. In March 1941, the Krakow Jewish community has been forced to live in "the Ghetto", where money no longer has any meaning. Several elders agree to invest in Schindler's factory and the DEF (Deutsche Emailwarenfabrik) is born—a place where large quantities of pots are manufactured. To do the work, Schindler hires Jews (because they're cheaper than Poles), and the German army becomes his biggest customer.

In March 1943, Germany's intentions towards the Jews are no longer a secret. The Ghetto is "liquidated", with the survivors being herded into the Plaszow forced labor camp. Many are executed, and still others are shipped away by train, never to return. During this time, Schindler has managed to ingratiate himself with the local commander, Amon Goeth, a Nazi who kills Jews for sport. Using his relationship with Goeth, Schindler begins to secretly campaign to help the Jews, saving men, women, and children from certain death.

Case Study: Stereotypes and Prejudice in *Zootopia*

Try to analyze the following case with the knowledge you have just learned. Here are some questions that may help you:

(1) People tend to compare the city of Zootopia to American society. Why?
(2) What stereotypes are embodied on Judy the rabbit and Nick the fox?
(3) Can prejudice and racism be seen in *Zootopia*?

Disney's *Zootopia* takes on prejudice in different forms. The main character, Judy Hopps, is a tiny, female bunny who didn't grow up in the big city. As such, when she joins a police force dominated by large, powerful male characters (of varying animal species) who are "street smart", no one thinks she's good for anything other than a lowly position as a meter maid.

The movie opens with 9-year-old Judy Hopps, a European rabbit performing a play on the city of Zootopia. Judy wants to be a police officer. Her career choice is laughed at by pretty much everyone, including her parents, who say she'll never be on the force since rabbits are cute and can't be cops; only predators can be cops. Judy graduates from the police academy and walks into the Zootopia Police Department headquarters. She gets assigned to parking ticket duty by Chief Bogo

on account of her small size. While on patrol she meets the red fox, Nick Wilde, a con artist.

Judy abandons her parking maid post the next day when a weasel tries stealing what appears to be beet roots. After an ensuing chase, during which she saves an arctic shrew, Judy captures the thief. Instead of being praised, she's reprimanded by Bogo for abandoning her post. Before Judy can get fired from the force, a North American river otter barges in begging for Bogo to get the police looking for her missing husband. Judy volunteers and the furious Bogo gives her 48 hours to find the otter before she's thrown off the force. The rabbit enlists the help of Wilde, and after an adventure, the pair finds the otter. However, the otter has gone savage and is being kept with many other savage animals. Still, Judy and Wilde gather video evidence of the whole thing, and after escaping by falling off a waterfall, the two save the day.

The story doesn't end there, however. During a press conference, Judy implies the predators have gone savage due to their genes. Panic spreads across Zootopia as prey, 90% of the population, become terrified and hostile towards predators, 10% of the population. Judy, having realized her work has made everything worse, resigns. Later, at her parents' carrot farm, she discovers going savage isn't a natural process brought on by DNA, but rather an artificial process brought on by essential drugs. Judy goes back to Zootopia, finds Nick, and together they find the criminal who's making the predators go savage.

The most brilliant part of *Zootopia* isn't its somewhat original plot, definitely original setting, or its gorgeous animation, though all of those are certainly strengths of the movie. It's how it handles its anti-discrimination theme. At first, it's easy to draw parallels between the real world of America and the Zootopia world. The animals are divided into two major groups—predators and prey. Predators make up 10% of the population, and prey makes up 90%.

When Judy is told she can't be a police officer because she's a rabbit, it's pretty much the same thing as Jackie Robinson was told that he can't play baseball because he's black. Nick Wilde reveals prey can be bullies too. In a moment of vulnerability for the character, he reveals he wanted to join the world's equivalent of the boy scouts. However, because he's a predator, the other members—all prey—slapped a muzzle on him and kicked him out. Wilde then confesses the only reason why he became a con artist was that the world stereotyped him as a mischievous, nefarious creature. And if he can't beat them, he might as well join them.

After Judy declares predators' going savage is wired into their DNA, racist acts really start to become prevalent. The harmless receptionist Clawhauser gets moved to records because citizens don't want to have a predator be the first thing people see. When Judy is riding the subway, a mother and her daughter, both prey, sit next to a tiger minding his own business. When the mother notices who's sitting next to her daughter, she pulls her away from the tiger who is just listening to music. What makes this so brilliant is that Disney isn't saying prejudice only comes from one side. Throughout *Zootopia* we see acts of prejudice by both predators and prey. This dual-sided racism reflects real life. The only way to truly overcome racism isn't to lash out with more racism, but to try and understand each other. And while we have our own limits in what we can do, we should be supportive of each other to build everyone up, rather than putting one group down to support our own.

6.3 Racism

6.3.1 Brief Introduction to Racism

According to race scholars Howard Winant and Michael Omi, racism results in an unequal distribution of power on the basis of race. The n-word (negro, nigger) was used historically and is still used today to cast black people as second-class citizens who do not deserve, or who have not earned the same rights and privileges enjoyed by others in American society. This makes it racist.

"I have a dream", fifty years ago, on August 28, 1963, American civil rights leader Martin Luther King, Jr., uttered those words in his most famous speech. Using that captivating refrain, King expressed his dream, or hope, that one day people would enjoy life free from racial discrimination or racism. Sadly, racism in the form of discrimination still persists in society now. A case in point is that blacks have traditionally suffered from higher rates of unemployment than whites. Black unemployment is often nearly twice as high as the white unemployment rate. Do blacks simply not take the initiative that whites do to find work? Studies indicate that, in actuality, discrimination contributes to the black-white unemployment gap.

6.3.2 Four Main Types of Racism

The word "racism" comes in different types, which makes it much more complex. There are four major types of racism.

1. Subtle Racism

To begin with, racism doesn't just concern a dominant racial group obviously oppressing minorities. There's subtle racism or racial microaggressions. It's like the form of discrimination that people of color most often experience.

Victims of subtle racism may find themselves snubbed by waitstaff in restaurants or salespeople in stores who believe that people of color aren't likely to be good tippers or able to afford anything expensive, just as Oprah Winfrey described about one of her shopping experiences in which the shop clerk thought she was a black person and couldn't afford expensive items and thus refused to show her the bag.

Targets of subtle racism may find that supervisors, landlords, etc., apply different rules to different people. For example, an employer might run a thorough background check on an applicant of color, while accepting a job applicant from a prospective white employee with no additional documentation. So racial prejudice is the driving force behind subtle racism.

Ignoring people of certain races is another example of subtle racism. When a Mexican woman enters a store waiting to be served, the employees may behave as if she's not there, continuing to rifle through store shelves or sorting through papers. Soon afterward, a white woman enters the store, and the employees immediately wait on her. They serve the Mexican woman only after they wait on her white counterpart. The covert message sent to the Mexican customer is "You're not as worthy of attention and customer service as a white person is."

2. Colorism Within Minority Groups

There's also colorism within minority groups in which lighter-skinned people discriminate against their darker-skinned counterparts. Colorism is often viewed as a problem that's unique to communities of color. It occurs when minorities discriminate against those with darker skin than they have.

For years in the black community, lighter skin was viewed as superior to darker skin. Anyone with skin color that was lighter than a brown paper lunch bag was welcomed into elite organizations in the black community, while darker skinned blacks were excluded. Colorism also exists outside of the African-American community. In Asia, sales of skin whitening products remain sky high.

3. Internalized Racism

Internalized racism is an issue as well. It occurs when minorities experience self-hatred because they've taken to heart the ideology that dubs them as inferior.

In American society in which blonde hair and blue eyes are still widely regarded as ideal and stereotypes about minority groups persist, it's not hard to see why some people of color suffer from internalized racism.

In this form of racism, people of color internalize the negative messages spread about minorities and come to loathe themselves for being "different".

They may hate their skin color, their hair texture and other physical features or intentionally marry interracially so their children won't have the same ethnic traits that they do. They may simply suffer from low self-esteem because of their race— performing poorly in school or in the workplace because they believe their racial background makes them inferior. Michael Jackson was long accused of suffering from this kind of racism because of the changing color of his skin and plastic surgeries.

4. Reverse Racism

Reverse racism is arguably the hottest form of racism in the 21st century. Reverse racism refers to anti-white discrimination. It's not that reverse racism is a huge problem in the U.S., it's that people keep claiming that they've been victims of this form of racism in which whites fall prey to discrimination. The U.S. Supreme Court has decided so in a few landmark cases, such as when white firefighters in New Haven, Connecticut, were prohibited from being promoted because their minority counterparts didn't qualify for promotions as well.

Not only social programs but also people of color in positions of power have generated cries of "reverse racism". A number of prominent minorities have been accused of being anti-white.

6.3.3 Causes and Effects of Different Types of Racism

1. Causes and Effects of Subtle Racism

Members of racial minority groups are much more likely to be the victims

of subtle racism, also known as everyday racism, covert racism, or racial microaggressions. This sort of racism has a damaging effect on its targets, many of whom struggle to see it for what it is.

A study conducted by San Francisco State University professor Alvin Alvarez identified everyday racism as subtle, commonplace forms of discrimination, such as being ignored, ridiculed or treated differently. Alvarez, a counseling professor, explains, "These are incidents that may seem innocent and small, but cumulatively they can have a powerful impact on an individual's mental health."

Annie Barnes further illuminates the matter in her book *Everyday Racism: A Book for All Americans*. She identifies such racism as a "virus" of sorts exhibited in the body language, speech, and isolating attitude of racists, among other behavior. Due to the covertness of such behavior, victims of this form of racism may struggle to determine for certain if bigotry is at play.

In *Everyday Racism: A Book for All Americans,* Barnes tells the story of Daniel, a black college student whose apartment building manager asked him not to listen to music on his earphones while strolling the premises. Supposedly, other residents found it distracting. The problem? "Daniel observed that a white youth in his complex had a similar radio with earphones and that the supervisor never complained about him."

Based on their fears or stereotypes of black men, Daniel's neighbors found the image of him listening to earphones off-putting but made no objections to his white counterpart doing the same thing. This gave Daniel the message that someone with his skin color must adhere to a different set of standards, a revelation that made him uneasy.

While Daniel acknowledged that racial discrimination was to blame for why the manager treated him differently, some victims of everyday racism fail to make this connection. These people only invoke the word "racism" when someone blatantly commits a racist act such as using a slur. But they may want to rethink their reluctance to identify something as racist. Although the notion that talking about racism too much makes matters worse is widespread, the study found the opposite to be true. "Trying to ignore these insidious incidents could become taxing and debilitating over time, chipping away at a person's spirit," Alvarez explained.

When we think of racism only in extremes, we allow subtle racism to continue wreaking havoc on people's lives. In an essay called "Everyday Racism, White Liberals and the Limits of Tolerance", anti-racist activist Tim Wise explains, "Since hardly anyone will admit to racial prejudice of any type, focusing on bigotry, hatred, and acts of intolerance only solidifies the belief that racism is something 'out there', a problem for others, 'but not me', or anyone I know."

Wise argues that because everyday racism is much more prevalent than extreme racism, the former reaches more people's lives and causes more lasting damage. That's why it's important to make an issue out of racial microaggressions.

2. Causes and Effects of Colorism Within Minority Groups

The repercussions of colorism should not be underestimated. While many discussions focus on how it plays out interpersonally, like in romantic relationships, colorism also has severe consequences at a systemic level. Let's dive into different ways colorism can manifest.

Perhaps one of the most infamous examples of colorism is the paper bag test that was used throughout black communities in the United States. Basically, light skin became associated with a high social status. To keep their social clubs pure, light-skinned black people would hold up a paper bag to someone's skin. If you were darker than the paper bag, you were too dark to participate.

Colorism dramatically shapes people's experiences with carceral institutions. In 2011, researchers from Villanova University in Philadelphia analyzed the prison sentences of 12,158 women who were incarcerated between 1995 and 2009. They found that those who were seen as lighter-skinned received sentences that were, on average, 12% shorter than dark skinned women.

However, sentences aren't the only thing influenced by colorism—even whether you get arrested or not is also impacted by skin color. In 2018, a study by Ellis Monk, a Harvard sociology professor, found that, when accounting for differences like gender and education levels, black people have a 36% chance of being jailed at some point in their lives. But if they were dark skinned, that chance jumped to almost 66%.

"To put it bluntly, while being black (and poor) may already predispose one to have a higher probability of contact with the criminal justice system and harsher treatment... being perceived as blacker intensifies this contact further and may increase the harshness of one's treatment by the criminal justice system as an institution," Monk wrote in the study.

Colorism has long been linked to restrictive beauty standards. Those who embrace colorism not only tend to value lighter-skinned people over their darker-

skinned counterparts but also view the former as more intelligent, noble, and attractive than dark-skinned people.

Actresses Lupita Nyong'o, Gabrielle Union, and Keke Palmer have all spoken about how they desired lighter skin because they thought darker skin made them unattractive. This is especially telling given that all of these actresses are widely considered to be good-looking, and Lupita Nyong'o earned the title of *People* magazine's Most Beautiful in 2014. Rather than acknowledging that beauty can be found in people of all skin tones, colorism narrows beauty standards by deeming only light-skinned people as beautiful and everyone else as less than.

3. Causes and Effects of Internalized Racism

While some people of color grew up in diverse communities where racial differences were appreciated, others felt rejected due to their skin color.

Being bullied because of ethnic background and encountering harmful messages about race in greater society may be all it takes to get people of color to begin loathing themselves. For some, the impetus to turn racism inward occurs when they see white people receiving privileges denied to people of color.

"I don't want to live in the back. Why do we always have to live in the back?" a fair-skinned black character named Sarah Jane asks in the 1959 movie *Imitation of Life*. Sarah Jane ultimately decides to abandon her black mother and pass for white because she "wants to have a chance in life". She explains, "I don't want to have to come through back doors or feel lower than other people."

In the classic novel *Autobiography of an Ex-colored Man*, the mixed-race protagonist first begins to experience internalized racism after he witnesses a white mob burn a black man alive. Rather than empathize with the victim, he chooses to identify with the mob. He explains, "I understood that it was not discouragement or fear, or search for a larger field of action and opportunity, that was driving me out of the negro race. I knew that it was shame, unbearable shame."

To live up to Western beauty standards, people suffering from internalized racism may attempt to alter their appearance to look more "white". For those of Asian descent, this could mean opting to have double eyelid surgery. For African Americans, this could mean chemically straightening one's hair and weaving in extensions. Also, people of color from a variety of backgrounds use bleach creams to lighten their skin.

But not all people of color who alter their physical appearance do so to look "whiter". For example, many black women say they straighten their hair to make it more manageable and not because they're ashamed of their descent. Some people turn to bleach creams to even out their skin tone and not because they're trying to uniformly lighten their skin.

Over the years, a variety of derogatory terms have cropped up to describe those suffering from internalized racism. They include "Uncle Tom" "sellout" "pocho" or "whitewashed". While the first two terms are typically used by black people, "pocho" and "whitewashed" have circulated among immigrants of color to describe people who have assimilated to white, Western culture, with little knowledge of their native cultural heritage. Also, many nicknames for those suffering from internalized racism involve foods that are dark on the outside and light on the inside such as "Oreo" for black people; "Twinkie" or "banana" for Asians; "coconut" for Latinos; or "apple" for Native Americans.

Put-downs such as "Oreo" are controversial because many black people recount being called the racial term for doing well in school, speaking standard English or having white friends, not because they didn't identify as black. All too often this insult demeans those who don't fit into a box. Accordingly, many black people who are proud of their descent find this term hurtful.

While such name-calling hurts, it persists. So, who might be called such a name? Multiracial golfer Tiger Woods has been accused of being a "sellout" because he identifies himself as "Cablinasian" (白黑印亚太) rather than as black. Cablinasian is a name Woods devised to represent the fact that he has Caucasian, black, American Indian, and Asian descent. Woods has not only been accused of suffering from internalized racism because of how he racially identifies but also because he's been romantically involved with a string of white women, including his Nordic ex-wife. Some people view this as a sign that he's uncomfortable with being a person of color. The same has been said about actress and producer Mindy Kaling, who's faced criticism for repeatedly casting white men as her love interests on the sitcom *The Mindy Project*.

People who refuse to date members of their own racial group may, in fact, suffer from internalized racism, but unless they declare this to be true, it's best not to make such assumptions. In any case, children may be more likely to admit to suffering from internalized racism than adults. A child may openly yearn to be white, while an adult will likely keep such wishes internalized for fear of being judged. Those who serially date whites or refuse to identify as a person of color may be accused of suffering from internalized racism but so are people of color who espouse political beliefs considered detrimental to minorities.

4. Causes and Effects of Reverse Racism

What makes white racism distinct? Because American institutions haven't traditionally been anti-white, the argument that whites can be truly victimized by reverse racism is difficult to make. Still, the assertion that reverse racism exists has persisted since the late 20th century when the government implemented widespread programs to make up for historic discrimination against ethnic minorities. In 1994, *Time* magazine ran an article about a small minority of Afrocentrists known as "melanists" (黑人主义者) who posit that those with an abundance of dark-skin pigment, or melanin, are more humane and superior to lighter-skinned people, not to mention prone to having paranormal powers such as ESP (Extra Sensual Perception) and psychokinesis. The idea that one group of people is superior to another based on skin color certainly fits the dictionary definition of racism. Yet, the melanists had no institutional power to spread their message or subjugate lighter-skinned people based on their racist beliefs. Moreover, because the melanists spread their message in predominantly black settings, it's likely that few whites even heard their racist message, let alone suffered because of it. Melanists lacked the institutional influence to oppress whites with their ideology.

"What separates white racism from any other form…is its ability…to become lodged in the minds of and perceptions of the citizenry," Wise explains. "White perceptions are what end up counting in a white-dominated society. If whites say Indians are savages, then by God, they'll be seen as savages. If Indians say whites are mayonnaise-eating Amway salespeople, who the hell is going to care? And such was the case with the melanists. No one cared what they had to say about the melanin-deprived because this fringe group of Afrocentrists lacked power and influence."

It occurs when institutions favor ethnic minorities over whites. If we include institutional power in the definition of racism, it's virtually impossible to argue that reverse racism exists. But as institutions attempt to compensate ethnic minorities for the racism of the past via affirmative action programs and similar policies, the government has found that whites have experienced discrimination. Although no study ever shows that this is the case, believers of reverse racism contend that crimes against whites committed by blacks are not only crimes against property or persons but constitute a hate crime. They claim it is similar to others' experience when they suffer crimes due to their belongingness to a particular race, minorities, or gender.

Without presenting any data or evidence, except anecdotal ones, they propagate the myth that crimes committed by blacks against whites are widespread throughout America. Worse, they present it as proof that blacks hate the whites. All in all, they firmly believe that there are crimes against whites because they are hated. Rather than allow the white firefighters to promote, the city of New Haven dismissed the test results for fear that minority firefighters would sue if they weren't also promoted. Chief Justice John Roberts argued that the events in New Haven amounted to racial discrimination against whites because the city would not have refused to promote black firefighters if their white counterparts had performed poorly on the qualifying exam.

Not all whites who find themselves excluded as institutions try to right past wrongs feel victimized. In a piece for *The Atlantic* called "Reverse Racism, or How the Pot Got to Call the Kettle Black", a legal scholar Stanley Fish described being ruled out of an administrative position at a university when the powers decided that a woman or ethnic minority would be a better candidate for the job. Fish explained "Although I was disappointed, I did not conclude that the situation was 'unfair', because the policy was obviously... not intended to disenfranchize white males. Rather, the policy was driven by other considerations, and it was only as a by-product of those considerations—not as the main goal—that white males like me were rejected. Given that the institution in question has a high percentage of minority students, a very low percentage of minority faculty, and an even lower percentage of minority administrators, it made perfect sense to focus on women and minority candidates, and within that sense, not as the result of prejudice, my whiteness and maleness became disqualifications."

Fish argues that whites who find themselves excluded when white institutions try to diversify mustn't protest. Exclusion, when the goal is not racism but an attempt to level the playing field, can't compare to the centuries of racial subjugation that people of color experienced in U.S. society. Ultimately, this kind of exclusion serves the greater good of eradicating racism and its legacy.

6.3.4 Ways to Cope with Racism

If we have proof or a strong hunch that we're being treated differently, ignored or ridiculed based on race, make it an issue. According to Alvarez' study, which

appears in the April 2010 issue of *Journal of Counseling Psychology*, men who reported incidents of subtle racism or confronted those responsibly, lowered amounts of personal distress while boosting self-esteem. On the other hand, the study found that women who disregarded incidents of subtle racism developed increased levels of stress. In short, speak out about racism in all its forms for the sake of your mental health.

While colorism is often thought of as a problem that exclusively afflicts communities of color, that's not the case. Europeans have prized fair skin and flaxen hair for centuries, and blonde hair and blue eyes remain status symbols for some people. When the conquistadors first traveled to the Americas in the 15th century, they judged the indigenous people they saw on their skin color. Europeans would make similar judgments about the Africans they enslaved. Over time, people of color began to internalize these messages about their complexions. Light skin was deemed superior, and dark skin, inferior. In Asia, though, fair skin is said to be a symbol of wealth and dark skin, a symbol of poverty, as peasants who toiled in the fields all day typically had the darkest skin.

If a child is born with dark skin and learns that dark skin is not valued by his peers, community, or society, he may develop feelings of shame. This is especially true if the child is unaware of colorism's historical roots and lacks friends and family members who shun skin color bias. Thus, it's important to let children and adult people develop an understanding of racism and classism, which will make them understand that no one's skin color is innately good or bad.

It's difficult to tell if someone suffers from internalized racism simply based on their friends, romantic partners or political beliefs.

To eradicate racism, it's important to understand the different types of racism that affect society. Whether you're experiencing racial microaggressions or helping a child to overcome internalized racism, staying educated on the issue can make a difference. To end racism, we must combat it everywhere it lives and thrives. We must confront it in ourselves, in our communities, and in our nation. Learn about the racism and practice empathy. Listen to and trust those who report racism, because anti-racism begins with basic respect for all people. Step in when you see racism occurring, and disrupt it in a safe way. An individual can do a greater good in fighting against racism. And what's important is that people can all act up and do something to make the world a better place for the entire human race.

Case Study: Justice for George Floyd

Read the following passage. Try to answer these questions:

(1) What are the causes of the death of George Floyd?

(2) Why did people conduct "Black Lives Matter" protest?

George Floyd was declared dead on May 25, 2020 after Chauvin, a Minneapolis police officer, who is white, pressed his knee against Floyd's neck for about nine minutes, ignoring the black man's cries that he couldn't breathe and holding his position even after Floyd went limp as he was handcuffed and lying on his stomach. Floyd's death sparked violent protests in Minneapolis and beyond, and led to a nationwide reckoning on systemic racism. In the aftermath of George Floyd's death, protests have broken out nationwide in America, including Black Lives Matter (BLM) Movement. Black Lives Matter claimed, "Right now, Minneapolis and cities across our country are on fire, and our people are hurting—the violence against black bodies is felt in the ongoing mass disobedience, all while we grapple with a pandemic that is disproportionately affecting, infecting, and killing us."

Chauvin is charged with second-degree unintentional murder and second-degree manslaughter, and a panel of judges from appeals court ruled that the judge must consider reinstating a third-degree murder charge that he dismissed last fall. Three other officers, all of whom were also fired, face trial in August on charges of aiding and abetting the second-degree murder and manslaughter.

The systemic racism is the cause of the tragic death of George Floyd and the following protests. Racist behavior and beliefs—even when they are subconscious or semi-conscious—fuel structural inequalities of race that fill society. The racial prejudices represented in racial discrimination are manifested in the disproportionate policing, arrest, and imprisonment of black men and boys (and increasingly black women); in racial discrimination in hiring practices; in the lack of media and police attention devoted to crimes against black people as compared with those committed against white women and girls; and, in the lack of economic investment in predominantly black neighborhoods and cities, among many other problems that result from systemic racism.

Racism in the United States has been a major issue since the colonial era and the slave era. Legally sanctioned racism imposed a heavy burden on Native Americans, African Americans, Asian Americans, and Latin Americans. The most prominent and notable form of American racism (other than imperialism against Native Americans) began with the institution of slavery, during which Africans were enslaved and treated as property. Prior to the institution of slavery, early African and non-white immigrants to the colonies had been regarded with equal status, serving as slaves alongside whites. After the institution of slavery, the status of Africans was stigmatized, and this stigma was the basis for the more fatal anti-African racism that persisted until the present. African Americans were treated like second-class citizens. Many people in the U.S. continue to have prejudice against other races. In the view of the U.S. Human Rights Network, a network of scores of U.S. civil rights and human rights organizations, discrimination spreads in all aspects of life in the United States, and extends to all communities of color.

What should people do to ease the bad impacts of racism? As Martin Luther King, Jr. made clear, we cannot have true justice as long as we value "a negative peace which is the absence of tension to a positive peace which is the presence of justice". And as Michelle Obama puts, "It's up to all of us—black, white, everyone—no matter how well-meaning we think we might be, to do the honest, uncomfortable work of rooting (racism) out; It starts with self-examination and listening to those whose lives are different from our own. It ends with justice, compassion, and empathy that manifest in our lives and on our streets."

6.4 Stereotypes, Prejudice & Intercultural Communication

6.4.1 Interrelationship Among Stereotypes, Prejudice & Discrimination

We have discussed stereotypes, prejudice, and discrimination, which often play a major role when communication occurs between people of different races or cultural backgrounds. These terms, stereotype, prejudice, discrimination, and racism are all considered as cultural biases. Thus, we need to understand their interrelationship and analyze why they are considered as barriers in intercultural communication.

Walter Lippmann (1889—1974), American writer, reporter, and political commentator, first introduced the word "stereotype" in 1922 to describe judgment made about others on the basis of their ethnic group membership. Today, this term is more broadly used to refer to judgments or beliefs made on the basis of any group membership. The sign for the Japanese in American Sign Language is a twist of the little finger at the corner of the eye to denote a slanted eye. And it applies to all Asians. Although you may think of stereotypes as being negative judgments, they can also be positive. Some people hold positive stereotypes of other individuals based on their professional group membership. For example, some people assume that all doctors are intelligent and wise.

The strong link between stereotypes and prejudice should be obvious. Prejudiced thinking is dependent on stereotypes and is a fairly normal phenomenon. Prejudice refers to negative attitudes towards other people that are based on inflexible stereotypes. Prejudiced attitudes include irrational feelings of dislike and even hatred for certain groups, biased perceptions and beliefs about the group members that are not based on direct experiences and first-hand knowledge, and a readiness to behave in negative and unjust ways toward members of the group.

While calling someone a "dumb blonde" might result in feelings of frustration, irritation, discomfort, or even anger for the person targeted by the insult, it's rare that there would be further negative implications. There is no research to suggest that hair color affects one's access to rights and resources in society, like college admission, the ability to buy a home in a particular neighborhood, access to employment, or the likelihood that one will be stopped by the police. This form of prejudice, most often manifested in bad jokes, may have some negative impact on the butt of the joke, but it is unlikely to have the same kinds of negative impacts that racism does.

Then a new term "discrimination" should be introduced here. Whereas prejudice refers to people's attitudes or mental representations, the term "discrimination" refers to the behavioral manifestations of that prejudice. Thus discrimination can be thought of as prejudice "in action". Discrimination can occur in many forms. From the extremes of segregation and apartheid to biases in the availability of housing, employment, education, economic resources, personal safety, and legal protection, discrimination represents unequal treatment of certain individuals solely because of their membership in a particular group.

Teun A. van Dijk, a Dutch discourse analyst, has conducted a series of studies

of people's everyday conversations as they discussed different racial and cultural groups. Van Dijk concludes that when individuals make prejudicial comments, tell jokes that belittle and dehumanize others, and share negative stereotypes about others, they are establishing and legitimizing the existence of their prejudice and are laying the "communication groundwork" that will make it acceptable for people to perform discrimination acts.

Race scholars Howard Winant and Michael Omi define racism as a way of representing or describing race that creates or reproduces structures of domination based on essentialist categories of race (Omi & Winant, 1987). In other words, racism results in an unequal distribution of power on the basis of race. Because of this, using the "n-word" does not simply signal prejudice. Rather, it reflects and reproduces an unjust hierarchy of racial categories that negatively impact the life chances of people of color.

Using the offensive terms such as the previously mentioned "racial slur"—a term popularized by white Americans during the era of African enslavement—encapsulates a wide swath of disturbing racial prejudices. The wide-sweeping and deeply detrimental implications of this term and the prejudice it reflects and reproduces make it vastly different from suggesting that people with blonde hair are dumb. The "n-word" was used historically, and is still used today, to perpetuate systemic inequalities based on race. This makes the use of this term "racist", and not simply prejudiced, as defined by sociologists.

Though racism is often used synonymously with prejudice and discrimination, the social attributes that distinguish it from these other terms are oppression and power. The word "racism" itself can evoke very powerful emotional reactions, especially for those who feel that the oppression and exploitation stem from racist attitudes and behavior. For example, for members of the African American, Asian American, Native American, and Latino cultures, racism has created a social history shaped by prejudice and discrimination.

Racism is the tendency by groups in control of institutional and cultural power to use it to keep members of groups who do not have access to the same kinds of power at a disadvantage. Racism oppresses entire groups of people, making it very difficult, and sometimes virtually impossible, for their members to have access to political, economic, and social power.

6.4.2 Impacts of Stereotype and Prejudice on Intercultural Communication

Cultural biases are based on normal human tendencies to view ourselves as members of a particular group and to view others as not belonging to that group.

Status, power, and economic differences heavily influence all intercultural contacts. Cultural biases are a reminder that all relationships take place within political, economic, social, and cultural contexts. As we live in a world where interactions with people from different cultures are common features of daily life, the intercultural challenges for all of us are to be willing to tackle with the consequences of prejudice, discrimination, and racism at the individual, social, and institutional levels.

Many people believe that creating the opportunity for personal contacts fosters positive attitudes towards members of other groups. Yes, it's true. The international "sister city" programs, wherein a Chinese city pairs itself with a city in another country, encourages the residents of both cities to visit and stay in one another's home.

Sometimes, of course, intercultural contact does overcome the obstacles of culture distance, and positive attitudes do emerge. Unfortunately, there is a great deal of historical and contemporary evidence to suggest that contact between members of different cultures does not always lead to good feelings. In fact, under many circumstances such contact only reinforces negative attitudes or may even change a neutral attitude into a negative one.

To explain it, stereotypes and prejudice both have negative effects on intercultural communication. If a stereotype is very common, people may assure that it is true. Even people who are the subjects of certain stereotypes may eventually believe it too. Stereotypes can have a negative effect when people use them to interpret behavior. Prejudice can have very serious effects too, for it can lead to discrimination. Historically in the United States, there was a lot of prejudice against people who had recently immigrated. After the huge wave of immigration that followed the Potato Famine in Ireland, there was much prejudice against Irish people in the United States because earlier immigrants worried that the new immigrants would take their jobs.

Summary

This chapter discussed the cultural perception process and its relationship with the intercultural communication process, particularly in terms of stereotypes, prejudice, discrimination, and racism.

A stereotype is an assumption. A stereotype means assuming that a group of people who share some characteristics also share certain attributes. In other words, when someone assumes something about us because of one part of our identity, it is a stereotype. Stereotypes are often negatively impactful, overly simplistic, dangerous, and unfair. Prejudice is a belief. Prejudice is when someone has a belief (usually negative) about a person or group based on a stereotype. The belief is usually based on a person's membership (or assumed membership) in a certain group. Prejudice also divides people based on stereotypes. Discrimination is an action. Discrimination is when someone acts on his or her prejudiced beliefs. It can also be systemic, like the policies and practices put in place to assimilate First Nations, Inuit, and Métis peoples.

Cultural biases are based on normal human tendencies to view ourselves as members of a particular group and to view others as not belonging to that group. Status, power, and economic differences heavily influence all intercultural contacts. Cultural biases are a reminder that all relationships take place within political, economic, social, and cultural contexts. Stereotypes and other forms of biases can overshadow the strategic benefits of diversity by preventing all employees from contributing to work processes. Companies that do not address internal biases might also face costly discrimination claims.

With the influences of globalization, we are becoming global citizens which means that we cannot avoid making contacts with people from different countries and different cultures. Intercultural communication is turning into the common features of our daily life. In such settings, it is all too easy for us to become trapped by invisible barriers or biases in global communication. Thus, the intercultural challenges for all of us is to be willing to grapple with the consequences of prejudice, discrimination, and racism at the individual, social, and institutional level.

Let's end this chapter with a quotation from Burke in 1935, "A way of seeing is also a way of not seeing—a focus on Object A involves a neglect of Object B." Similarly, in intercultural communication settings, it is all too easy to become trapped by invisible barriers or biases to communication. The only way to "escape" is to learn to see them and avoid making the communication mistakes that come from them.

Exercises

Questions for Review

1. Can you use real-life examples to further illustrate the four basic kinds of gender stereotypes?

2. Stereotypes can be seen in two different dimensions. Can you briefly describe them?

3. Can you explain the reasons and possible influences of stereotypes?

4. Can you briefly describe the causes of prejudice and its possible effects?

5. Can you use real-life examples to further illustrate the four main types of racism?

6. Can you explain the interrelationship among stereotypes, prejudice, and racism?

7. How do cultural biases influence intercultural communication?

Problems and Application

1. Based on the format used in analyzing the movie *Zootopia*, choose one or more of the following movies to conduct an in-depth analysis on stereotypes and prejudice. These movies include *Crash, Guess Who's Coming to Dinner, Pride and Prejudice*, and *To Kill a Mocking Bird.*

2. Our world is confronting the COVID-19 pandemic. As of May 2020, the World Health Organization declared there are more than three million confirmed cases of COVID-19 in 213 countries, areas, and territories. The outbreak of COVID-19 has sent billions of people into lockdown, health services into crises, and economies into turmoil worldwide. While anxiety and fear about the pandemic have been widespread, racist incidents have also occurred, particularly in the United States. The COVID-19 pandemic has brought Asian discrimination and racism back in full force there. Make a research on what has happened to Asian community during the pandemic in America. Then use this question as a starter, "Do the events that happened to Asian people in America during the pandemic relate to prejudice?" to analyze the reasons behind this phenomenon.

3. It's clear that no one will connect the Chinese to the famous movie *Titanic*, let alone the racism against Chinese people. However, *Titanic* should also be a movie about Chinese. *The Six* is a documentary that tells the unknown story of the six Chinese survivors of the eight Chinese passengers on board

Titanic. Through the work of the team of researchers—led by historian Steven Schwankert—the central mysteries of their story are revealed. Watch this documentary and answer the following questions. How did they survive the accident at such a high rate and, afterwards, why did they disappear from the history books so completely within 24 hours of arriving in the U.S.? While most of the 700 or so survivors of Titanic were warmly welcomed and treated in their home countries, and to this day are regularly covered in the press on Titanic anniversaries, the Chinese on Titanic were never interviewed, and never claimed by relatives, making their experience unique. Why is it so?

4. Stereotypes and prejudice are commonly seen topics in literature. Among them is *Monster* by Walter Dean Myers. The questions for discussion are as follows: What does O'Brien's assessment imply about the American justice system? Why do you think the book is called *Monster*?

Chapter 7

Identity

Learning Objectives

After learning this chapter, you should be able to:

1. understand the concepts of personal identity, social identity, and cultural identity;

2. know Henri Tajfel's social identity theory and the three stages of social identity awareness;

3. identify the three stages of the formation of cultural identity based on Jean S. Phinney's Three-Stage Model of Ethnic Identity Development;

4. provide examples of major types of cultural identity;

5. identify and employ strategies to tackle with identity threat and identity crisis.

How to define ourselves? Why do people like to look down on others in order to maintain their self-esteem? When entering a different culture/country, why would people encounter cultural identity crisis? To answer all of these questions, we have to know the concepts of personal identity, social identity, and cultural identity.

In this chapter, we will focus on the term "identity". What is identity? To talk about our identity, we try to answer the question, "Who am I?" Identity in terms of ethnicity, race, minority group status, gender, and sexual orientation is often contrasted with class consciousness—group self-awareness in terms of belonging to the same socioeconomic group. Some anthropologists write of the emergence of a new "identity" politics as distinct from an older "class" politics. This distinction sometimes suggests that people have to choose between uniting for social and political action primarily on the grounds of common membership in perceived ethnic, racial, minority, gender, sexual orientation, or environmental groups rather than on the grounds of membership in a similar socioeconomic group.

We have different kinds of identity: personal identity, national identity, social identity, cultural/racial identity, class identity, familial identity, gender identity, sexual identity, cultural identity, etc. All these identities are formed beyond our control, at least partly. This explains why some contemporary theories say that we have multiple identities and that our identities are split. Among those, personal identity, social identity, and cultural identity are the three heat-discussed ones.

7.1 Personal Identity

Out of all of these inter-related kinds of identities, we form our personal sense of identity. Usually, we loudly articulate and/or defend a certain kind of identity unless it is strongly related to our beliefs or unless it is threatened.

Personal identity can be defined as the persistent and continuous unity of the individual person normally attested by continuity of memory with present consciousness. Personal identity, in metaphysics, is the problem of the nature of a person's identity and its persistence through time (Gendler, 2009).

John Locke (1632–1704) was one of the greatest philosophers in Europe at the end of the 17th century. Locke grew up and lived through one of the most extraordinary centuries of English political and intellectual history. Locke's monumental *An Essay Concerning Human Understanding* (1689) is one of the first great defenses of modern empiricism and concerns itself with determining the limits of human understanding in respect to a wide spectrum of topics.

He discussed a problem that had not before received sustained attention: personal identity. Assuming one is the same person as the person who existed last week or the person who was born many years ago, what fact makes this so? Locke was careful to distinguish the notion of sameness of person from the related notions of sameness of body and sameness of man, or human being. Sameness of body requires identity of matter; sameness of human being depends on continuity of life; but sameness of person requires something else. Locke's proposal was that personal identity consists of continuity of consciousness. One is the same person as the person who existed last week or many years ago if one has memories of the earlier person's conscious experiences. Locke's account of personal identity became a standard and highly contested position in subsequent discussions.

Personal identity consists of those characteristics that set one apart from others in his or her in-group, those things that make one unique, and how one sees oneself. Cultural influences also come into play when we determine personal identity. People from individualistic cultures try to demonstrate their personal identity in their dress and appearance, while students of collectivistic cultures tend to wear the same brand shoes in a similar fashion because it is important to blend in.

Personal identity deals with philosophical questions that arise about ourselves by virtue of our being people. This contrasts with questions about ourselves that arise by virtue of our being living things, conscious beings, material objects, or the like. Many of these questions occur to nearly all of us now and again: What am I? When did I begin? What will happen to me when I die? Others are more difficult to understand. They have been discussed since the origins of Western philosophy, and most major figures have had something to say about them.

Outside of philosophy, "personal identity" usually refers to properties to which we feel a special sense of attachment or ownership. Someone's personal identity in this sense consists of those properties he or she takes to define him or her as a person or make him or her the person he or she is, and which distinguish him or her from others. The precise meaning of these phrases is hard to be defined clearly. To have an "identity crisis" is to become unsure of what one's most characteristic properties are —of what sort of person, in some deep and fundamental sense, one is. This "personal identity" contrasts with ethnic or national identity, which consists roughly of the ethnic group or nation that one takes oneself to belong to and to which one attaches great importance.

One's personal identity in this sense is contingent and temporary: The way a person defines himself or herself as a person might have been different, and can vary from one time to another. It could happen that being a philosopher and a parent belong to his or her identity, but not being a man and living in Yorkshire, while someone else has the same four properties but feels differently towards them, so that being a man and living in Yorkshire belong to his or her identity but not being a philosopher or a parent. And these attitudes are all subject to change.

Depending on how the term is defined, it may also be possible for a property to belong to someone's "identity" without him or her actually having it: If I become convinced that I am Napoleon, being an emperor could be one of the properties central to the way I define myself, and thus an element of my identity, even though my belief is false. The "Who am I?" question, sometimes called the characterization question, is what determines someone's personal identity in this sense.

Case Study: The Ship of Theseus

In this case, there are two questions you need to answer:

(1) Is there a paradox in the story of "The Ship of Theseus"? What is it?
(2) How can "The Ship of Theseus" help to solve the problem of who we are?

In ancient Greece, there was a legendary king named Theseus who supposedly founded the city of Athens. Since he fought many naval battles, the people of Athens dedicated a memorial in his honor by preserving his ship in the port. This "ship of Theseus" stayed there for hundreds of years. As time went on, some of the wooden planks of Theseus' ship started rotting away. To keep the ship nice and complete, the rotting planks were replaced with new planks made of the same material.

This is the original puzzle: Over the years, the Athenians replaced each plank in the original ship of Theseus as it decayed, thereby keeping it in good repair. Eventually, there was not a single plank left of the original ship. So, did the Athenians still have one and the same ship that used to belong to Theseus?

But we can liven it up a bit by considering two different, somewhat modernized, versions. On both versions, the replacing of the planks takes place while the ship is at sea. We are to imagine that Theseus sails away, and then systematically replaces each plank on board with a new one. He carries a complete supply of new parts on board as his cargo. Now we can consider these two versions of the story:

Simple version: Theseus completely rebuilds his ship, replaces all the parts, and throws the old ones overboard. Does he arrive on the same ship as the one he left on? Of course it has changed.

Complex version: Like the simple version, but with one addition—the Scavenger is following Theseus in another boat. He picks up the pieces Theseus throws overboard, and uses them to rebuild his boat. The Scavenger arrives in port in a ship composed of precisely the parts that compose the ship Theseus has used. He docks his ship right next to the one that Theseus docks.

Now we have: A = the ship on which Theseus started his voyage.

B = the ship created during the voyage and sailed into a port by Theseus.

C = the ship the Scavenger finished his voyage on.

Our problem is to sort out the identity (and non-identity) relations among A, B, and C. The only "obvious" fact is that B isn't C. After all, they are berthed side by side in the harbor, so they can hardly be one and the same ship. Beyond that, there are two alternatives.

The understanding of identity and persistence may require the Mereological Theory of Identity (MTI), i.e., the view that the identity of an object depends on the identity of its component parts. MTI tells us that A = C. The ship on which Theseus started his voyage, namely A, is identical to the ship on which the Scavenger finished his voyage, namely C. So we have two ships: one (A) that was sailed out by Theseus and (C) sailed in by the Scavenger, and another one (B) that was created (out of new parts) during the voyage and was sailed into port by Theseus.

The alternative is to abandon MTI and hold that A = B. On this account, we still have two ships, but their identity and non-identity relations are different: One ship (A) was sailed out by Theseus and (B) sailed in by Theseus, and another one (C) was created (out of used parts) during the voyage and was sailed into a port by the Scavenger.

Scholars tend to use the story "The Ship of Theseus" to further discuss the issue of personal identity.

The paradox was introduced in this Greek legend. The ship whereby Theseus and the youth of Athens returned from Crete (克利特岛) had thirty oars, and was preserved by the Athenians down even to the time of Demetrius Phalereus, for they took away the old planks as they decayed, putting in new and stronger timber in their places, in so much that this ship became a standing example among the philosophers,

for the logical question of things that grow; one side holding that the ship remained the same, and the other contending that it was not the same. Theseus' paradox is a thought experiment that raises the question of whether an object that has had all of its components replaced remains fundamentally the same object. It has a very simple yet similar idea of illusions like soul and identity which emerged in some of the complex systems (e.g., humans).

With the understanding of what "The Ship of Theseus" is about, it's time for us to think about how it can help us solve the problem of who we are. In a similar scenario as in the story of "The Ship of Theseus", a person is going from point A to point B and then things fall apart catastrophically on the way, yet he or she finally makes it here. So he or she can think: "Well, I'm who I was." This would be one kind of his or her identity, that is: "I'm the person I thought I was." If this way of thinking blows apart, then he or she is in a very terrible place and he or she may think: "Oh, I'm the sort of person who's in this terrible place." That's another form of his or her identity. And then he or she may think: "I'm not the old person or the person who was in the catastrophe, I'm the new person." But the problem is the new person can fall apart, too.

But then there's a third way of thinking. This is a better way of thinking. This person may hold the following thoughts: "I'm not this, or this, or this, I'm the process by which the transformation occurs. I know something, it's not quite right. It collapses, it causes trouble or the collapse, but I regroup, I learn, I regenerate, I put myself back together and it happens again and it happens again. But each time it happens, maybe, you're a little wiser, you're a little more put together."

Thus, according to the third way of thinking, our identity should be seen as an ongoing process. Rather than a static snapshot, we should embrace a flowing sense of self, whereby we are perpetually re-framing, re-organizing, re-thinking and re-considering ourselves.

7.2 Social Identity

Here's a common scenario in our daily life. Steven, a leading football player at school, and his team lost their football game and he felt very upset. He thought his team is better than his rival and could have won. Have you ever thought why people always think that their group is better than other groups? Social identity and its relative theories may give us some insights.

7.2.1 Understanding of Social Identity

Social identity is a person's sense of who they are based on their group memberships. Tajfel & Turner (1979) proposed that the groups (e.g., social class, family, football team, etc.) which people belonged to were an important source of pride and self-esteem. Groups give us a sense of social identity—a sense of belonging to the social world. We divide the world into "them" and "us" based upon a process of social categorization. We see the group to which we belong (the in-group) as being different from the others (the out-group), and members of the same group as being more similar than they are.

Henri Tajfel proposed that stereotyping is based on a normal cognitive process: the tendency to group things together. In doing so we tend to exaggerate both the differences between groups and the similarities of things in the same group. This is known as in-group (us) and out-group (them). The central hypothesis of social identity theory is that group members of an in-group will seek to find negative aspects of an out-group, thus enhancing their self-image (Tajfel, 1979).

Just as shown in Figure 7.1, people in the nation as the left ship belongs, come up with a bunch of positive words and expressions, to build up a good self-image. While, on the other hand, they take the other nation (as the right ship represents) as an out-group, using negative words to form a bad image of this out-group nation.

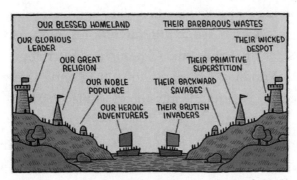

Figure 7.1   An Example of In-Group Bias (McLeod, 2019)

One's self-concept is a collection of beliefs about oneself that includes elements such as academic performance, gender roles, sexuality, and racial identity. Generally speaking, self-concept embodies the answer to "Who am I?" Self-esteem reflects a person's overall subjective emotional evaluation of his or her own worth. It is a judgment of oneself as well as an attitude towards the self. Self-esteem involves beliefs about oneself, such as "I am competent", "I am worthy", as well as emotional states like triumph, despair, pride, and shame (McDonald et al., 2012).

Prejudiced views between cultures may result in racism; in its extreme forms, racism may result in genocide, such as that occurred in Germany with the Jews, in Rwanda between the Hutus and Tutsis and, more recently, in the former Yugoslavia between the Bosnians and Serbs.

Social categorization is one explanation for prejudiced attitudes (i.e., "them" and "us" mentality) which leads to in-groups and out-groups.

7.2.2 Henri Tajfel and His Social Identity Theory

Have you ever wondered why we like to form and identify with a particular group? What kind of influence does our group membership have on our intergroup behavior? Why do we often favor those who are like "us" and discriminate against those who are not included with us?

Psychologists believe that intergroup behavior differs qualitatively from individual behavior. They have also done some very interesting experiments to explore such questions. One of the most famous ones is called the Minimal Group Paradigm, which, as its name suggests, explored the minimal conditions for discrimination based on group membership. In the experiment, people who joined the study were put randomly into groups invented by the experimenters. The "groups" have no real-life basis and participants did not know each other beyond their assigned group labels. Sometimes, they did not even meet or interact with each other at all. However, when asked to allocate rewards, most participants tended to favor those of the same artificially created group and discriminated against those of different groups. This finding of in-group favoritism and out-group discrimination led to the development of social identity theory (Tajfel, 1971; Tajfel, 1982; Tajfel & Turner, 1986).

Henri Tajfel was a British social psychologist, best known for his pioneering work on the cognitive aspects of prejudice and social identity theory. Tajfel and his student John Turner's social identity theory explains that part of a person's concept of self comes from the groups to which that person belongs. An individual does not have a personal self-hood, but multiple selves and identities associated with their affiliated groups.

Tajfel (1979) proposed that there are three mental processes involved in evaluating others as "us" or "them", namely, "in-group" and "out-group". An in-group is a social group to which a person psychologically identifies as being a member. By contrast, an out-group is a social group with which an individual does not identify. Thus, we have an "us" vs. "them" mentality when it comes to our in-groups and their respective out-groups. These take place in a particular order. The three mental processes are social categorization, social identification, and social comparison.

Social identity theory aims to specify and predict the circumstances under which individuals think of themselves as individuals or as group members. The theory also considers the consequences of personal and social identities for individual perceptions and group behavior.

7.2.3 Three Stages of Social Identity Awareness

Social identity theory explains that one derives esteem from a group that they positively identify with, therefore they favor it. They allocate more resources to the in-group to maximize the difference between their in-groups and out-groups in order to achieve such identifications. This is a psychological basis for "ethnocentrism", a common concept in intercultural communication.

The term "ethnocentricity" originated with William Sumner, after he observed people distinguish or discriminate between their in-groups and out-groups. Psychology tells us about the concepts of in-groups and out-groups, where one tends to agree with the beliefs and actions of one's in-group (such as one's race, religion, or ethnicity) and judge or have biased opinions about the out-groups (such as other religions or ethnicities).

Ethnocentricity refers to a belief that your culture or ethnic group is superior to others. Ethnocentric individuals are biased in that they draw conclusions about other cultural groups based on their own cultural values, norms, and traditions. Ethnocentric individuals use their own ethnic groups as the standard by which they judge other cultures. We tend to immediately judge other cultures as "bad" or "wrong" based upon their actions, if their values are not aligned with our own beliefs. Does this concept seem familiar to you? We all do it, sometime or other, mostly not even realizing that we're being ethnocentric at that moment.

Here's an example of ethnocentrism—Nazi Germany. This is one of the worst, most extreme, and most tragic examples of ethnocentrism. Hitler believed that Jews, as well as people belonging to some other communities were all inferior to his ethnicity, and did not deserve to live. He had thousands and thousands of innocent people slaughtered in concentration camps, only because they weren't of his "pure" race, which was, according to him, superior among all. Though ethnocentrism is not

always this extreme, history does tell us stories about how the concept and prejudice that arose from it, took such a turn for the worse, and had horrible consequences.

Ethnocentrism might seem similar to ethnic pride, which is having pride for one's culture and values, but there is a very fine line separating the two. Ethnocentrism is a widely observed belief that one's own ethnic group is superior to other ethnic groups. This process of favoring one's in-group happens in three stages: social categorization, social identification, and social comparison, as mentioned earlier, and their concepts will be explained in details as follows.

1. Social Categorization

The first is social categorization. We categorize objects in order to understand and identify them. In a very similar way, we categorize people (including ourselves) in order to understand the social environment. We use social categories like the black, white, Australian, Christian, Muslim, student, bus driver, etc. because they are useful.

If we can assign people to a category, it tells us things about those people. Similarly, we find out things about ourselves by knowing what categories we belong to. We define appropriate behavior by reference to the norms of groups we belong to, but we only do this when we can tell who belongs to our group. An individual can belong to many different groups.

Categorization is the idea that humans all categorize each other, sometimes subconsciously, creating a set of natural groups. Describing someone as a woman, a business person, a wheel chair user, and so forth is creating a series of categories. These categories play into personal identity and the perception of the identities of others. Personal identification with a specific group and the development of an in-group mentality is also involved.

2. Social Identification

In the second stage, social identification, we adopt the identity of the group we have categorized ourselves as belonging to. If, for example, we have categorized ourselves as students, the chances are that we will adopt the identity of a student and begin to act in the ways we believe students act (and conform to the norms of the group). There will be an emotional significance to our identification with a group, and our self-esteem will become bound up with group membership.

One interesting thing to note is that people can be part of multiple groups, and the part of their identity that is most dominant can change, depending on which group they are associating with. For example, a Chinese man who belongs to a professional organization of surgeons may feel that the nationality part of his identity is dominant when he is among other Chinese people, confirming his in-group identity, and that the surgeon aspect of his identity is dominant when he is among other surgeons or in the hospital.

3. Social Comparison

The final stage is social comparison. Once we have categorized ourselves as part of a group and have identified with that group, we then tend to compare that group with other groups. If our self-esteem is to be maintained, our group needs to compare favorably with other groups.

Comparison is also a key part of social identity theory. Once people have categorized themselves and others, they can start to compare themselves. People generally want to create favorable comparisons that make their own groups appear superior. This plays into psychological distinctiveness, the desire to be unique within a group identity, and to be viewed positively when compared with others. The Chinese surgeon, for example, may derive self-esteem from the knowledge when he is compared with a surgical nurse; he may be viewed as superior because of his more advanced job title.

Figure 7.2 will help us better understand the basic ideas of social identity theory.

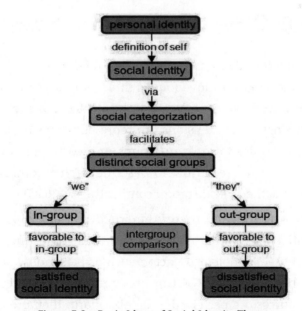

Figure 7.2   Basic Ideas of Social Identity Theory

Social identity theory is widely cited for providing a basis for how we perceive

and interact within and across groups. Hopefully these theoretical ideas help us in practice to better consider some of our own identity responses in certain contexts.

Just to reiterate, in social identity theory, the group membership is not something foreign or artificial which is attached onto the person; it is a real, true and vital part of the person. It is critical to understanding prejudice, because once two groups identify themselves as rivals, they are forced to compete in order for the members to maintain their self-esteem. Competition and hostility between groups are thus not only a matter of competing for resources like jobs but also the result of competing identities.

Again, it is crucial to remember in-groups are groups we identify with, and out-groups are ones that we don't identify with, and may discriminate against. A social identity is the portion of an individual's self-concept derived from perceived membership in a relevant social group. To put it simply, it is people's sense of who they are based on their group membership. People always put themselves in a social group, especially introducing themselves or asking others who they are. For example, you would introduce yourself like this, "Hi, I'm Lucy, and I am a college student." Or we may hear others introduce themselves like this, "I am a teacher", "I am a banker", etc.

7.2.4 Realistic Group Conflict Theory: Intergroup Conflict

Between the borders of Pakistan and India lies a fertile valley known as Kashmir. Since 1947, India and Pakistan have fought three wars over this valuable territory. Unfortunately, the wars have contributed to hostilities and prejudice experienced by people on both sides. These tensions are representations of intergroup conflict. As learned above, attitudes towards in-groups and corresponding out-groups are negatively reciprocally related. How to describe such intergroup conflicts and tensions? The answer is the realistic group conflict theory (RGCT).

RGCT is a well-established theory emerged in the 1960s to describe how perceived competition for limited resources can lead to hostility between groups. Unlike theories that use psychological factors such as personality or value differences to explain conflict and prejudice, RGCT focuses on situational forces outside the self. When valuable resources are perceived to be abundant, then groups cooperate and exist in harmony. However, if valuable resources are perceived as scarce (regardless of whether they truly are), then these groups enter into competition, and antagonism ensues between them. The resources in question can be physical (such as land, food, or water) or psychological (such as status, prestige, or power).

With the belief that competition exists for hostile feelings and discriminatory needs, one group may put the belief into action in their behavior. For example, if ethnic group A believes that members of ethnic group B pose a threat to them by "stealing jobs", then regardless of whether this is true, ethnic group A will feel resentment and hostility. The extent to which ethnic group A holds any power to follow through on its hostile feelings determines if unfair or discriminatory behavior toward ethnic group B will occur. At the very least, negative stereotypes about the other group will be created and mistrust and avoidance will result. How long and how severe the conflict will become is determined by the perceived value and scarcity of the resource in question. (Tajfel & Turner, 1986)

RGCT is unique because it does not discuss any personal features of the individuals engaged in the conflict. Other psychological theories use personality factors (such as authoritarianism) or ideologies (such as social dominance orientation) to explain why these hostilities exist. In RGCT, if individuals in a group believe that the two groups share a zero-sum fate, meaning that the other group's success feels like a failure or loss for one's own group, then no matter what outside group members say or do, feelings of resentment and discriminatory behavior will result. As the conflict unfolds, the members of each group will close ranks with their fellow members and will come to believe that their fate is connected with each other. (Jackson, 1993)

Case Study: Robbers Cave Experiment

Try to analyze this case with the knowledge you have just learned. Here are some questions that may be helpful.

(1) Did this experiment support Muzafer Sherif's idea that intergroup conflict occurs when two groups are in competition for limited resources?

(2) How did this experiment demonstrate the realistic group conflict theory?

In the mid-1950's Muzafer Sherif and others carried out the Robbers Cave Experiment on intergroup conflict and cooperation as a part of research program at the University of Oklahoma. The field experiment involved two groups of twelve-year-old boys at Robber's Cave State Park, Oklahoma, America. The twenty-two

boys in the study were unknown to each other and all from white middle-class backgrounds. They all shared a Protestant, two-parent background. The boys were randomly divided by the researchers into two groups, with efforts being made to balance the physical, mental, and social talents of the groups. Neither group was aware of the other's existence.

Phase 1: In-group Formation (5–6 Days)

The members of each group got to know one other, social norms developed, leadership and group structure emerged. At the camp, the groups were kept separate from each other and were encouraged to bond as two individual groups through the pursuit of common goals that required cooperative discussion, planning, and execution. During this first phase, the groups did not know of the other group's existence. The boys developed an attachment to their groups throughout the first week of the camp, quickly establishing their own cultures and group norms, by doing various activities together like hiking, swimming, etc. The boys chose names for their groups, The Eagles and The Rattlers, and stenciled them onto shirts and flags.

Phase 2: Group Conflict (4–5 Days)

The new-formed groups came into contact with each other, competing in games and challenges, and competing for control of territory. Sherif now arranged the "competition stage" where friction between the groups was to occur over the next 4–6 days. In this phase it was intended to bring the two groups into competition with each other in conditions that would create frustration between them. A series of competitive activities (e.g. baseball, tug-of-war, etc.) were arranged with a trophy being awarded on the basis of accumulated team score. There were also individual prizes for the winning group such as a medal and a multi-bladed pocket knife with no consolation prizes being given to the "losers". The Rattlers' reaction to the informal announcement of a series of contests was absolute confidence in their victory. They spent the day talking about the contests and making improvements on the ball field, which they took over as their own to such an extent that they spoke of putting a "Keep Off" sign there. They ended up putting their Rattler flag on the pitch. At this time, several Rattlers made threatening remarks about what they would do if anybody from The Eagles bothered their flag.

Situations were also devised whereby one group gained at the expense of the other. For example, one group was delayed getting to a picnic and when they arrived the other group had eaten their food. At first, this prejudice was only verbally expressed, such as taunting or name-calling. As the competition went on, this expression took a more direct route. The Eagles burned the Rattlers' flag. Then the next day, the Rattlers' ransacked The Eagles' cabin, overturned beds, and stole private property. The groups became so aggressive with each other that the researchers had to physically separate them. During the subsequent two-day cooling off period, the boys listed features of the two groups. The boys tended to characterize their own in-group in very favorable terms, and the other out-group in very unfavorable terms. Keep in mind that the participants in this study were well-adjusted boys, not street gang members. This study clearly shows that conflict between groups can trigger prejudice attitudes and discriminatory behavior. This experiment confirmed Sherif's realistic conflict theory.

Phase 3: Conflict Resolution (6–7 Days)

Sherif and his colleagues tried various means of reducing the animosity and low-level violence between the groups. They now arranged for the introduction of a number of scenarios presenting superordinate goals which could not be easily ignored by members of the two antagonistic groups, but the attainment of which was beyond the resources and efforts of one group alone. These scenarios were played out at a new location in the belief that this would tend to inhibit recall of grievances that had been experienced at Robbers Cave.

Typical Cases

(1) The Drinking Water Problem

The first superordinate goal to be introduced concerned a common resource used by both groups. Their water supply had suddenly stopped flowing. All of the drinking water in the camp came from a reservoir on the mountain north of the camp. The water supply had failed and the camp staff blamed this on "vandals". Upon investigations of the extensive water lines by the Eagles and the Rattlers as separate groups, they discovered that an outlet faucet had a sack stuffed into it. Almost all the boys gathered around the faucet to try to clear it. Suggestions from members of both groups concerning effective ways to unblock the obstruction were thrown in from all sides simultaneously which led to cooperative efforts clearing the obstacle itself. The joint work on the faucet lasted over 45 minutes. When the water finally came on there was common rejoicing. The Rattlers did not object to having the Eagles get ahead of them when they all got a drink, as the Eagles did not have canteens with them and were thirstier. No protests or "Ladies first" type of remarks were made.

(2) The Problem of Securing a Movie

The next superordinate goal to be introduced was a favorite feature-length movie for boys of their age. Two movies had been chosen in consultation with children's movie experts and brought to the camp along with other stimulus materials. In the

afternoon, the boys were called together and the staff suggested the possibility of watching either "Treasure Island" or "Kidnapped": Both groups yelled approval of these movies. After some discussion, one Rattler said, "Everyone that wants Treasure Island raise their hands." The majority of members in both groups gave enthusiastic approval to "Treasure Island" even though a few dissensions were expressed to this choice. Then the staff announced that securing the movie would cost $15 and the camp could not pay the whole sum. After much discussion it was suggested that both groups would pay $3.50 and the camp would pay the balance. This was accepted even though, as a couple of homesick Eagles had gone home, the contribution per person per group was unequal.

At supper that night there were no objections to eating together. Some scuffling and sticking chewing gum on each other occurred between members of the two groups, but it involved fewer boys on both sides than were usually involved in such encounters. Other problem-solving superordinate goals introduced in this phase included the joint use of a tug-of-war rope, and both groups of boys "accidentally" came across a stuck-in-a-rut truck that was carrying food for both groups. In the event the joint pursuit of such superordinate goals saw a lessening of intergroup conflict. At breakfast and lunch on the last day of camp, the seating arrangements were considerably mixed up insofar as group membership was concerned.

(3) Critical Evaluation

Sherif is credited as one of the most important social psychologists of his time and he argued that intergroup conflict (i.e., conflict between groups) occurs when two groups are in competition for limited resources. His idea is supported by evidence from the Robbers Cave Experiment. In the second phase of the study, the boys were introduced to the other group and were required to engage in a series of competitive activities. Rewards and prizes were handed out to the winning team. Sherif and his colleagues purposely set up these games and rewards so that the boys would have reason to compete intensely. (Tajfel, 1981)

This experiment is also a demonstration of the realistic group conflict theory. In the 2-week experiment involving white, middle-class, 12-year-old boys at a summer camp, the boys, at first, interacted only with their own group members because Sherif wanted them to develop a sense of group identity. The boys did develop a group identity and called themselves the Eagles or the Rattlers. In the second phase of the study, the boys engaged in a series of competitive activities. During these fierce competitions, both groups became suspicious of and hostile toward one another. As tensions increased, the boys demonstrated allegiance to their group by discouraging one another from establishing friendship across group lines. No one wanted to be seen as a traitor, so the boys stuck to their own groups. Hostility increased to the point that physical fights and acts of vandalism broke out. Despite direct interventions by adults, the two groups could not seem to reconcile. (Tajfel et al., 1971)

As time went, unity was restored only when Sherif and his colleagues created situations requiring both groups of boys to depend on each other to achieve important goals equally valued by both groups. In other words, harmony was restored when both groups were equally invested in achieving a goal that required everyone's help and cooperation in tasks like solving the drinking water problem and the problem of securing a movie. After completing a series of such tasks requiring interaction and everyone's involvement, positive behavior toward the other group members increased. The boys began to behave more like individuals rather than group members and formed friendship across group lines. Psychologically, they began as two distinct groups, but when the perception of threat was replaced by cooperation and interdependence, the groups reestablished themselves as one large group. Therefore, the group distinctions made between Eagles and Rattlers disappeared and everyone felt as if they belonged to the same group. (Jackson, 1993)

7.2.5 Identity Threat

According to social identity theory, group members may experience different kinds of identity threats. Group-status threat occurs when the perceived competence of the group is devalued. Group members may also experience various forms of social identity threats, one of which takes place when the moral behavior of their group is called into question. The latter form of threat is sometimes experienced even by group members who can in no way be held personally accountable for their group's behavior, for citizens of a certain country may feel guilty or shameful for crimes committed by their country long before they were born.

Group members can also experience social identity threat when they think that their group is not sufficiently acknowledged as a separate entity with unique characteristics. Such group-distinctiveness threat is experienced when different groups of people are included in larger, more inclusive groups, nations, or organizations, such as members of linguistic minorities who strive for political autonomy or workers in a small company that is taken over in an organizational merger. In addition, categorization threat occurs when individuals are treated as

group members at times when they would prefer not to be, as when a woman who is a lawyer is addressed in court on the basis of her gender instead of her profession. Acceptance threat occurs when individuals fail to gain acceptance and inclusion in the groups of which they consider themselves members, such as when a manager of Asian descent is not invited to join a local Asian business club.

To cope with identity threat, group members will respond differently depending on the degree to which they identify with the group. In addition to the perceived characteristics of the social structure (and the opportunities and restrictions implied), the psychological significance of group membership and the loyalty and commitment to the group and its members also determine how people cope with identity threat.

Case Study: Emily in Paris

Try to analyze this case with the knowledge you have just learned. Here are some questions that may be helpful:

(1) How will you illustrate Emily's French colleagues?
(2) Was Emily well accepted by her French colleagues?
(3) Did the differences between Emily and her French colleagues spark tensions?

Emily in Paris became Netflix's biggest comedy series of the year, with 58 million households sampling the freshman series during the first month of its debut in 2020. This comedy series follows Emily (Lily Collins), an American 20-something from Chicago, who is hired by a marketing firm, based in Paris, to provide the company with an American perspective on things. The series centers around the career challenges she faces, the new friends she meets, and the ups-and-downs of her love life.

After Emily made her way to report to the company, she was humiliated. First, the receptionist pretended that he didn't understand her English. Then she was satirized by her supervisor that she couldn't speak French. Finally, the CEO pointed out with a smile that he didn't think they French had anything to learn from Americans. They didn't value her as an asset to the company.

On her first official workday, Emily got up early and went to work. But she waited downstairs for two hours before a colleague slowly appeared on his bicycle.

Emily: I arrived here at 8:30 a.m.! Where were you?

Colleague: We start to work at 10:30 a.m.

When her supervisor stepped in the office on her high-heeled shoes, Emily looked at her clock and it was 11:15 a.m.! Emily was very excited to share her new ideas with Patricia, the head of new media publicity, and hoped she would accept her ideas, but Patricia was extremely resistant and ran away from her. At noon, Emily invited her colleagues to have lunch together, and they refused her for various reasons. So she went to the park alone and ate a sandwich on the bench. Later, on her way back to the company, she found all her colleagues eating and chatting in the restaurant. When they came back to the company, they called her face to face a hillbilly.

After work, one nice colleague ran into her and couldn't help inculcating her not to work so hard, because they French only work to enjoy life instead of living to work.

The series presents "Frenchness" as a national identity that is very much stereotyped and essentialized. This notion of national identity contradicts our contemporary idea of a globalized and multicultural world. Emily is sent to give an American point of view in a luxury marketing firm, but she can't speak French and struggles to get along with her colleagues as she attempts to adjust their French culture to the American way. She is confronted with mean Parisians（巴黎人）, aggressively flirtatious Frenchmen, lazy and smoking colleagues, and many more stereotypical characters.

Emily is very dedicated to her job and her every move is career-oriented. She is also considered rude for not being able to interact with others in French language and in French way of being. When she describes this to her French colleague, he answers with "you live to work; we work to live". This puts an essentialized version of American culture in opposition to the French one. Clearly, Emily wasn't welcomed and accepted by her French colleagues. They isolated her and were mean to her. They thought of her as the out-group and were reluctant to accept anything from Emily and American culture. There's tension between Emily and her French colleagues. They refused to talk to her about her marketing proposals. They isolated her from their lunch party. They even called her in an impolite way. Thus, cultural identity differences do spark tensions. There are more examples in history, for example, in early America, Caucasians and Africans co-existed in owner-slave relationships where Africans were viewed as uncivilized. World War II involved the Holocaust where Nazi troops killed over 6 million Jewish people because the Germans felt they were "racially superior". Both instances involved racial and cultural identities, an issue that exists in many communities and nations today.

7.3 Cultural Identity

Humans are complex creatures, whose identities include gender, religion, race, age, geographical orientation, and ethnic or cultural identification. In fact, many Americans are currently living multicultural lives in the 21st century.

7.3.1 Definition of Cultural Identity

In an increasingly diverse society and interconnected global world, awareness of cultural identity is essential to effective cross-cultural communication. Maintaining one's cultural identity and values in a changing and multicultural world requires both awareness and effort. Also, understanding and celebrating cultural identity can boost pride and self-esteem.

Then, what's cultural identity? To talk about identity, we try to answer the question: Who am I? We all might have asked the same questions to ourselves at a certain time. Identity consists roughly of those attributes that make one unique as an individual and different from others. Or it is the way one sees or defines oneself. Cultural identity is bureaucratic or self-ascribed membership in a specific culture. Cultural identity is the identity or feeling of belonging to a group. It is part of a person's self-conception and self-perception and is related to nationality, ethnicity, religion, social class, generation, locality, or any kind of social group that has its own distinct culture.

In this way, cultural identity is both the characteristic of the individual and the culturally identical group of members sharing the same cultural identity. Cultural identity can be expressed through certain styles of clothing or other aesthetic markers. Every culture has a particular style of dress. For example, Indian women wear sari. Dhoti and kurta is supposed to be the native Indian dress for men. How people wear their hair can also be an indicator of their cultural identity. As you can see from the long-haired Zeus (2nd century AD), in ancient Greece, long male hair was a symbol of wealth and power, while a shaven head was appropriate for a slave. Historically, East Asian cultures viewed long hair as a sign of youth and aesthetic beauty. The types of food people eat can also indicate their identity. For example, tribes that are gatherers mainly look for natural food sources. Hunters bring meat to the table. Ethnic groups that live along the coast may gain the majority of their nutrients from seafood. For example, the seafaring Bajau, commonly called "sea gypsies" living in the waters surrounding Indonesia, Malaysia, and the Philippines, make their living from fishing.

People's cultural identity is multifaceted because they are all of many overlapping communities. They may be the speakers of one native language or citizens of the same city. They may be members of the same sports teams, churches or political groups. They may also be fellow students of one same university or co-workers of the same profession or occupation, etc.

Cultural identity is important in intercultural communication, because there are cultural differences in the structures of expectations to identity. Each community implies certain types of culture which might be shared with other members and which communicators must seek to infer as they interact. Just as how Chinese and American people interpret the color red, when people from different cultures come in contact, if one perceives himself or herself in one way, and the people with whom he or she interacts perceive him or her in another way, serious problems can arise.

Case Study: *The Guasha Treatment*

Try to analyze this case with the knowledge you have just learned. Here are some questions that may be helpful:

(1) The misunderstanding obviously comes from the Americans' understanding of *Guasha*. What's their interpretation of *Guasha*?

(2) How can you identify the characters' cultural identities? Are they the same to each other?

(3) What do you think we should do to avoid such problems in cross-cultural communication when participants are empowered with different cultural identities?

The Guasha Treatment is a Chinese movie released in 2001, which is about cultural conflicts experienced by a Chinese family in the U.S. The Chinese immigrant, Xu Datong succeeded in his career after many years of struggle in America. However, an incident changed his happy life. Datong's father gave a simple Chinese medicine therapy called Guasha to his grandson, Dennis, which left bruise marks on his skin and the American doctor mistook it as child abuse behavior. The Children Welfare Bureau started a lawsuit about the behavior of Dennis' father and took action to protect Dennis. In the court, Datong lost his

mind and he finally lost custody of his son. The family went through hell when the child was taken away by the child protection agency. Meanwhile, the grandfather left America because he found that the living environment was really not suitable for him, as he felt that a simple, harmless treatment like *Guasha*, which was so common in China, was treated as child abuse in America. Furthermore, he could not communicate in English. Finally, with joint efforts, the child was able to return home and the family was reunited.

This movie exhibits an episode of a Chinese immigrant family's life in America. With the notion and misunderstanding of *Guasha* in America, the movie uncovers the conflicts and later the understanding of Chinese and Western cultures, indicating the trend of cultural clash and integration. The Americans consider *Guasha* as abuse rather than a medical therapy.

The main character Xu Datong's father represents typical Chinese identity in the movie. He treats little Dennis with *Guasha* when Dennis gets sick, which foreshadows the following conflict between the two cultures. The social worker Margaret represents typical American identity. The bruise left by *Guasha* is thought by them as a proof of abuse, which conforms to the American thinking pattern of evidence first. Datong represents the image of Chinese immigrants in America who tried hard to integrate into American life. At first, he identifies himself as an American when he receives the award. However, the rooted Chinese culture influences his behavior and thought subconsciously. Datong's cultural identity as a Chinese has been varied, and the hybrid of cultural identities eventually brings him harsh cultural conflicts.

In a word, not accepting cultural identities, people would create limited worldviews and perceptions of others (Tisdell et al., 2001). According to Tisdell & Tolliver (2003), cultural identity development can help people withstand oppression and be motivated to support social transformation. In the movie, Datong's boss and friend Mr. Quinlan went to the Chinatown and experienced *Guasha* himself and helped to get Denis back. So, one of the ways to work toward understanding cultural identity is to ask and answer questions instead of shying away from issues.

7.3.2 Major Types of Cultural Identities

We want to point out that one actually consists of multiple identities. As the situation varies, we may choose to emphasize one or more of our identities. For instance, at work, our occupational and organizational identity is paramount, but when visiting our parents, we are first a son or a daughter. As we have indicated, identity is dynamic and multifaceted. In this section we will examine a few of our many identities and illustrate how culture influences each.

1. Ethnic Identity

Ethnicity or ethnic identity is derived from a sense of shared descent, history, traditions, values, similar behavior, area of origin, and in some instances, language. A shared language constitutes an additional dimension of its ethnic identity. For example, the Roma (or Gypsies), who speak Romany, scattered across Eastern and Western Europe.

In the U.S. the ethnicity of many Americans is tied to their ancestors' home of origin before immigrating to the United States, such as Germany, Italy, Mexico, China, or other places. Generations subsequent to the original immigrants often refer to themselves using linguistic terms such as "German-American", "Italian-American", "Mexican-American" or "Chinese-American". The hyphen both separates and connects the two cultural traditions.

Also, in the United States, immigrants often grouped together in a particular region to form ethnic communities, such as Chinatown in San Francisco and Little Italy in New York. Those with a Euro-American descent, who are members of the U.S. dominant culture, will often simply refer to themselves as "just Americans" or even "white Americans" .

2. Gender Identity

Gender identity is quite different from biological sex or sexual identity. Gender is a socially constructed concept that refers to how a particular culture differentiates masculine and feminine social roles. For instance, the appearance of American men in the 1960s and 1970s was characterized by long hair, often with beards or mustaches.

Language is another means of expressing gender differences. In Japanese, certain words are traditionally used exclusively by women, while men employ entirely different words to express the same meaning.

A culture's gender norms can also influence career decisions. For instance, males make up less than 6% of nurses in the United States. Why? This disparity is because most people consider nursing to be a woman's career.

3. National Identity

It refers to nationality, which the majority of people associate with the nation

where they were born. But national identity can also be acquired by immigration and naturalization.

People who have taken citizenship in a country different from their birthplace may eventually begin to adopt some or all aspects of a new national identity, depending on the strength of their attachment to their new homeland. People who have been living permanently in another nation may retain a strong connection to their homeland.

As we can see, national identity usually becomes more pronounced when people are away from their home country. Just as when asked where they are from, international travelers normally respond with their national identity—e.g., "We are from Canada." Strong feelings of national identity are often on display at international sporting events, such as the World Cup or the Olympics.

4. Regional Identity

With the exception of very small nations like Andorra (安道尔), Lichtenstein (列支敦士登), or Monaco (摩纳哥), every country can be divided into a number of different geographical regions, and often those regions reflect varying cultural traits.

The cultural contrasts among these regions may be manifested through ethnicity, language, accents, dialects, customs, food, dress, or different historical and political legacies. Residents of these regions use one or more of those characteristics to demonstrate their regional identity.

Although the total population of Belgium is just over 10 million, the country has three official languages—Dutch, French, and German. In the United States, residents of Alaska, California, and Texas offer prime examples of pride in regional identity. Another example, political division resulting from war has imposed different national identities on residents of the Democratic People's Republic of Korea and South Korea and divided regional identities.

5. Organizational Identity

In some cultures, a person's organizational affiliation can be an important source of identity. This is especially true in collectivistic cultures, but far less so in individualistic cultures.

For example, Mrs. Suzuki, an employee at the Tokyo Bank, would be introduced as " 私は東京銀行 (ぎんこう) の鈴木です " (I'm Suzuki from Tokyo Bank). In Japan, a person's organizational identity is so important that during introductions the company's name is given before the individual's name.

While in the United States, an individual is introduced first by his or her name, followed by the organization, like "I'm John from Facebook." These two examples offer insight into how collective cultures stress identity through group membership, and individualistic cultures emphasize individual identity.

6. Cyber and Fantasy Identity

The Internet allows individuals to construct cyber or virtual identities that are very different from their actual identities. Fantasy identity, which also extends across cultures, centers on characters from science fiction movies, comic books, and anime.

This will definitely draw our attention to cosplay, a popular practice nowadays among youngsters. It's a contraction of the words "costume" and "play", and simply means the practice of dressing up as a character from a movie, book, or video game, especially one from the Japanese genre of manga and anime. Every year people attend domestic and international conventions devoted to these subjects.

7.3.3 Formation of Cultural Identity: Jean S. Phinney's Three-Stage Model of Ethnic Identity Development

As we all know, a range of cultural complexities structure the way individuals operate with the cultural realities in their lives.

Cultural identities are influenced by several different factors such as one's religion, ancestry, skin color, language, class, education, profession, skill, family, and political attitudes. All these factors contribute to the development of one's identity.

Although the formation of cultural identity is a complex process, it develops in a pattern process. Jean S. Phinney's three-stage model of ethnic identity development is a widely accepted view of the formation of cultural identity. In this model, cultural identity is often developed through a three-stage process: unexamined cultural identity, cultural identity search, and cultural identity achievement.

Stage 1: The Unexamined Cultural Identity Stage

During the first stage, the unexamined cultural identity stage, one's cultural characteristics are taken for granted, and consequently there is little interest in exploring cultural issues.

Young children, for instance, typically lack an awareness of cultural differences and the distinguishing characteristics that differentiate one culture from another. As

children grow older, however, they become mindful of categories and who belongs to a particular culture. Parents, the media, social memberships, and other sources play a role in helping individuals understand what is meant by cultural identity.

Also, some people may not have explored the meanings and consequences of their cultural membership but may simply have accepted preconceived ideas about it that were obtained from parents, the community, the mass media and others. As a result, some individuals may unquestioningly accept the prevailing stereotypes held by others and may internalize common stereotypes of their own culture and of themselves.

Scholars have suggested that the cultural identities of many European Americans, in particular, have remained largely unexamined, which is a consequence of the power, centrality and privilege that the European American cultural group has had in the United States.

Examples of thoughts in this stage are listed below. A European American exclaims, "I don't have a culture. I'm just an American." A Mexican American puts, "My parents tell me about where they lived, but what do I care? I've never lived there." And an African American says, "Why do I have to learn who the first black woman was to do this or that? I'm just not too interested."

Stage 2: The Cultural Identity Search Stage

The second stage, cultural identity search stage, involves the process of exploration and questioning about one's culture in order to learn more about it and to understand the implications of membership in that culture.

By exploring the culture, individuals can learn about its strengths and may come to a point of acceptance both of their culture and of themselves. For some individuals, a turning point or crucial event precipitates this stage, whereas for others it just begins with a growing awareness of other cultures and reinterpretation of everyday experiences.

This stage is characterized by growing awareness in social and political forums and a desire to learn more about culture. Such learning may be characterized by an increased degree of talking with family and friends about descent, visiting museums, reading of relevant cultural sources, enrolling in school courses, or attendance at cultural events. This stage might have an emotional component, of varying intensity, which involves tension, anger, and perhaps even outrage directed toward other groups.

Here are more examples of thoughts in this stage. A Mexican American says, "I want to know what we do and how our culture is different from others." A Japanese

American puts, "There are a lot of non-Japanese people around me, and it gets pretty confusing to try and decide who I am." An African American exclaims, "I think people should know what black people had to go through to get to know where we are now."

Stage 3: The Cultural Identity Achievement Stage

Then it comes to the third stage, cultural identity achievement stage. This stage competes the whole process of cultural identity formation. It's characterized by a clear, confident acceptance of oneself and an internalization of one's cultural identity.

People in this stage have developed ways of dealing with stereotypes and discrimination so that they do not internalize others' negative perceptions and are clear about the personal meanings of their culture. This usually leads to an increase in self-confidence and positive psychological adjustment.

We'll certainly also list some examples of thoughts in this stage to further explain it. Let's look at the following words. A Japanese American says, "My culture is important and I am proud of what I am. Japanese people have so much to offer." An African American puts in this way, "It used to be confusing to me, but it's clear now. I am happy being black."

Case Study: *Fresh Off the Boat*

Fresh Off the Boat is an American sitcom created by Nahnatchka Khan which was debuted from ABC on February 4, 2015 and concluded on February 21, 2020. The story is based on the memoir of the same name by Eddie Huang. It is set in the 1990s and revolves around Eddie and his family that moves to suburban Orlando. After moving to Orlando from Washing, D.C.'s Chinatown, 11 years old, hip-hop loving Eddie and his immigrant family experience culture shock in this comedy about pursuing the American Dream. It talks about a man who struggles to gain a sense of cultural identity while raising his kids in a predominantly white, upper-middle-class neighborhood. *Fresh Off the Boat* struggles with a great many issues that Asians have had to face, and continue to face today. The common repeating theme in *Fresh Off the Boat* is the struggle that immigrant families go through when they move to America.

The Huang family consists of five members: Louis the father, Jessica the mother and their three sons who are Eddie the eldest and his two younger brothers, Emery

and Evan. In one of the episodes, Marvin, one of their white neighbors, pointed out that he often forgot they were Chinese. Jessica observed just how far their family had changed to fit in with their whitewashed surroundings as she finally became close with her neighbors and Louis considered joining a country club. The conflict of this episode revolved around the Huang family's appreciation of the American culture that they had assimilated into, including both the luxury and the leisure of life in the middle class, against Jessica's desire to reconnect with the Chinese culture that had defined both her and Louis' work ethics. As Louis began to enjoy his visits to the country club both for its luxury and for its business opportunity, he and other family members began to resist Jessica's push to maintain Chinese culture.

Jessica was very concerned, so she began to make changes at home, for instance, making Chinese food, speaking Mandarin, and instilling Chinese culture into her children, asking them to examine their Chinese identity. However, the children obviously didn't want to do so. The eldest son refused to be an ambassador to show China and Chinese culture on World Culture Day at school. Instead, he wanted to join the Jamaican culture exhibition group. Jessica sent them to a Chinese school after class to learn Chinese. The children were at a loss. Eddie especially resisted learning Chinese while his two younger brothers just wanted to do well to please their mother and put their homework on the refrigerator to show off at home. Just when their mother was about to give up, Eddie was irritated by one of his classmates who made fun of China on World Culture Day at school, and safeguarded China and Chinese culture by educating his classmates about China. As a result, he failed to complete his task of Jamaican culture exhibition and got an F. But his mother was proud of him and posted his failing report card on the refrigerator at home.

After reading and watching this series, here are some questions for you:

- Did the three boys care about their Chinese root?
- What did their mom Jessica do to remind of their awareness of Chinese identity?
- Why did Jessica put Eddie's World Culture Day report on the refrigerator even if he got an F?
- Can you analyze the formation of Eddie's cultural identity based on Jean S. Phinney's three-stage model of ethnic identity development?

While the perceived benefits of assimilating into white culture are displayed extensively throughout the show, like social acceptance, business success, and less judgment received from white neighbors, the Huangs have to constantly battle within themselves to determine their identity in a rapidly globalizing world today. During the episode, clearly, the three boys didn't care about their Chinese root at the beginning, particularly Eddie, the eldest one. However, at last, a significant change can be viewed on Eddie for he started to defend Chinese culture. His two little brothers showed urge in learning Chinese language mainly to please their mom. Thus, no self-motivation in searching their cultural identity can be sensed from these two.

Jessica came to the realization that they had assimilated so far into American culture that their kids were starting to lose perspective of the ancestral culture that they came from. Jessica's epiphany compounded through several events: Marvin's mentioning that they seem like an average American family to him, Evan's requesting to know how to say "Can you say that in English" in Mandarin, and the fact that she cooked mac and cheese with bacon bits for dinner.

There's a significant change on Eddie. He defended China and grew cultural awareness of his Chinese root. That made Jessica very proud of him. It's highly possible that she put his report up on the refrigerator as a reminder of the whole family about their cultural identity and about who they are.

During the first stage, the unexamined cultural identity stage, one's cultural characteristics are taken for granted, and consequently there is little interest in exploring cultural issues. The three boys typically lack an awareness of their Chinese cultural root. Also, some people may not have explored the meanings and consequences of their cultural membership but may simply have accepted preconceived ideas about it that were obtained from parents, the community, the mass media, and others. Examples of thoughts in this stage are listed below. "My parents tell me about where they lived, but what do I care? I've never lived there." "Why do I have to learn the language? I'm just not too interested." Thus, it's clear that Eddie was in this stage at the beginning. The second stage, the cultural identity search stage, involves the process of exploration and questioning about one's culture in order to learn more about it and to understand the implications of membership in that culture. This stage might have an emotional component of varying intensity, which involves tension, anger, and perhaps even outrage directed toward other groups. Eddie got angry when his teammates started to mess about China and stood up to it defending Chinese culture. Thus, Eddie moved to the second stage afterwards.

Summary

People's identities identify who they are, what they are like, their social connections, and the groups to which they belong. For example, if Steve tells others that he's a white male social psychologist living in England who is married with two sons and a granddaughter and plays drums in a faculty garage band, all these racial, gender, occupational, relational, and group identities tell others a lot about himself. In addition to reflecting who we are and where we plug into the world, our identities influence our behavior and our reactions to events. We filter what happens through the lens of our identities—so our identities determine what's important to us and what we pay attention to. And they also guide our behavior and emotions.

As illustrated, an individual may have different kinds of identity, like personal identity, national identity, social identity, racial identity, class identity, familial identity, gender identity, cultural identity, etc. Among those, personal identity, social identity, and cultural identity are the three heat-discussed ones. Personal identity deals with philosophical questions that arise about ourselves by virtue of our being people (or, as lawyers and philosophers like to say, persons). This contrasts with questions about ourselves that arise by virtue of our being living things, conscious beings, material objects, or the like. Many of these questions occur to nearly all of us now and again: What am I? When did I begin? What will happen to me when I die? They have been discussed since the origins of Western philosophy (Olson, 2003).

Social identity relates to how we identify ourselves in relation to others according to what we have in common. Social identity can provide people with a sense of self-esteem and a framework for socializing, and it can influence their behavior. In addition to how you view yourself, social identity also influences how other people treat you. People form a cultural identity when they subconsciously interpret and incorporate signals from the world around them into their own identity so they can belong. Therefore, a person's cultural identity is a critical piece of his or her personal identity (and worldview) that develops as he or she absorbs, interprets, and adopts (or rejects) the beliefs, values, behavior, and norms of the communities in his or her life. Our cultural identity can evolve, as culture is ever-evolving and dynamic (Wilson, 2018). The Jean S. Phinney's three-stage model of ethnic identity development is a widely accepted view of the formation of cultural identity, in which cultural identity is often developed through three stages: unexamined cultural identity, cultural identity search, and cultural identity achievement.

Although people's identities serve important functions, they also create a slew of problems (Marilynn, 1999). One problem is people's identities usually reflect ways in which they differ from other people. Every time one thinks of some part of his or her identity, he or she implicitly distinguishes himself or herself from others (Turner, 1975). If a person's identity includes being religious, a marathon runner, or a cattle rancher, those identities reflect a difference between them and other people who are not religious, runners, or ranchers. Then, the in-group and out-group come into being (Sherif & Sherif, 1953). People may allocate more resources to the in-group to maximize the difference between their in-group and out-groups in order to achieve such identifications. This is a psychological basis for "ethnocentrism", which is a widely observed belief that one's own ethnic group is superior to other ethnic groups (Sherif, 1966). This process of favoring one's in-group happens in the following three stages: social categorization, social identification, and social comparison. The realistic group conflict theory describes how perceived competition for limited resources can lead to hostility between groups, focusing on situational forces outside the self (Leary, 2019).

Exercises

Questions for Review

1.   What are the aspects that personal identity covers/studies?

2.   Can you name the scholar who has done a great contribution to the study of social identity?

3.   What are the characteristics of three stages discussed in social identity?

4.   Can you briefly describe the possible situations in which people may encounter identity threat?

5.   What are the aspects that cultural identity covers/studies?

6.   Cultural identity can be presented in different aspects and can be captured in different real-life scenarios. Can you list some examples of various types of cultural identities?

7.   Can you provide examples to further explain the characteristics of each stage in ethnic identity development?

Problems and Application

1. A person's identity is shaped by many different aspects. Family, culture, friends, personal interests, and surrounding environments are all factors that tend to help shape a person's identity. Please draw a mind-map to illustrate your personal identity.

2. While the world is struggling to control COVID-19, China has managed to control the pandemic rapidly and effectively. Summarize what China's identities are presented in combating the pandemic.

3. Globalization has made it very easy for people to learn and practice other peoples' culture and traditions. Multiculturalism is one of the effects of globalization. However, some people argue that it wipes out the uniqueness and difference between various cultures. It makes great cities like Paris, New York, or London look and feel exactly the same. It makes biracial and multi-racial people struggle in defining their cultural identities. Analyze the reasons why these people are struggling with their identities, and then give some feasible and practicable solutions.

Chapter *8*

Globalization and Global Citizenship

Learning Objectives

After learning this chapter, you should be able to:

1. understand the concept of globalization and global citizenship;

2. know three aspects of globalization as well as their benefits and drawbacks;

3. know the content of global citizenship education;

4. understand themes, outlooks, and skills needed for global citizenship.

In the past, most human beings were born, lived, and died within a limited geographical area, never encountering people of other cultural backgrounds. Such an existence, however, no longer prevails in the world. The wheel of human history has moved us forward from isolation to integration. It is very easy to find situations in which members of once isolated groups of people have to communicate with others of different cultural groups. An increasing number of companies expand their operations beyond national borders. Internationalization will involve locating new facilities in countries that provide a cheap labor force and preferential tax treatment. Entrepreneurs can no longer afford to simply communicate well within their own cultures. The influence of globalization and cross-cultural interaction in recent years has influenced the types of communication skills needed in many ways. People nowadays need to understand the impact of culture on manners of speaking and body language, the necessity of long-distance cooperation, and how to use modern technology to communicate with people on the other side of the Earth. Understanding the impact of globalization can help us to think about intercultural communication more deeply.

Before we start this chapter, there are some questions for you:

(1) Have you ever been to any foreign restaurants? What do you know about it?

(2) Have you ever seen the movie *Kung Fu Panda*? What is the most impressive part for you? Do you like it? Why or why not?

8.1 Globalization

8.1.1 Overview of Globalization

Two thousand years ago, the trade routes of the Silk Road carried merchants, goods and travelers from China through Central Asia and the Middle East to Europe and represented the wave of globalization. Nowadays, the influence of globalization can be experienced by simply walking down our "local" high street, where "local" goods and services are displayed alongside "global" goods and services. We encounter the "globe" in the clothes we wear, the music we listen to, the television programs and movies we watch, and the Internet sites we visit.

The term "globalization" comes from the word "globalize", meaning the emergence of an international network of economic systems. From its earliest usages in the 1930s to its popularity in the 1980s, globalization has aroused heated discussion over its definition.

1. Definition of Globalization

Globalization is the process of international integration arising from the interchange of world views, products, ideas and other aspects of culture. Humans have interacted over long distances for thousands of years. Philosophy, religion, language, arts, and other aspects of culture spread and mix as nations exchange products and ideas. In both the 15th and 16th centuries, Europeans made important discoveries in their exploration of the oceans, including the start of transatlantic travel to the "New World" of the Americas. Global movement of people, goods, and ideas expanded significantly in the following centuries. Early in the 19th century, the development of new forms of transportation (such as the steamship and railroads) and telecommunications that "compressed" time and space, allowed for increasingly rapid rates of global interchange. In the 20th century, road vehicles, intermodal transport, and airlines made transportation even faster. The coming of electronic communications, most notably mobile phones and the Internet, connected billions of people in new ways. The International Monetary Fund (IMF) identified four basic aspects of globalization: trade and transactions, capital and investment movements, migration and movement of people, and the dissemination of knowledge. Further, environmental challenges such as global warming, cross-boundary water and air pollution, and over-fishing of the ocean are linked with globalization. Globalizing processes affect and are affected by business and work organization, economies, socio-cultural resources, and the natural environment. Understanding globalization and the phenomena of globalization in our daily life enables us to be rational consumers, responsible citizens, and critical individuals.

2. Three-Tiered Conception of Globalization

According to Angela W. Little (1996), globalization is a three-tiered concept (as shown in Figure 8.1), including economic globalization, political globalization and cultural globalization, in which economic globalization is the base and core, political globalization is the reaction of economic globalization at the political or governmental level, while cultural globalization is the byproduct of economic globalization.

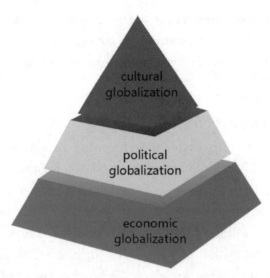

Figure 8.1　Three-Tiered Conception of Globalization (Little, 1996)

For Your Information

Angela W. Little and Three-Tiered Conception of Globalization

The three-tiered conception of globalization is put forward by Angela W. Little in "Globalization and Educational Research: Whose Context Counts?" which is published in *International Journal of Educational Development*. This paper relates contemporary educational research to processes of globalization. It points out that while the activity of educational research is essentially cultural, its production is also economic.

Angela W. Little is Professor Emerita at the Institute of Education, University of London where she held the Chair of Education and International Development between 1987 and 2010. She was previously a fellow of the Institute of Development Studies at the University of Sussex. Throughout her career she has combined academic and professional work and has collaborated with many universities, bilateral and multinational agencies and national education ministries.

She is the author and editor of ten books, seven special issues of journals, book chapters, journal articles and reports on the themes of education for all, globalization and education, pedagogy, multigrade teaching, assessment and qualifications and the political economy of education reform. She has directed twelve comparative research projects in countries across Africa, Asia, Europe and Latin America, supervised thirty-four research students to successful completion of their doctorates, and written and directed two movies. She is a fellow of the Academy of Social Sciences.

In recent years, with the increasing attention of countries around the world to global ecological problems, there is also a voice to enlarge the dimensions of globalization. Someone argues that there are four dimensions of globalization: economic, political, cultural and ecological. Ecological globalization covers population growth, access to food, worldwide reduction in biodiversity, human-induced climate change and global environmental degradation.

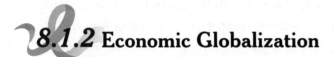

8.1.2 Economic Globalization

1. Definition of Economic Globalization

According to Joshi (2009), economic globalization is the increasing economic integration and interdependence of national, regional, and local economies across the world through an intensification of cross-border movement of goods, services, technologies and capital. To put it simply, it's the world's money being spread around as goods, products, and technology that are sent from one country to another. Economic globalization is the reason why one can go to the local superstore and buy products from all over the world. For example, people in Europe and Africa can also buy products made in China.

International commodity markets, labor markets, and capital markets make up economic globalization. Economic globalization is a worldwide phenomenon. One popular activity under globalization is international trade, in which products and services are exchanged between or among nations. Many allied countries supply resources to each other that the other countries do not have. These resources can cover imported products, technology, and even human labor. Many countries that have abundant natural resources rely on this trading system to market their unique local products and, in turn, improve their economic state. Thus countries' economic situations can depend significantly on other countries. International trade has been practiced for centuries, as evidenced by the Silk Road that connects Asia and Europe for trading purposes.

The spread of multinational corporations such as McDonald's has accompanied the rise of economic globalization. These corporations have a headquarter in one country, but have offices or factories in various other countries. That's the reason why intercultural communication is so important in business context.

2. Impact of Economic Globalization

Economic globalization has both advantages and disadvantages. Advocates said that the phenomenon increases a country's productivity with increased job opportunities and possible higher salaries. This can lead to economic growth and a higher standard of living. The reliance of countries on each other has also led to better chances of international peace. It has also paved the way for cultural awareness and understanding, largely through the help of technology. Economic growth accelerated and poverty declined globally with the process of globalization. India and Bangladesh, once among the poorest countries in the world, have greatly narrowed inequality because of their economic expansion ratio due to globalization. Globalization increases market, trade and investment potential as well as resource accessibility of firms. It has become easier for firms to outsource their production to different locations to gain benefits from location advantage. Firms are able to reach out and serve many new untapped markets around the globe. Liberal movements of financial and human capital also facilitate their business transactions.

One negative result is that natural resources are depleted at a faster rate, since the demand of raw materials has increased among many countries. Although globalization enhances a firm's market opportunities, it also increases the amount and level of competition faced by such firms. Firms operating at different levels—domestic, regional, international and global—are now competing against one another.

All in all, the trend of economic globalization is a double-edged sword. It brought not only opportunities but also challenges to each country. Whether economic globalization has positive or adverse effects, no one can doubt the phenomenon's influence and impact on today's global development. We should keep pace with this tendency and maximize our development as possible as we can.

With 40 years of reform and opening up, China has gone through dramatic changes to become the world's second-largest economy. China is the world's largest manufacturer and trader of goods and has the largest foreign exchange reserves. China's destiny has never been tied so closely with the world's fate. President Xi Jinping expressed the view of anti-protectionism in his keynote speech at the World

Economic Forum in Davos in January 2017. Xi's strong defense of globalization and free trade is vastly supported around the world. This is just one example to prove that China's development and changes help maintain and boost economic globalization.

 8.1.3 Political Globalization

1. Definition of Political Globalization

According to Steger (2003), political globalization refers to the intensification and expansion of political interrelations across the globe. It is the reaction of economic globalization at the political or governmental level. It is when governmental action takes place at a global level, where responsibilities, such as the welfare of citizens and economic growth, are acted upon by an international political body. In the past, governments typically served the citizens of their own nations, but now, the world is much more globally connected, which means politics often takes place in a globally connected setting. Political globalization is mainly manifested in two aspects: Politics from one country goes to the world and world politics shows multi-polarization.

The former refers to the fact that politics from one country goes to the world and has close link to international politics. Domestic politics has to obey the international politics.

The latter means that since the end of World War Ⅱ, the world's political structure has changed. Multi-polarization is developing forward continuously and a number of political entities have appeared, such as the European Union (EU), the Association of Southeast Asian Nations (ASEAN), the African Union, etc.

There are many examples of political globalization, like the EU, where political integration makes multiple nations together. Because the nations of the world have become much more connected, there is a growing prevalence of intergovernmental agencies, like the IMF, WTO and the UN. Political activity has transcended the old barriers of national divisions, where global agencies, international organizations and worldwide political movements have become much more common. The new challenges of global warming, social inequality, and terrorism are further indicators of how globalized politics may be integral to the shaping of future international policies.

2. Impact of Political Globalization

The advantages of political globalization can be concluded as follows.

Firstly, political globalization deepens international dependency between countries, making the political interference, especially armed intervention increasingly unpopular internationally, and it is favorable to achieve peace. Secondly, political globalization deepens the ties between countries. The heads of states often have some political friendly visits, which led to the rapid development of economic and cultural industries, and this is an important opportunity for developing countries. Thirdly, some common political values and political systems are valued by people, and common political rules have increasingly become truly international. Therefore, the various political systems tend towards democratization, legalization, and modernization.

Although the political exchanges between the countries continue to strengthen and the political system continues to innovate, there are still some Western developed capitalist countries trying to put the majority of developing countries into the political system in order to maintain a dominant position in the world. Hegemonism (霸权主义) and power politics interfere other countries' internal affairs, and stir up political trouble.

8.1.4 Cultural Globalization

1. Definition of Cultural Globalization

Cultural globalization is the byproduct of economic globalization. According to James (2006), it refers to the transmission of ideas, meanings and values around the world in such a way as to extend and intensify social relations. Cultural globalization began in the Era of Discovery during the 16th century. The processes of commodity exchange carry cultural meanings around the globe. For example, the expeditions of early European explorers introduced potato into Europe from South America, which had profound effects on the European diet. This process is marked by the common consumption of cultures that has been spread by the Internet, popular culture media, and international travel. Decade by decade, telephones, radio, jet air travel, and television media spread information around the world with increasing efficiency. By the end of the century, the Internet had made it possible for ordinary people on opposite sides of the Earth to connect instantly and cheaply, whether for the purpose of conducting business or for personal communication.

Pop entertainment culture is the best example of cultural globalization. Young people in Moscow dance in ways that are similar to those in Reykjavik and Tokyo. Japanese animations are watched in Chicago, and Mexican soap operas are enjoyed by viewers in Manila. The newest release of a musical group can spread worldwide quickly through a variety of video sharing websites; celebrity personalities achieve global pop icon status through the same means. It is easier than ever before for people from different cultures to find common interests. Foremost among cultural globalization's proponents is big business, since the more culture becomes globalized, the easier it is for businesses to sell their products in other countries. Certain goods, such as soft drinks or portable electronics, are sold all over the world. Many brand names are just as famous in Madras (former name of Chennai) as in New York. Economic globalization goes together with cultural globalization, and it is sometimes pointed out that cultural globalization is more commercial-driven than country-driven.

Kung Fu Panda is a typical example of cultural globalization by mass media. It was produced by DreamWorks Animation and distributed by Paramount Pictures. The movie became DreamWorks' biggest opening for a non-sequel movie, the highest grossing animated movie of the year worldwide. It was also well received in China. It made nearly ¥110 million by July 2, 2008, becoming the first animated movie to make more than ¥100 million in Chinese box offices. The accurate positioning, clever ideas, colorful animation, and professional operation contribute to its popularity. But the most important is that the cartoon integrated the Chinese cultural elements into Western spirits successfully.

2. Two Perspectives of Cultural Globalization

There are two perspectives of cultural globalization: One is hybridization, and the other homogenization. From the first view, cultural globalization is a long-term historical process of bringing different cultures into interrelation. Religious movements were among the earliest cultural forces to globalize. Christianity, Islam, and Buddhism have taken root and influenced local cultures in places far from their origins. It was the rapid technological developments of the 20th century that speeded up the process greatly, and which really caused people to begin taking globalization as a broad concept. Hybridization is one of the most important cultural aspects of America, a region long known as the "new continent". The mixture is such that it is impossible to take the region and its people as anything less than a hybrid of different cultures.

To understand hybridization better, we will take *Kung Fu Panda* again as

an example. In this movie, American culture and Chinese culture are perfectly integrated. Po, a giant panda, is a Kung Fu fanatic who idolizes the Furious Five, living in a daydream all day. But when he is accidentally chosen by Master Oogway to become the Dragon Warrior and has the opportunity to realize his dream, he has to face himself truely. Master Shifu did everything he could to force the panda to quit, but Po did not give up. At last, he made great progress and defeated Tai Lung to become a real Dragon Warrior. The touching inspirational story actually is a typical one about American dream. That is, everyone has his or her own potential. As long as you work hard, you can achieve prosperity. The concepts of "the chosen one" and individual heroism also come from American culture. At the same time, there are many Chinese elements in the movie, such as acupuncture, firework, Chinese lantern, kite, writing brush, chopsticks, and so on. Furthermore, many lines also reflect Chinese wisdom, especially the lines of Master Oogway. This represents the inner peace which Taoism admires very much.

An alternative perspective on cultural globalization emphasizes the transfiguration of worldwide diversity into a pandemic of Westernized consumer culture, that is, homogenization. Some critics argue that the dominance of Western culture influencing the entire world will ultimately result in the end of cultural diversity. This process, understood as cultural imperialism, is associated with the destruction of cultural identities, dominated by a homogenized and Westernized consumer culture. Today, with the development of technology and information, the growth of the mass media industry has largely influenced individuals and societies across the globe. Since the 1930s, Hollywood has aimed at the holy position of the movie and television industry. Now, with the accelerating process of globalization, the movie industry in all around the world is developing rapidly, like Bollywood in India and many studio cities in China.

Although it's beneficial in some ways, this increased accessibility may affect negatively a society's individuality. With information being so easily distributed throughout the world, cultural meanings, values, and tastes face the risk of becoming homogenized. As a result, the strength of identity of individuals and societies may be weakened. For example, sushi is available in Germany as well as in Japan, potentially reducing the demand for "authentic" French pastry.

3. Impact of Cultural Globalization

The ultimate consequence of cultural globalization is a world that seems smaller, and in which interactions take place more rapidly. The new widespread cultural awareness could help reduce bigotry and discrimination, and might even smooth international relations as a whole. At the same time, it may also bring destructive effects. The critics of cultural globalization often argue against its destructive effects on national identities. They warn that unique cultural entities may vanish, and those languages spoken by small populations could be at an increased risk of extinction. The specific values, traditions, and history—the identity—of a culture could disappear. They fear the threat of dominant, industrialized cultures overtaking and replacing indigenous ones, silencing new and different ideas.

We should look at it objectively with an open and analytic mind. All in all, cultural globalization has benefits as well as drawbacks. As the largest developing country in the world, China will be influenced profoundly by this trend. Steak, salad, and many Western foods have swept the country. Going to Western restaurants becomes a fashion. But at the same time, dumplings and noodles from China are holding more and more people's appetite in Western countries. Cultural globalization more or less enriches our life by not only broadening our horizons but also providing a way for intercultural communication. People no longer need to travel abroad in order to experience other countries' life with the foreign arts as well as commodities surrounding them. There are both opportunities and challenges for China. The positive aspects mean that cultural globalization provides the opportunity for China to introduce the foreign advanced culture. At the same time, Chinese culture will walk into the world. The government has already taken steps in promoting the traditional Chinese culture, one of which is that more than 100 Confucius Institutes have been set up abroad to showcase China's cultural heritage. Moreover, more and more young people start to make short videos about Chinese traditional culture and China's development on Tiktok or YouTube. In this way, they take part in the activities to preserve and promote Chinese culture, which has contributed to a sense of national unity and pride.

The past 40 years have proved that the reform and opening up is the only path that China should have traveled. Now the second decade of the century is over and China is already capable of helping other developing countries in the world, which is the very embodiment of economic globalization and its cultural significance. China is a responsible big country by any standard. We are taking the global responsibilities and aiding other developing countries based on our own development standard and competence. All in all, China's development and success are based on the trend of globalization and will reinforce the trend as well.

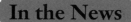

In the News

Applause for China's Generous Vision Is Heard Around the World

The Belt and Road Initiative (BRI) has been welcomed and supported by the world's major emerging and industrial economies, as well as by international organizations, which sent high-profile representatives to the two-day Belt and Road Forum for International Cooperation in Beijing.

The forum, which concluded on Monday, hosted representatives from more than 130 countries, which together account for more than two-thirds of the world's population and 90% of global GDP.

Expected to help promote the common prosperity of the international community, the forum was supported by both developing and emerging countries, as well as the leading industrial developed economies, or G7 (Group of Seven).

Representatives from Brazil, Russia, India and South Africa—the BRICS organization—as well as other emerging economies, such as Indonesia, Mexico, and Türkiye, attended the forum.

Russian President Vladimir Putin said the China-led Belt and Road Initiative was timely, as it promises to boost economic cooperation and exchanges.

Italian Prime Minister Paolo Gentiloni said the initiative was perhaps the most important modern infrastructure project underway in the world today.

"Bringing the Chinese economy closer through this gigantic infrastructure operation is enormously interesting to Italy," Gentiloni said.

The United States sent a delegation led by Matt Pottinger, special assistant to the president and senior director for Asia at the U.S. National Security Council. White House spokesman Sean Spicer said on Friday that the Belt and Road "is a major trade initiative" and "we're going to continue to work with them".

Toshihiro Nikai, secretary-general of Japan's ruling Liberal Democratic Party, led the Japanese delegation.

British Chancellor of the Exchequer Philip Hammond, the special envoy of Prime Minister Theresa May, and German Minister for Economics and Energy

Brigitte Zypries, the special envoy of Chancellor Angela Merkel, attended the forum.

"Britain stands ready to work with all participating countries to make the Belt and Road a success," Hammond said.

Former French Prime Minister Jean-Pierre Raffarin, the special envoy of the president, said during the forum that President Emmanuel Macron supports the initiative as an effective way to solve the world's myriad problems.

"Macron wants to send the message to China that he supports the initiative. France is very interested in the initiative, which will develop Eurasia," Raffarin said.

Heads of major international organizations, such as the United Nations, the World Bank and International Monetary Fund, were also present at the event.

Peter Thomson, president of the UN General Assembly, said the Belt and Road Initiative brings enormous benefits to all countries involved and serves as a major drive of the global transformation emerging with the UN 2030 Agenda for Sustainable Development.

World Bank President Jim Yong Kim said the initiative is a "most remarkable" drive to fulfill the aspirations of people in less-developed regions that are in dire need of investment.

IMF Managing Director Christine Lagarde said the initiative adds new economic flavors by creating infrastructure projects based on 21st-century expertise and governance standards.

Roberto Azevedo, director-general of the World Trade Organization, said the initiative will help build an infrastructure network that facilitates trade. "Infrastructure is essential. Lack of a proper transportation network is at the top of the trade cost list, and the Belt and Road is hugely important in responding to this need."

Case Study: The Belt and Road Initiative

Read the following passage and try to answer the questions:

(1) What are the benefits of the Belt and Road Initiative?

(2) What is the significance of the Belt and Road Initiative to the whole world?

The Belt and Road Initiative—China's proposal to build a Silk Road Economic Belt and a 21st Century Maritime Silk Road in cooperation with related countries—was unveiled by Chinese President Xi Jinping during his visits to Central and Southeast Asia in September and October 2013. The initiative focuses on promoting policy coordination, connectivity of infrastructure and facilities, unimpeded trade, financial integration, and closer people-to-people ties through a consultative process and joint efforts, with the goal of bringing benefits to all.

The initiative covers primarily East Asia, Southeast Asia, South Asia, West Asia, Central Asia, and Central and Eastern Europe. It reflects a convergence of interests and an increasing need for regional and global cooperation. The response from these countries has been enthusiastic.

The Belt and Road Initiative has driven new advances in opening up. By the end of 2018, China had signed more than 150 cooperation agreements with 106 countries and 29 international organizations from Asia, Europe, Africa, Latin America and the Caribbean, and South Pacific, and carried out industrial cooperation projects with more than 30 countries. The UN General Assembly and Security Council have made reference to the initiative in some of their resolutions. General Assembly resolution 2344, for instance, called on the international community to increase regional economic cooperation through the Belt and Road Initiative.

The Belt and Road Initiative is China's original form for global development, which is based on the concept of each country contributing to the "common destiny of all nations" and mankind's "shared future". By focusing on "global connectivity" through massive investments in infrastructure, linking China to the rest of the world through its land and maritime Silk Road, China has presented the world with a new model for development—in effect, redefining globalization. The initiative is China's contribution to a new kind of co-existence and sustainable development, and an alternative to the old-style Western globalization. The initiative operates across economic, political, cultural, social, and ecological sectors, while being based on a firm communications infrastructure.

In the political sphere, enhancing policy coordination is regarded as a guarantee for implementing the initiative. Policy coordination seeks to identify and expand shared interests, enhance mutual political trust, reach new cooperation consensus, and integrate economic development strategies and policies. This would be achieved by inter-governmental cooperation through a multi-level inter-governmental macro policy exchange and communication mechanisms. Moreover, political cooperation, in the form of policy coordination, plays an important part in all other areas such as trade policies, investment policies, and financial policies.

In social and cultural area, the Belt and Road Initiative emphasizes developing people-to-people bond and cultural exchange, including extensive cultural and academic exchanges, personnel exchanges and cooperation, media cooperation, youth and women exchanges and volunteer services.

In the economic area, the document lists three main goals and relevant policies. The first is to facilitate connectivity, which mainly means the connectivity of infrastructure constructions, including international trunk passageways, infrastructure network connecting all sub-regions in Asia, and between Asia, Europe and Africa, low-carbon infrastructure and other energy infrastructure. Moreover, the proposal also emphasizes the connectivity of technical standard systems, which is an important institution for global interconnectedness.

The second economic priority is unimpeded trade and investment. Investment and trade are two means by which the people in different parts of the world are connected. The Belt and Road Initiative also seeks to facilitate investment and trade by removing investment and trade barriers, including by opening free trade areas, enhancing customs cooperation, improving bilateral and multilateral cooperation, implementing WTO Trade Facilitation Agreement, improving customs clearance capability, improving the coordination of cross-border supervision procedures, lowering non-tariff barriers, speeding up investment facilitation, expanding mutual investment areas, deepening investment in agriculture, forestry, manufacturing and emerging industries, and so on.

The third economic goal is to promote financial integration, including the deepening of financial cooperation, the building of a currency stability system, an investment and financing system and a credit information system.

Even though the Belt and Road Initiative is a strategic action launched by the Chinese government, it has global influence; its contents are consistent with the structural tendencies of the globalization process, and its mechanisms have taken into account of the concerns, interests, actions and interactions of multiple agents at multiple spheres and levels. It is not just a regional policy, but a global strategy, whose potential impact on global economy cannot be overlooked.

The Belt and Road initiative has opened a new chapter in the history of China's all-round opening up. Focusing on connectivity in the fields of policy communication, infrastructure connectivity, unimpeded trade, monetary circulation and understanding between peoples, the initiative marks China's fundamental transformation from being a mere participant to a shaper of globalization, and that the situation is changing from one where China opens up to the outside world, to one where the world opens itself to China.

Moreover, through the connectivity among Europe, Africa, and Asia, this initiative will revive hinterland and marine civilizations, help developing countries shake off poverty, and promote the sustained and successful rise of emerging countries, so as to rectify the traditional logic of globalization.

Now it's your turn to analyze another case. Try to think about what opportunities and challenges Chinese fast food chain "Kung Fu" will meet in the background of economic globalization.

Kung Fu Catering Management Co., Ltd., established in 1994, currently possesses over 300 restaurants as the Chinese fast food chain with most restaurants and the biggest size.

In recent years, locally branded fast food chains are making an impromptu resurgence. Rather surprisingly, given what a huge hit Western chains were when they first opened in China, the passion for McDonald's is beginning to wane and some KFCs are even closing down. But fast food fans need not fear, as the Kung Fu chain is quickly taking up the slack. Kung Fu, which opened its first branch in 1994, now operates 90 restaurants in Guangdong, 300 across China, and hopes to become the top Chinese fast food chain in the country within 5 years. Relying heavily on the Bruce Lee brand, the menu consists of steamed dishes with fresh ingredients and simple seasoning, such as pork ribs with soybean sauce, chicken with mushroom, beef with pickled vegetable, etc., all priced between ¥22 and ¥29. The restaurant chain believes that a Cantonese-style steamed meal is a healthier alternative for customers.

8.2 Global Citizenship

With the growing trend of globalization, citizens all over the world are more likely to live in one extended family. Easterners or Westerners, young or old, male or female, should contribute to its harmonious construction and development.

8.2.1 Definition of Global Citizenship

The term "citizenship" refers to an identity between a person and a city, state, or nation and his or her right to work, live, and participate politically in a particular geographic area. When combined with the term "global", it typically defines a person who places a "global community" above his or her identity as a citizen of a particular nation or place.

The ideas include the following:

- One's identity goes beyond geography or political borders.
- The human community on the Earth is interdependent.
- Humankind is essentially one.

The idea is that one's identity transcends geography or political borders and that responsibilities or rights can be derived from membership in a broader class: "humanity".

This does not mean that such a person denounces or gives up his or her nationality or other local identities, but such identities are given "second place" to their membership in a global community (Israel, 2012). The term has been used in education and political philosophy and has enjoyed popular use in social movements such as the "World Citizen" movements. The famous scientist Albert Einstein described himself as a world citizen and supported the idea throughout his life.

An interesting feature of globalization is that, while the world is being internationalized, it's also being localized at the same time. The world shrinks as the local community (village, town, city) takes on greater and greater importance. This is reflected in the term "glocalization", a combination of the words "global" and "local". If this trend is true, it seems global citizens may be the glue that holds separate entities together. Put it another way, global citizens are people who can travel within these various boundaries and somehow still make sense of the world through a global lens.

8.2.2 Core Themes of Global Citizenship

There are five core themes of global citizenship, which can help us understand it more deeply.

1. Fairness and Equality

All people are created equal and all should have an equal opportunity to succeed. Social fairness and equality are the interests of all aspects. People's internal contradiction should be correctly handled. Social fairness and equality

should be protected and realized. Everyone wants to get the maximum benefits. At this time, the society needs a standard which we follow to ensure everyone has access to the benefits—this is the rule. Only to ensure that the various members of the society have equal opportunities can we maintain social stability. Therefore, fairness and equality are the foundation on which the development of our society depends.

2. Rights and Responsibilities

Rights are legal, social, or ethical principles of freedom or entitlement; that is, rights are the fundamental normative rules about what is allowed of people or owed to people. According to some legal systems, they are social conventions or ethical theory. Rights are of essential importance in such disciplines as law and ethics, especially theories of justice. Responsibilities here refer to social responsibilities. Social responsibility is an ethical framework and suggests that an entity, whether an organization or individual, has an obligation to act for the benefit of the society at large. Social responsibility is a duty every individual has to perform so as to maintain a balance between the economy and the ecosystems.

3. Conflict and Peace

Although in the modern world, peace and development have become two major themes, religious conflicts or local wars still exist. The war brought us hunger, death, poverty, and made our society decay, so we should avoid war and defend our peace.

4. Sustainable Living

Sustainable living is a lifestyle that attempts to reduce an individual's or society's use of the Earth's natural resources and personal resources. Practitioners of sustainable living often attempt to reduce their carbon footprint by changing methods of transportation, energy consumption, and diet. Proponents of sustainable living aim to conduct their lives in ways that are consistent with sustainability, in natural balance and respectful of humanity's symbiotic relationship with the Earth's natural ecology and cycles.

5. Identity and Belonging

In the previous chapters, we have known that an identity is who or what a person or thing is. It is a self-representation of our interests, relationships, social activity and much more. Our sense of identity and belonging is impacted by various factors, including our experiences, relationships, and environment. Discovering our identity is a challenging journey, for identity is never static. Everyone struggles with his or her identity. Others only see our true identity when we are confident with ourselves.

Our identity determines where we belong. It is difficult to possess a sense of belonging when we are unsure of our own identity. Everyone needs a sense of belonging.

8.2.3 Outlooks of Global Citizenship

The themes mentioned above decide that we should adopt the following outlooks of global citizenship: open to new ideas; commitment to justice, peace, rights, responsibilities, and sustainability; desire to make a difference; positive sense of identity; sense of interdependence.

Studies of the psychological roots of global citizenship have found that people high in global citizenship are also high in the personality traits of openness to experience and agreeableness from the big five personality traits and high in empathy and caring. Oppositely, the authoritarian personality and mental illness are all associated with less global human identification. Some of these traits are influenced by heredity as well as by early experiences, which, in turn, are likely to influence individuals' receptiveness to global human identification.

Not surprisingly, those who are high in global human identification are less prejudiced toward many groups, and care more about international human rights, worldwide inequality, global poverty, and human suffering. They attend more actively to global concerns, value the lives of all human beings more equally, and give more in time and money to international humanitarian causes. They tend to be more politically liberal on both domestic and international issues. They want their countries to do more to alleviate global suffering.

Following a social identity approach, some scholars tested a model showing the outcomes of global citizenship identification. It includes six broad categories of prosocial behavior and values, including intergroup empathy, valuing diversity, social justice, environmental sustainability, intergroup helping, and responsibility to act.

8.2.4 Skills Needed for Global Citizenship

Basically, there are eight skills that a global citizen should have: critical

thinking, communicating, taking action, collaborating, creative thinking, conflict resolution, empathy, and self-awareness. We should do more social practice and experience different cultures to improve these skills.

To be a qualified global citizen means to think and act on global terms. As the hope and backbone of the country, contemporary Chinese college students should always bear in mind issues of common concern, such as energy crisis, environment pollution, global warming, terrorism, etc. Actions speak louder than words. Qualified global citizens will take action in their daily life by using recyclable materials, saving water, electricity and other natural resources, and respecting other people and their values. Only when we share responsibility, care about and collaborate with each other, can we realize our dreams and live harmoniously as global citizens.

In the News

This App Plants Trees When People Make Lower-Carbon Choices

What if you could turn a good deed into a new tree? An award-winning mobile app game from China does just that, and is responsible for more than 120 million trees being planted in some of the country's most arid regions. Since its launch in 2016, over half a billion people have used Ant Forest to convert lower-carbon activities such as using public transport into real trees. The game is helping China lead the way in re-greening the planet and is serving as a model for tree-planting schemes elsewhere.

The Ant Forest Model

"Ant Forest taps into the best of human ingenuity and innovation to create a better world," says Inger Andersen, Executive Director of the United Nations Environment Program—which in 2019 gave the project the UN's top environmental award.

So How Does It Work?

To start with, Ant Forest has plenty of potential players, being part of

China's Alipay mobile payments app, which is used by more than a billion people. Each time a user performs a lower-carbon activity, such as paying a utility bill online or cycling to work, he or she is rewarded with "green energy points". However, rather than immediately spending those points on a real tree, Ant Forest turns its users into game players. The green energy points "grow" into a virtual tree on each of the users' app. And users can share green energy with friends and see how their virtual forests compare with others. For every virtual tree grown, Ant Forest donates—and plants—a real one. And this gamification has had real-world impacts.

A Greening China

According to a study in Nature Sustainability, NASA satellites have revealed a 5% increase in global green leaf cover since the early 2000s—with China leading that growth. While a third of Chinese greening is due to the expansion of agriculture, 42% comes from projects to plant forests. According to the UN, Ant Forest has become the country's largest private sector tree-planting scheme—so the game is a big part of China's greening. And the locations for planting are expansive: arid areas of Northern China like parts of Inner Mongolia, Gansu and Shaanxi. Many of the 122 million Ant Forest trees have been planted in the areas that have become deserts.

However, there has been some criticism. In 2019, the journal, *Nature*, reported concerns that holding back deserts with trees could put pressure on water supplies. Scientists in China responded that local conditions are taken into account. Drought-resistant varieties, such as the "saxaul" (梭梭), are used by Ant Forest.

The project is certainly ambitious. In 2019, Alipay's parent company, Ant Financial Group, said the trees covered some 112,000 hectares. And there are sizeable spillover benefits too.

Environment and People

The young trees maintain and repair eroded soils, as well as lower global CO_2 levels.

Another major gain from the project has been employment. Ant Financial Group says 400,000 job opportunities have been created through Ant Forest, many for local farmers.

But if the trees are donated by Ant Financial, why not simply plant the

trees and cut out the virtual ones? The reason, as the UN puts it, is "significant behavioral change"; gamification has encouraged millions of people to adopt lower-carbon lifestyles.

The success of the project has now led to a similar initiative in the Philippines, launched by the mobile payments provider, GCash. The project is an encouraging step, according to the UN's Andersen. "Although the environmental challenges we face are daunting," she says, "we have the technology and the knowledge to overcome them and fundamentally redesign how we interact with the planet."

Case Study: Ant Forest and Building a Community with a Shared Future for Mankind

Read the following passage and try to analyze it by answering the questions:

(1) How does Ant Forest work?

(2) Can you analyze this case with the knowledge of global citizenship?

When the Alipay Ant Forest users take a step to reduce their emissions, such as by biking or public transportation to work, limited usage of paper and plastic, online payment of utility bills, and buying sustainable products, they are rewarded with "green energy points" each time. These green energy points grow into a virtual tree on the user's app, which Alipay matches by planting a real tree or protecting a conservation area, in partnership with local NGOs (non-governmental organizations). The publicity generated is creating a virtuous cycle whereby more and more residents are encouraged to adopt low-carbon and energy-saving lifestyles. This model is turning doing good into an everyday action. Protecting the environment is no longer an empty slogan, but a daily activity that everyone can do. In this way, Ant Forest motivates more than half a billion people to adopt an eco-friendly and greener lifestyle, thus greatly contributing to ecological protection with the help of digital technology.

This innovative method easily accepted by the younger generations is helping those born after the year 1995 to become more aware of and to take action in environmental protection. Things growing in the Ant Forest are not only trees, but also the spirit of exploration and innovation of the Chinese youth. Alipay Ant Forest shows how technology can be applied to foster massive individual efforts to tackle climate change, which represents a meaningful step towards the Sustainable Development Goal 13— "taking urgent action to combat climate change and its impacts". It is also in line with the Chinese government's strategy of transforming the nation into a "green economy". To accomplish this objective, the country is taking aggressive action in expanding its green coverage.

In March 2013, for the first time, the concept of "building a community with a shared future for mankind" was formally put forward to the world by Chinese President Xi Jinping during his speech at the Moscow State Institute of International Relations. What is the relationship between Ant Forest and this notion?

Sustainable living is one of the core themes of global citizenship. According to the United Nations, almost two-thirds of the world's population would experience acute "water-stressed" conditions. A third of the planet's fertile land has become extinct due to land degradation in the last 40 years. Unless governments, businesses, and people all come together to form a focused team, it's difficult to contain global warming and its ensuing impact. Going by the warnings of climate scientists, the planet is at a tipping point which could result in unparalleled natural disasters unless urgent actions are taken immediately.

One of the key ideas in the notion of "building a community with a shared future for mankind" is to increase inter-civilization exchanges to promote harmony, inclusiveness, and respect for differences. This notion also lays stress on protecting our ecosystem and to put Mother Nature first. Under the notion of "building a community with a shared future for mankind", President Xi calls on world powers to promote open, innovative, and balanced development that benefits all.

We can see the notion is in accordance with the concept of global citizenship. Ant Forest is a typical project to awake people's global awareness by encouraging them to live a greener life. Initiatives like Ant Forest tap into the best of human ingenuity and innovation to create a better world. It is a meaningful practice to realize the notion and a practical way to make our own effort to be a global citizen.

China aims to reduce net carbon emissions to zero by 2060. Along with a target for carbon emissions to peak before 2030, it is critical to the fight against global climate change. China has long been committed to reforestation to improve its environment and tackle climate change. We can search the relative information on the Internet and find out what measures China has taken to realize its commitment and think about what we can do in our daily life.

8.3 Global Citizenship Education

The world faces global challenges, which require global solutions. These interconnected global challenges call for far-reaching changes in how we think and act for the dignity of fellow human beings. It is not enough for education to produce individuals who can read, write, and count. Education must cultivate an active care for the world and for those with whom we share it. Education must also be relevant in answering the big questions of the day. Technological solutions, political regulation or financial instruments alone cannot achieve sustainable development. We should transform the way people think and act. Education must fully assume its central role in helping people to forge more just, peaceful, tolerant, and inclusive societies. It must give people the understanding, skills, and values they need to cooperate in resolving the interconnected challenges of the 21st century. Hence, global citizenship education (GCE) has significant meaning in today's globalized world.

8.3.1 Definition of Global Citizenship Education

Global citizenship education is a form of civic learning that involves students' active participation in projects that address global issues of a social, political, economic, or environmental nature (UNESCO, 2017). In education, the term "global citizenship" is most often used to describe a worldview or a set of values towards which education is oriented. It has been linked with awards offered for helping humanity. Teachers are being given the responsibility of being social change agents. Within the educational system, the concept of GCE is beginning to substitute movements such as multicultural education, peace education, human rights education, education for sustainable development, and international education.

Global citizenship consists of voluntary practices oriented to human rights, social justice, and environmentalism at the local, regional, and global levels. Unlike national citizenship, global citizenship does not denote any legal status or allegiance to an actual form of government. The emergence of regional economic blocs, supranational political institutions such as the European Union, and the advancement of information and communication technologies, has caused governments to try to prepare national populations to be competitive in the global job market. This has led to the introduction of GCE programs at primary, secondary, and third levels, but also at independent NGOs, grass-root organizations, and other large-scale educational organizations, such as UNESCO (Dill, 2014).

In the present era of globalization, the recognition of global interdependence on the part of the general public has led to a higher degree of interest in global citizenship education. Though modern schooling may have been oriented to education suitable for the nation states throughout the 19th and 20th centuries, in the 21st century, citizenship is understood in global terms, so that schooling might improve the individual nation's global competitiveness. Many universities worldwide have responded to the need for a globally oriented education by sending their students to study abroad in increasing numbers, and some have announced that this will soon become a compulsive degree requirement.

Many governments now also promote GCE for the cohesion of society. The large numbers of people migrating across national borders mean that the diversity of ethnic, religious, and linguistic groups, has raised complex and difficult questions about citizenship, human rights, democracy, and education. In addition, global issues related to sustainability, such as the world's future energy arrangements, have also been incorporated into the domain of global citizenship education.

The two main elements of GCE are "global consciousness", the moral or ethical aspect of global issues, and "global competencies", or skills meant to enable learners to compete in the global job market. The promotion of GCE is a response by governments and NGOs to the emergence of supra-national institutions, regional economic blocs, and the development of information and communications technologies. These have all resulted in the emergence of a more globally oriented and collaborative approach to education.

8.3.2 Pedagogical Features of Global Citizenship Education

In an increasingly interconnected and interdependent world, GCE is seen as a transformative pedagogy that can empower learners to resolve growing global challenges, and build a more just and sustainable world. Most educators agree that "global citizenship is a learned and nurtured behavior", and the most widely used classroom strategy for developing global skills is project-based learning. This

teaching technique can be used in the case of almost any school subject. Educators see it as an important method for developing the tools—technical and emotional—for success in the global society. With the aim of nurturing students' potential to be both learners and citizens, the project-based approach has been used successfully in community-based learning (Melaville et al., 2006).

Another important pedagogical feature of GCE is learning through communicative practices outside the classroom. According to Catalano (2013), if students are encouraged to see themselves as political agents, educators assume they are more likely to acquire the knowledge, skills, and abilities that enable them to become agents of change. Another important element of the student-centered participatory nature of GCE means that students, through their engagement with others via Social Network Services, create their own forms of global citizenship through dialog, learning, and action (Bourn, 2009). This is an important element, for example, in the activities of grass-root organizations like Global Issues Network (GIN), which involves students and teachers in projects that address global issues such as human rights, trade rules, and deforestation. Such student-driven, student-led projects combine both the "global consciousness" and "global competencies" aspects of GCE.

International organizations have developed a powerful GCE discourse, elements of which can be seen in national education policy and school practice, yet with different emphasis between countries as a result of diverse socio-economic, political and historical contexts. Global citizenship includes development of knowledge, understanding, skills, and values, such as learning about a globalized world, learning for life and work in a global society, and learning through global contexts.

The most important features of global citizenship education are voluntary action that can extend from local to international collectives, the practice of cultural empathy, and a focus on active participation in social and political life at the local and global levels. Enabling young people to participate in shaping a better, shared future for the world is at the heart of global education. From these actions, the students and schools can develop awareness of a global issue, embrace the need to change, engage in personal or global action and reflect on learning.

All in all, developing global citizenship is about recognizing our responsibilities towards each other and the wider world. The outcome will be that our children and young people as global citizens, are able to take up their place in the world, contribute to it confidently, successfully, and effectively, and understand the rights and responsibilities of living and working in a globalized world.

Australia's GCE Program

The Australian Curriculum sets out the core knowledge, understanding, skills, and general capabilities important for all Australian students. It describes what all young Australians are to be taught as a foundation for their future learning, growth and active participation in the Australian community. There is great accordance between global education and the Australian Curriculum.

The curriculum aims to develop global citizens through promotion of open mindedness and a willingness to take action for change, respecting and valuing diversity, and being active in the development of a peaceful, just, and sustainable world. The general capabilities particularly relevant to global education are:

- critical and creative thinking;
- ethical behavior;
- personal and social competence;
- intercultural understanding.

Here are some programs they have been doing:

Protecting the local creek is designed for third-year students of primary schools. Students tested the temperature, stream flow, pH and salt levels of their local creek, and then developed a plan to protect the creek, which included planting trees and native grasses and many other practical measures. This program developed students' awareness of both the effect of people's behavior on the environment and their ability to exercise their civic rights. Behavioral changes were noted as a result of the students' work: Rubbish levels went down and environmental interest increased.

Case Study: Making a Multicultural School

Read the following passage and try to analyze it with the knowledge of GCE.

School: Glen Waverley Primary School, Victoria, Australia

Year levels: Year F–6

Number of students involved: 500

Impetus for Action

Glen Waverley Primary School has students from 35 different nations, predominantly Sri Lanka, India, China, and South Korea. There is high mobility as many families are business migrants. The school has worked closely with the Global Education Project to develop a whole-school approach to multicultural and global citizenship perspectives across the curriculum.

Action

The school's Welcoming New Families to Our School policy outlines expectations to ensure all families feel comfortable and are able to settle in smoothly. Families are conducted on school tours with interpreters (when possible), provided a welcome pack of information and maps, and invited to a welcome afternoon tea. Where needed, parents are enrolled in English language classes and linked to welfare organizations. Within a month of arrival, new families are contacted by the Student Wellbeing Leader or principal and class teacher. They are linked to parents who have children in the same year level(s) as their children.

Around the school, there are displays of flags and welcome signs in a variety of languages. School assemblies include performances by the Chinese choir, Indian, Sri Lankan and Greek dancing, and music on a traditional Chinese instrument like a zither. Children are greeted in different languages and major cultural festivals such as Chinese New Year and Diwali (印度排灯节) are celebrated.

During Cultural Diversity Week, the Victorian Multicultural Commission chairperson, Chin Tan, invited all children to turn to their neighbor and say hello in their neighbor's language. Manal greeted everyone in an African language, "With my thoughts I greet you; with my words I greet you; with my heart I greet you; I have nothing up my sleeve". After the assembly, Chin was interviewed by Senudi and Sithumya in the TV studio with Steven recording. The interview was played at an assembly and on the TV in the lobby.

Community members have provided professional learning for staff about the background of the students and their countries of origin, family values and expectations. They are actively involved in supporting classroom and whole-school activities.

In the classroom, new students are paired with a buddy who will look after them. Teachers draw upon the experience of living in different countries in their curriculum. The school has undertaken a broad range of initiatives with a multicultural and global focus, including work with UNICEF (United Nations International Children's Emergency Fund) ambassadors and Childfund Connect to make digital connections with children in Vietnam, Timor Leste (东帝汶), Laos, and Sri Lanka.

Each grade level undertakes units of work with a global focus and staff to nurture their students' sense of social responsibility and active citizenship. Students are encouraged to apply this lens to their school work, helping them to understand that they have a part to play in making positive changes in their own community and the world.

In 2012, the school was recognized for its outstanding effort in working to serve the multicultural and wider community with an Excellence in Multiculturalizm Award.

This project is an excellent example of GCE. As we know, the two main elements of GCE are "global consciousness" and "global competencies". The purpose of the project is to develop a whole-school approach to multicultural and global citizenship perspectives. The measures such as providing welcome pack and co-partner can not only cultivate children's global awareness, but also improve their intercultural communication skills. School assemblies are a good chance to learn about a globalized world through global contexts.

The most important features of global citizenship education are voluntary action, the practice of cultural empathy, and a focus on active participation in social and political life at the local and global levels. In this case, we can find not only students themselves but also the teaching staff and the parents are taking part in all kinds of local and international activities actively. Students engage with others from various cultures by project-based approach, community-based learning and communicative practices outside the classroom. These facts illustrate the pedagogical features of GCE.

Now here is a case to help you know more about GCE. You can analyze how this kind of project realizes the objective of GCE and what kind of pedagogical method is used.

Here is one example of Webster University's Global Citizenship Program. The program prepares students for future professional success through a set of undergraduate degree requirements that will help them confront global challenges, and provides them with the skills necessary to generate permanent solutions.

Highlights: Italy and Greece

Program Length:10 Days

Day by Day Itinerary

Day 1—Athens

Afternoon arrival at Athens airport. After collecting your luggage and clearing customs, you will be met by your Travel Director. Board your private motor coach and transfer to your hotel. Get your first impressions of Athens during an orientation walk.

Day 2—Athens

Enjoy a morning guided visit of the city including the Acropolis and the Parthenon. Then view the Agora, followed by a visit to the Acropolis Museum. Later, enjoy an evening of Greek culture. Eat local cuisine while watching local dancers perform to traditional music. You will learn some of the dance steps so that you can participate as well.

Day 3—Kalambaka Area

This morning drive to Delphi for a guided visit of the mythical site that was home of the fabled oracle. Also included is the Archaeological Museum, featuring artifacts unearthed during local excavations. Continue the drive north to the Kalambaka area, known for the spectacular Meteora rocks that rise high above the town.

Day 4—Overnight Ferry

This morning ascend Meteora to see the stunning UNESCO World Heritage site that comprises the local monasteries dating as far back as the 14th century. The visit includes entry to two of the monasteries where you will immerse yourselves in the local ancient religious traditions. Continue to the port city of Igoumenitsa to board the overnight ferry bound for the Italian port of Ancona.

Day 5—Ravenna

Welcome to Italy. Arrive at the port and continue to Ravenna to admire the UNESCO-listed Byzantine mosaics in the Basilica of Sant' Apollinare. Overnight in Ravenna.

Day 6—Tuscany

This morning drive to Florence, the birthplace of the Renaissance in Italy. A local expert will guide you around the highlights of the city such as Ghiberti's Baptistry Doors, Santa Croce and the beautiful Duomo. After some free time in the city, continue to the countryside of Tuscany for your overnight.

Day 7—Tuscany

This morning, visit an organic farm in the Tuscan countryside where you will learn about local agriculture, and help out on the farm. You'll pick your own produce and learn to make a traditional Italian farm to table lunch (lunch is included). Later, explore the city of Lucca, which is known for it well-preserved Renaissance walls encircling its historic city center and its cobblestone streets, enjoy some free time to shop, and eat your share of gelato.

Day 8—Rome

Your first stop today is in Assisi where St. Francis founded the Franciscan Friars. Take a walk through the beautiful hilltop town and visit the Basilica to admire the frescoes by Giotto. Later continue to Rome, and enjoy a beautiful evening walk around the Piazza Navona, the Spanish Steps and the Trevi Fountain.

Day 9—Rome

A local guide will introduce you to the smallest state in the world, Vatican City, situated in Rome. This is the home of the Pope but also home to almost 1,000 other residents. You'll visit Michelangelo's Sistine Chapel, and Saint Peter's Basilica. Later, you'll take an interactive cooking lesson on the art and tradition of tiramisu making. Tonight, join our farewell dinner!

Day 10

Transfer to the airport for return flight.

More to Read

Globalization: Its Origin, Process, and Impact
by Yang Boxu

The book is divided into two parts. The first part analyzes the causes of globalization from the aspects of society, politics, and economy. The second part discusses the influence of globalization from the perspectives of political economy, sociology, and communication. In other words, the book will reexplain why the world started, how it moved, and where it headed. The book is comprehensive, informative, and instructive. It is well worth reading for the beginners who are interested in globalization.

In the first chapter of this book, the theoretical problems involved in globalization are further discussed on the basis of Marx's related views. Chapter

Two deals with the evolution of Western corporations. Chapter Three points out that the scale of a company and the scope of the market are the basis of social change. Chapter Four discusses the evolution of consumer culture in capitalist society, the role of media, and globalization.

The fifth chapter points out that in the era of economic globalization, if we can't make the majority of people rich quickly, if we rest at the level of "Made in China" and neglect "Created in China", it means the end of our nation or our national culture. Chapter Six tells us that before companies form a global alliance, they have already been united and politically ready in their home countries. Chapter Seven discusses the reorientation of social relations in the era of globalization. This positioning is based on multinational corporations as the core positioning. Chapter Eight discusses the relationship between the different media and the capitalist economy.

Grave New World: The End of Globalization, the Return of History
by Stephen D. King

Combining historical analysis with current affairs, economist Stephen D. King provides a provocative and engaging account of why globalization is being rejected, what a world ruled by rival states with conflicting aims might look like, and how the pursuit of nationalist agendas could result in a race to the bottom. King argues that a rejection of globalization and a return to "autarky" (自给自足) will risk economic and political conflict, and he uses lessons from history to estimate how best to avoid the worst possible outcomes.

In this book, the author has written a brilliant summary of how Westerners got where they are. He provides a history of globalization and suggests Western world may be at a turning point. He believes that globalization in the West may be in trouble. The book ends with a few recommendations on how to prevent the wave of protectionism and populism that threaten the global regime. To follow this book better, readers need requisite knowledge of economics, finance or political economy. However, if you are interested in modern history, the book involves the major world political, economic, financial, military events since modern times and the author interprets these events from the perspective of globalization.

Summary

If we want to be a good intercultural communicator, we should live at the moment while looking towards the future. Anyone who is familiar with current news can tell us something about how the world is shrinking into the chip of a smart phone or computer while some states expand their boundaries over mountains and sea. That is why we should understand how the tide of globalization has swiped around our planet and how to be a qualified global citizen.

This chapter mainly talks about the concept of globalization and its three tiers, including economic globalization, political globalization, and cultural globalization. Economic globalization is the increasing economic integration and interdependence of national, regional, and local economies across the world through an intensification of cross-border movements of goods, services, technologies, and capital. Political globalization is when governmental action takes place at a global level, where responsibilities, such as the welfare of citizens and economic growth, are acted upon by an international political body. Cultural globalization is the rapid movement of ideas, attitudes, and values across national borders.

Other important concepts in this chapter are global citizenship and global citizenship education. The two main elements of GCE are "global consciousness" and "global competencies". As an individual, if we want to be a global citizen, we also should know the principles and core themes of GCE; we also need to practice the skills that a global citizen should have.

Exercises

Questions for Review

1. What are the three tiers of the concept of globalization and what are the relationships between them?

2. What are the two perspectives of cultural globalization?

3. What are the benefits and drawbacks of economic globalization?

4. What are the advantages and disadvantages of political globalization?

5. What are the positive and negative effects of globalization?

6. What are the themes and outlooks of global citizenship?

7. What skills are needed for global citizenship?

Problems and Application

1. Here is a case about Australian GCE course—Sustainable Resource Use. How did this activity achieve the objectives of GCE?

School: Iona Presentation College, Perth, Western Australia

Year level: Year 11, Geography

Number of students involved: 20

Impetus for action

A teacher from Iona Presentation College participated in the One World Center's Global Teaching advocates professional learning program, leading to the planning of a number of units of globally focused classroom work, including the one described below.

Action

As part of our geography unit we focused on sustainable resource use around the world, including studies of a number of slum areas in different places. We explored the idea that demographics, population growth, values, culture and government intervention are important building blocks for sustainable resource use.

We looked at the extraction of non-renewable resources through the mining process and rehabilitation practices. We investigated silver- and tin-mining in Bolivia, its impact on locals and the activities of advocacy groups. We compared this to iron-ore mining in the Pilbara of Western Australia. Students were able to see how companies were held more accountable in Australia and the impact of their sustainable management practices. Also, through looking more closely at slum areas, students were able to identify the challenges faced by those communities as well as what other communities have to learn from the systems and practices undertaken in places showcased by documentaries such as *Welcome to Lagos and Slumming It.*

We also looked at the renewable resource activity of forestry and timber production. We participated in a sustainable forest field trip at the Wellington Discovery Forest EcoEducation center where we went on a night walk to observe the vast diversity of the forest. The students made comparisons between forestry in pine plantations and native woodlands in Western Australia and Indonesia.

Students examined key demographic figures: education, infant mortality rate, wealth, GDP, distribution of income, and population. From this they concluded that Australia has the ability to enforce sustainable practices, whereas in Indonesia and Bolivia there were more difficulties in balancing the need to attract global companies with the protection of local people and the environment.

Students evaluated their own consumption patterns and the imbalance of wealth around the world. They presented well-researched and thought-provoking persuasive speeches recognizing the importance of researching the facts about corporations, the complexities involved, and the difficulty of balancing economic growth and sustainability.

They now have more respect for the ease of their lives and have taken steps to improve their own carbon footprints and impact on the environment. I know that if they had a chance, they would love to visit some of the places they learned about and take the opportunity to investigate how people with so little can live quite amazing lives.

References

李杰群 . 2002. 非言语交际概论 . 北京：北京大学出版社 .

老甲 . 2017. 嫩模吉吉眯眼模仿佛像，网友怒批：种族歧视 . 新浪网，9 月 1 日 . 来自新浪网站 .

施婷婷 . 2013. 进电梯后人们会像 "散点" 一样站位 . 金陵晚报，1 月 30 日 . 来自新浪新闻网站 .

Abbas, T. 2022. Examples of ageism and its types at workplace. *ChangeManagementInsight*. Retrieved May 3, 2022, from ChangeManagementInsight website.

ACLU. 2021. Justice for George Floyd and Daunte Wright. *ACLU*. Retrieved May 19, 2021, from ACLU website.

Afifi, W. A. & Johnson, M. L. 2005. The nature and functions of tie-signs. In V. Manusovt (Ed.), *The Sourcebook of Nonverbal Measures: Going Beyond Words*. Mahwah: Lawrence Erlbaum Associates Publishers, 189–198.

Akande, S. 2018. We often ignore these 3 everyday examples of prejudice against women. *PulseNg*. Retrieved May 23, 2018 from PulseNg website.

Andersen, P. A. 1999. *Nonverbal Communication: Forms and Functions.* Mountain View: Mayfield.

Alexander, P. 1985. *Ideas, Qualities and Corpuscles: Locke and Boyle on the External World.* Cambridge: Cambridge University Press.

Andersen, P. A. & Andersen, J. F. 2004. Measures of perceived nonverbal immediacy. In V. Manusovt (Ed.), *The Sourcebook of Nonverbal Measures: Going Beyond Words*. Mahwah: Lawrence Erlbaum Associates Publishers, 113–126, 189–198.

Baker, W. 2012. From cultural awareness to intercultural awareness: Culture in ELT. *ELT Journal, 66*(1): 62–70.

Bednarz, F. 2010. Building up intercultural competences: Challenges and learning processes. In F. Bednarz & M. G. Onorati (Eds.), *Building Intercultural Competencies: A Handbook for Professionals in Education, Social Work, and Health Care*. Leuven: Acco, 39.

Bennett, M. J. 1993. Towards ethnorelativism: A developmental model of intercultural sensitivity. In R. M. Paige (Ed.), *Education for the Intercultural Experience* (2nd ed.). Yarmouth: Intercultural Press, 21–71.

BlackLivesMatter. 2020. Impact report. *BlackLivesMatter*. Retrieved November 3, 2021, from BlackLivesMatter website.

Blessing, A. & Lawrence, T. 2014. *Effects of Information Capitalism and Globalization on Teaching and Learning*. Hershey: Information Science Reference.

Bourn, D. 2009. Students as global citizens. In E. Jones (Ed.), *Internationalisation and the Student Voice: Higher Education Perspectives*. London: Routledge, 18–29.

Brewer, H. 2020. List of gender stereotypes. *HealthGuidance*. Retrieved April 30, 2020, from HealthGuidance website.

Butler, A. D. 2021. *White Evangelical Racism: The Politics of Morality in America*. Chapel Hill: The University of North Carolina Press.

Byram, M. 1989. *Cultural Studies in Foreign Language Education*. Cleveland: Multilingual Matters.

Canale, M. 1983. From communicative competence to communicative language pedagogy. In J. C. Richard & R. W. Schmidt (Eds.), *Language and Communication*. London: Longman, 2–14.

Catalano, T. 2013. Occupy: A case illustration of social movements in global citizenship education. *Education, Citizenship and Social Justice*, 8(3): 277–279.

Chi, R. B. 2015. Social identity theory. *Courses*. Retrieved April 18, 2015, from Courses website.

Chihiro, H. 2019. *Green Book:* A guide to shattering stereotypes. *IsshInternational*. Retrieved May 30, 2019, from IsshInternational website.

Chomsky, N. 1965. *Aspects of the Theory of Syntax*. Cambridge: Cambridge University Press.

Cole, N. L. 2020. What's the difference between prejudice and racism?—How sociology explains the two and their differences. *ThoughtCo*. Retrieved July 16, 2020, from ThoughtCo website.

Couzin-frankel, J. 2017. How can we blunt prejudice against immigrants? *ScienceOrg*. Retrieved May 17, 2017, from ScienceOrg website.

Cox, W. T. L., Abramson, L. Y., Devine, P. G. & Hollon, S. D. 2012. Stereotypes, prejudice and depression: The integrated perspective. *Perspectives on Psychological Science*, 7(5): 427–449.

DePaulo, P. J. 1992. Applications of nonverbal behavior research in marketing and management. In R. S. Feldman (Ed.), *Applications of Nonverbal Behavior Theories and Research*. Hillsdale: Lawrence Erlbaum Associates, 63–87.

Dill, J. S. 2014. *The Longings and Limits of Global Citizenship Education: The Moral Pedagogy of Schooling in a Cosmopolitan Age*. New York: Routledge.

Fiske, S. T. 1998. Stereotyping, prejudice and discrimination. In D. T. Gilbert, S. T. Fiske & G. Lindzey (Eds.), *The Handbook of Social Psychology*. New York: McGraw-Hill, 357–411.

Gendler, T. S. 2009. Personal identity and metaphysics. In A. Beckermann, B. P. McLaughlin & S. Walter (Eds.), *The Oxford Handbook of Philosophy of Mind*. New York: Oxford University Press

Ginsburg, R. B. 2022. Barriers & bias: The status of women in leadership. *AAUW*. Retrieved September 30, 2022, from AAUW website.

Graham, A. J. R. 2015. John-Locke: An essay concerning human understanding. *Britannica*. Retrieved January 21, 2015, from Britannica website.

Graham, M. V. 2021. Henri Tajfel, Polish-born British social psychologist. *Britannica*. Retrieved May 21, 2021, from Britannica website.

Guerrero, L. & Floyd, K. 2005. *Nonverbal Communication in Close Relationships*. Mahwah: Lawrence Erlbaum Associates.

Hall, E. T.1968. Proxemics, comments and replies. *Current Anthropology, 9*(2): 83–95.

Hall, E. T. 1976. *Beyond Culture*. New York: Anchor Books.

Hall, S. 1996. *Questions of Cultural Identity*. Beverly Hills: Sage.

Hans, A. 1982. *From Locke to Saussure: Essays on the Study of Language and Intellectual History*. Minneapolis: University of Minnesota Press.

Hans, A. 1994. Locke's influence. In V. Chappell (Ed.), *The Cambridge Companion to Locke*. Cambridge: Cambridge University Press, 252–289.

Hargie, O. 2011. *Skilled Interpersonal Interaction: Research, Theory, and Practice*. London: Routledge.

Heslin, R. & Apler, T. 1983. Touch: A bonding gesture. In J. M. Weimann & R. Harrison (Eds.), *Nonverbal Communication*. Beverly Hills: Sage, 47–76.

Hofstede, G. 1984. *Culture's Consequences: International Differences in Work-Related Values* (2nd ed.). Beverly Hills: Sage.

Hofstede, G., & Hofstede, G. J. 2005. *Cultures and Organizations—Software of the Mind*. New York: McGraw-Hill.

Houtrow, A. J. 2020. Handcuffed by racism. *Archives of Physical Medicine and Rehabilitation, 101*(12): 2256–2257.

Hymes, D. 1971. *On Communicative Competence*. Philadelphia: University of Pennsylvania Press.

Inzlicht, M., Tullett, A. M. & Gutsell, J. N. 2012. Stereotype threat spillover: The short- and long-term effects of coping with threats to social identity. In M. Inzlicht & T. Schmader (Eds.), *Stereotype Threat: Theory, Process, and Application.* New York: Oxford University Press, 108.

Israel, R. C. 2012. What does it mean to be a global citizen? *Kosmos.* Retrieved June 10, 2021, from Kosmos website.

Jackson, J. 1993. Realistic group conflict theory: A review and evaluation of the theoretical and empirical literature. *Psychological Record, 43*: 395–413.

James, P. 2006. *Globalism, Nationalism, Tribalism.* Thousand Oaks: Sage.

Jiang, N. 2018. "Fresh off the Boat" theme of cultural assimilation and identity. *SitesGateCh.* Retrieved September 22, 2018, from SitesGateCh website.

Jones, R. G. 2010. Putting privilege into practice through "intersectional reflexivity": Ruminations, interventions, and possibilities. *Reflections: Narratives of Professional Helping, 16*(1): 122–125.

Joshi, R. M. 2009. *International Business.* Delhi: Oxford University Press

Joshua, A. & Stelle, C. M. 2005. Stereotypes and the fragility of academic competence, motivation, and self-concept. In A. J. Elliot & C. S. Dweck (Eds.), *Handbook of Competence and Motivation.* New York: Guilford Press, 436–443.

Kafui, D. 2020. Revising the a priori hypothesis: Systemic racism has penetrated scientific funding. *Cell, 183*(3): 576–579.

Kendall, J. 2019. Young adult books. *ThoughtCo.* Retrieved July 09, 2019, from ThoughtCo website.

Kendi, I. X. 2017, January 21. Racial progress is real, but so is racist progress. *New York Times.*

Keneally, T. 1982. *Schindler's List.* New York: Simon & Schuster.

Khan, C. 2022. What are some examples of social class prejudices in *To Kill a Mockingbird? Enotes.* Retrieved September 30, 2022, from Enotes website.

Kluckhohn, F. & Strodtbeck, R. 1961. *Variations in Value Orientations.* Evaston: Row Perterson.

Knapp, M. & Hall, J. 2010. *Nonverbal Communication in Human Interaction* (7th ed.). Boston: Wadsworth Cengage Learning.

Leary, M. 2019. People's identities can separate them from others—or bring them together. *PsychologyToday.* Retrieved July 23, 2019, from PsychologyToday website.

Levin, N. 2019. Introduction to philosophy and the *Ship of Theseus. Ancient Philosophy Reader: An Open Educational Resource.* Chicago: N.G.E. Far Press.

Little, A. W. 1996. Globalisation and education research: Whose context counts? *International Journal of Educational Development, 16*(4): 427–438

Liu, J. H. 2012. A cultural perspective on intergroup relations and social identity. *Online Readings in Psychology and Culture, 5*(3): 5–7.

Lustig, M, W. & Koester, J. 2007. *Intercultural Competence: Interpersonal Communication Across Cultures.* Shanghai: Shanghai Foreign Language Education Press.

Lynch, M. 2021. 7 novels that encourage young adults to discuss racial issues. *TheEdAdvocate.* Retrieved June 4, 2021, from TheEdAdvocate website.

Macionis, J. J. & Gerber, L. M. 2011. *Sociology.* Toronto: Pearson Prentice Hall.

Man, J. 2021. Understanding reverse racism and its impact. *DiversityForSocialImpact.* Retrieved July 1, 2021, from DiversityForSocialImpact website.

Marilynn, B. B. 1999. The psychology of prejudice: In-group love or out-group hate? *Journal of Social Issues, 55*(3): 429–444.

Masequesmay, G. 2022. Sexism sociology. *Britannica.* Retrieved August 26, 2022, from Britannica website.

McDonald, M. M., Navarrete, C. D. & Vugt, V. M. 2012. Evolution and the psychology of intergroup conflict: The male warrior hypothesis. *Philosophical Transactions of the Royal Society, 367*: 670–679.

McLeod, S. A. 2008. Robbers Cave Experiment. *SimplyPsychology.* Retrieved October 4, 2008, from SimplyPsychology website.

McLeod, S. A. 2019. Social identity theory. *SimplyPsychology.* Retrieved October 24, 2019, from SimplyPsychology website.

Melaville, A., Berg, A. C. & Blank, M. J. 2006. *Community-based learning—Engaging students for success and citizenship.* Washington: Coalition for Community Schools.

Meso, A. 2021. Level mechanisms of racism in medicine. *The American Journal of Bioethics, 21*(2): 66.

Metts, S. & Planlap, S. 2002. Emotional communication. In M. L. Knapp & K. J. Daly (Eds.), *Handbook of Interpersonal Communication* (3rd ed.). Thousand Oaks: Sage, 339–373.

Michàlle, E. & Barak, M. 2008. Social psychological perspectives of workforce diversity and inclusion in national and global contexts. *ResearchGate.* Retrieved January, 2008, from ResearchGate website.

Nittle, N. K. 2018. Racial bias and discrimination: From colorism to racial profiling. *ThoughtCo.* Retrieved April 20, 2018, from ThoughtCo website.

Nittle, N. K. 2019a. Blockbusting: When black homeowners move to white

neighborhoods. *ThoughtCo*. Retrieved October 28, 2019, from ThoughtCo website.

Nittle, N. K. 2019b. Does reverse racism exist? *ThoughtCo*. Retrieved July 3, 2019, from ThoughtCo website.

Nittle, N. K. 2020. Persistent racial stereotypes in TV shows and movies. *ThoughtCo*. Retrieved December 13, 2020, from ThoughtCo website.

Nittle, N. K. 2021a. 5 common black stereotypes in TV and film. *ThoughtCo*. Retrieved March 6, 2021, from ThoughtCo website.

Nittle, N. K. 2021b. 5 examples of institutional racism in the United States. *ThoughtCo*. Retrieved March 13, 2021, from ThoughtCo website.

Nittle, N. K. 2021c. Difficulties faced by interracial couples historically and today. *ThoughtCo*. Retrieved March 3, 2021, from ThoughtCo website.

Nittle, N. K. 2021d. Understanding 4 different types of racism. *ThoughtCo*. Retrieved March 1, 2021, from ThoughtCo website.

Nittle, N. K. 2021e. Understanding racial prejudice. *ThoughtCo*. Retrieved March 11, 2021, from ThoughtCo website.

Nittle, N. K. 2021f. What is a stereotype? *ThoughtCo*. Retrieved February 4, 2021, from ThoughtCo website.

Nittle, N. K. 2021g. What is the definition of internalized racism? *ThoughtCo*. Retrieved March 1, 2021, from ThoughtCo website.

Nittle, N. K. 2021h. Why are the effects of colorism so damaging? *ThoughtCo*. Retrieved March 21, 2021, from ThoughtCo website.

Noonan, H. 1998. Animalism versus Lockeanism: A current controversy. *Philosophical Quarterly, 48*: 302–318.

Noonan, H. 2003. *Personal Identity* (2nd ed.). London: Routledge.

Noonan, H. 2010. The thinking animal problem and personal pronoun revisionism. *Analysis, 70*: 93–98.

Noonan, H. 2011. The complex and simple views of personal identity. *Analysis, 71*: 72–77.

Noonan, H. 2019. Personal identity: The simple and complex views revisited. *Disputatio, 11*: 9–22.

Olson, E. 2003. Personal identity. In S. Stich & T. Warfield (eds.), *The Blackwell Guide to the Philosophy of Mind*. Oxford: Blackwell, 84–107.

Omi, M. & Winant, H. 1987. *Racial Formation in the United States: From the 1960s to the 1980s*. New York: Routledge & Kegan Paul.

Peace, D. 2018. Monsooned project deadlines—The Indian yes and high context communication. *ShantiConsulting*. Retrieved October 3, 2022, from ShantiConsulting website.

Pease, A. & Pease, B. 2004. *The Definitive Book of Body Language*. New York: Bantam.

Peoples, J. & Garrick, B. W. 1988. *Humanity: An Introduction to Cultural Anthropology*. New York: West Publishing Company.

Peterson, J. 2021. 12 rules for life tour in Seattle: Facts, stories, and values. *JordanbPeterson*. Retrieved January 12, 2021, from JordanbPeterson website.

Prahl, A. 2019. *Pride and Prejudice* overview—literature's ultimate romantic comedy. *ThoughtCo*. Retrieved January 3, 2019, from ThoughtCo website.

Quattrone, G. A. & Jones, E. E. 1980. The perception of variability within in-groups and out-groups: Implications for the law of small numbers. *Journal of Personality and Social Psychology, 38*: 141–152.

Quinn, D. M., Kallen, R. W. & Spencer, S. J. 2010. Stereotype threat. In J. F. Dividio, M. Hewstone, P. Glick & V. M. Esses (Eds.), *The Sage Handbook of Prejudice, Stereotyping and Discrimination*. Thousand Oaks: Sage, 379–394.

Rebecca, L. F. & Volker, F. 2013. Culture matters: Individualism vs. collectivism in conflict decision-making. *Societies, 3*: 128–146.

Rokeach, M. 2017. Value theory and communication research: Review and commentary. *Annals of the International Communication Association, 5*(4): 7–28.

Sam, D. L. & Berry, J. W. 2010. Acculturation when individuals and groups of different cultural backgrounds meet. *Perspectives on Psychological Science, 5*(4): 472.

Sami, E. D. 2021. Reason for consult: Institutional racism. *The American Journal of Medicine, 134*(1):18–23.

Samovar, L. A., Porter, R. E., McDaniel, E. R. & Roy, C. S. 2019. *Communication Between Cultures* (9th ed.). Boston: Wadsworth Cengage Learning.

Schutz, W. 1958. *FIRO: A Three Dimensional Theory of Interpersonal Behaviour*. Oxford: Rinehart.

Schwartz, S. H. 1992. Universals in the content and structure of values: Theoretical advances and empirical tests in 20 countries. *Advances in Experimental Social Psychology, 25*: 1–65.

Schwartz, S. H., Verkasalo, M., Antonovsky, A. & Sagiv, L. 1997. Value priorities and social desirability: Much substance, some style. *British Journal of Social Psychology, 36*: 7–8.

Sherif, M. & Sherif, C. W. 1953. *Groups in Harmony and Tension: An Integration of Studies on Intergroup Relations*. New York: Harper.

Sherif, M. 1954. *Experimental Study of Positive and Negative Intergroup Attitudes Between Experimentally Produced Groups: Robbers Cave Study*. Norman: University of Oklahoma Book Exchange.

Sherif, M. 1956. Experiments in group conflict. *Scientific American, 195*(5): 54–59.

Sherif, M. 1958. Superordinate goals in the reduction of intergroup conflict. *American Journal of Sociology, 63*(4): 349–356.

Sherif, M. 1966. *In Common Predicament: Social Psychology of Intergroup Conflict and Cooperation*. New York: Houghton Mifflin.

Sherif, M., Harvey, O. J., White, B. J., Hood, W. R. & Sherif, C. W. 1988. *The Robbers Cave Experiment: Intergroup Conflict and Cooperation*. Middletown: Wesleyan University Press.

Sherif, M., Harvey, O. J., White, B. J., Hood, W. R. & Sherif, C. W. 1961. *Intergroup Conflict and Cooperation: The Robbers Cave Experiment* (Vol. 10). Norman: University of Oklahoma Book Exchange.

Slimbach, R. 2005. The transcultural journey. *Frontiers: The Interdisciplinary Journal of Study Abroad, 1*(1): 205–230.

Song, X. 2018. Hollywood movies and China: Analysis of Hollywood globalization and relationship management in China's cinema market. *Global Media and China, 3*(3): 177–194.

Steele, C. M. & Aronson, J. 1995. Stereotype threat and the intellectual test performance of African Americans. *Journal of Personality and Social Psychology, 69*(5): 797–811.

Steger, M. B. 2003. *Globalization: A Very Short Introduction*. Delhi: Oxford University Press

Stephan, C. W., Demitrakis, K. M., Yamada, A. M. & Clason, D. L. 2000. Women's attitudes toward men: An integrated threat theory approach. *Psychology of Women Quarterly, 24*: 63–73.

Stone, J., Lynch, C. I., Sjomeling, M. & Darley, J. M. 1999. Stereotype threat effects on black and white athletic performance. *Journal of Personality and Social Psychology, 77*(6): 1213–1227.

Swollow, D. 2010. The classic 5 stage culture shock model. *DrDeborahSwallow*. Retrieved October 6, 2022, from DrDeborahSwallow website.

Tajfel, H. 1978. *Differentiation Between Social Groups: Studies in the Social Psychology of Intergroup Relations*. London: Academic Press.

Tajfel, H. 1981. *Human Groups and Social Categories*. Cambridge: Cambridge University Press.

Tajfel, H. 1982. Social psychology of intergroup relations. *Annual Review of Psychology,*

33(1): 1–39.

Tajfel, H., Billig, M., Bundy, R. & Flament, C. 1971. Social categorization and intergroup behaviour. *European Journal of Social Psychology, 1*: 149–178.

Tajfel, H. & Turner, J. 1979. An integrative theory of intergroup conflict. In W. G. Austin & S. Worchel (Eds.), *The Social Psychology of Intergroup Relations.* Monterey: Brooks/Cole Publishing Company, 33–47.

Tajfel, H. & Turner, J. C. 1986. The social identity theory of intergroup behavior. In S. Worchel & W. Austin (Eds.), *Psychology of Intergroup Relations.* Chicago: Nelson-Hall, 7–24.

Tajfel, H., Turner, J. C., Austin, W. G. & Worchel, S. 1979. An integrative theory of intergroup conflict. *Organizational Identity: A Reader, 5*(1): 21–26.

Tareva, E. G., Schepilova, A. V., Tarev, B. V. 2017. Intercultural content of a foreign language textbook: Concept, texts, practices. *XLinguae Journal, 10*(3): 246–255.

Theodore, T. 2020. Prejudice vs stereotype: Definitions and examples. *PracticalPie.* Retrieved February 9, 2022, from *PracticalPie website.*

Tisdell, E. J., Tolliver, D. E. & Villa, S. 2001, June 10–11. *Toward a culturally relevant and spiritually grounded theory of teaching for social transformation and transformational learning.* Adult Education Research Conference, East Lansing, MI, USA.

Tisdell, E. J. & Tolliver, D. E. 2003. Claiming a sacred face: The role of spirituality and cultural identity in transformative adult higher education. *Journal of Transformative Education, 1*(4): 368–392.

Triandis, H. C. 2001. Collectivism: Cultural concerns. *International Encyclopedia of the Social and Behavioral Sciences, 52*(1): 2227–2232.

Turner, J. C. 1975. Social comparison and social identity: Some prospects for intergroup behaviour. *European Journal of Social Psychology, 5*: 5–34.

Turner, J. C. & Oakes, P. 1986. The significance of the social identity concept for social psychology with reference to individualism, interactionism and social influence. *British Journal of Social Psychology, 25*(3): 237–252.

UNESCO. 2017. *Schools in Action, Global Citizens for Sustainable Development: A Guide for Students. UNESCO.* Retrieved November 28, 2018 from UNESCO website.

Wagmeister, E. 2021. Emily in Paris creator says Emily will assimilate more to French culture in Season 2. *Variety.* Retrieved May 4, 2021, from Variety website.

Wallenfeldt, J. 2018. The *Green Book* travel guide. *Britannica.* Retrieved November 28, 2018 from Britannica website.

Wilson, V. 2018. What is cultural identity and why is it important? *Exceptional Futures.* Retrieved June 12, 2018, from ExceptionalFutures website.

Xi, J. P. 2020. *The Governance of China III*. Beijing: Foreign Language Press.

Xu, J. 2015, August 14. Are Our Kids Tough Enough: A documentary or a reality show? *China Daily*.

Xu, X. H. 2019 December 21. A very good way to tell China's story to the world. *China Daily*.

Zhang, M. 2019. How to tell Chinese stories effectively in a deeply globalized world? *CGTN*. Retrieved December 21, 2019, from CGTN website.

Zhao, Y. L. & Zeng, X. 2009. Communication differences in high context culture and low context culture. *Journal of Southwest University of Science and Technology*, *26*(2): 45–49.

Chen. D. N. 2013, April 19. Why where you stand in the lift reflects your social status. *China Daily*.